Interpretative Phenomenological Analysis

Interpretative Phenomenological Analysis

Theory, Method and Research

Jonathan A. Smith, Paul Flowers and Michael Larkin

Los Angeles | London | New Delhi
Singapore | Washington DC

First published 2009

Reprinted 2012

SAGE Publications Ltd
1 Oliver's Yard
55 City Road
London EC1Y 1SP

SAGE Publications Inc.
2455 Teller Road
Thousand Oaks, California 91320

SAGE Publications India Pvt Ltd
B 1/I 1 Mohan Cooperative Industrial Area
Mathura Road
New Delhi 110 044

SAGE Publications Asia-Pacific Pte Ltd
3 Church Street
#10-04 Samsung Hub
Singapore 049483

Library of Congress Control Number 2009924133

British Library Cataloguing in Publication data

A catalogue record for this book is available
from the British Library

ISBN 978-1-4129-0833-7
ISBN 978-1-4129-0834-4(pbk)

Typeset by C&M Digitals (P) Ltd., Chennai, India
Printed in Great Britain by CPI Group (UK) Ltd, Croydon, CR0 4YY
Printed on paper from sustainable resources

Contents

ONE

Introduction

Interpretative phenomenological analysis (IPA) is a recently developed and rapidly growing approach to qualitative inquiry. It originated and is best known in psychology but is increasingly being picked up by those working in cognate disciplines in the human, social and health sciences. This is a handbook offering a comprehensive guide to conducting research using IPA. It presents the theoretical underpinnings of the approach, a detailed guide to the stages of an IPA research project, and examples of high quality studies using the approach. We hope the book will be useful to people at different stages of their research careers, students interested in finding out more about IPA, people embarking on their first IPA study, and more experienced researchers wishing to widen their skills.

What is IPA?

IPA is a qualitative research approach committed to the examination of how people make sense of their major life experiences. IPA is phenomenological in that it is concerned with exploring experience in its own terms. The philosopher Edmund Husserl famously urged phenomenologists to go 'back to the things themselves', and IPA research follows his lead in this regard, rather than attempting to fix experience in predefined or overly abstract categories.

Of course, 'experience' is a complex concept, and we will be discussing it further throughout the book, but IPA researchers are especially interested in what happens when the everyday flow of lived experience takes on a particular significance for people. This usually occurs when something important has happened in our lives.

For example, imagine that you are about to take a swim in the sea on a hot summer day. You may not be mindful of the pebbles under your feet until you remove your shoes, and then find that you have to hobble the last few steps down to the waterline. You may not be aware of the warmth of the sun on your back, until you begin to anticipate your first bracing contact with the cold water. Momentarily then, you are made aware of the flow of your experience; for most of the time, however, you are simply immersed in it, rather than explicitly aware of it. Now imagine that the event has further significance for you: you have been a keen swimmer since childhood, but have not swum on a public beach for some years, since undergoing major surgery for a serious health problem. The anticipation of this swim takes on a host of additional meanings. Perhaps you are concerned about the visibility of scars or other changes to your bodily appearance. Perhaps you have been looking forward to this moment for some time, as a marker of recovery, and the return of a lost self. Perhaps you are simply wondering whether you will be able to remember how to swim! In any of these cases, the swim is marked for you as *an* experience, something important which is happening to you.

This illustration demonstrates a hierarchy of experience. At the most elemental level, we are constantly caught up, unselfconsciously, in the everyday flow of experience. As soon as we become aware of what is happening we have the beginnings of what can be described as 'an experience' as opposed to just experience. As Dilthey (1976) says:

> Whatever presents itself as a unit in the flow of time because it has a unitary meaning, is the smallest unit which can be called an experience. Any more comprehensive unit which is made up of parts of a life, linked by a common meaning, is also called an experience, even when the parts are separated by interrupting events. (p. 210)

Becoming aware of the pebbles or the heat of the sun might count as examples of the 'smallest unit' of 'an experience' for Dilthey, and it would be possible to conduct an IPA study on such experiences. More commonly, however, IPA is concerned with Dilthey's more 'comprehensive unit', where the experience has larger significance in the person's life, as in this case where the anticipation of the swim is connected to important events in the past and is signified as a marker of recovery.

We have given this example to show the wide range of what can be encompassed by a concern with experience and the way the levels relate to each other. In practice, hearing about this particular experience of anticipating the swim would be likely to come about during an interview with a participant taking part in a research study on the experience of major surgery and its impact on their life. The comprehensive unit would be the impact of surgery and it would be composed of a range of 'parts of a life': for example receiving the diagnosis from the doctor, preparing for surgery, recovery from pain, dealing with reactions from significant others, displaying the body in public. The parts are separated in time but 'linked with a common meaning' and the aim of the interview would be to recall the parts and their connections and discover this common meaning.

When people are engaged with 'an experience' of something major in their lives, they begin to reflect on the significance of what is happening and IPA research aims to engage with these reflections. So an IPA researcher might be interested in looking in detail at how someone makes sense of a major transition in their life – for example, starting work, having a first child, losing a parent – or they may wish to examine how someone makes an important decision – for example, whether to emigrate to a new country, or to take a genetic test, or to commit to an elite sport. Some of these experiences are the result of proactive agency on the part of the person, some come unexpectedly and are uncalled for. Some are discrete and bounded while others go on for a considerable period of time. Some will be experienced as positive, others are definitely negative. What they all have in common is that they are of major significance to the person, who will then engage in a considerable amount of reflecting, thinking and feeling as they work through what it means.

This attempt by the research participant to make sense of what is happening to them takes us to IPA's second major theoretical axis. It is an interpretative endeavour and is therefore informed by hermeneutics, the theory of interpretation. IPA shares the view that human beings are sense-making creatures, and therefore the accounts which participants provide will reflect their attempts to make sense of their experience. IPA also recognizes that access to experience is always dependent on what participants tell us about that experience, and that the researcher then needs to interpret that account from the participant in order to understand their experience.

It can be said that the IPA researcher is engaged in a double hermeneutic because the researcher is trying to make sense of the participant trying to make sense of what is happening to them. This captures the dual role of the researcher. He/she is employing the same mental and personal skills and capacities as the participant, with whom he/she shares a fundamental property – that of being a human being. At the same time, the researcher employs those skills more self-consciously and systematically. As such, the researcher's sense-making is second order; he/she only has access to the participant's experience through the participant's own account of it.

IPA is committed to the detailed examination of the particular case. It wants to know in detail what the experience for *this* person is like, what sense *this* particular person is making of what is happening to them. This is what we mean when we say IPA is idiographic. IPA studies usually have a small number of participants and the aim is to reveal something of the experience of each of those individuals. As part of this, the study may explore in detail the similarities and differences between each case. It is possible to move to more general claims with IPA but this should only be after the potential of the case has been realized.

IPA studies are conducted on relatively small sample sizes, and the aim is to find a reasonably homogeneous sample, so that, within the sample, we can examine convergence and divergence in some detail. Immediate claims are therefore bounded by the group studied but an extension can be considered through theoretical generalizability, where the reader of the report is able to assess the evidence in relation to their existing professional and experiential knowledge.

Data collection is usually (but not necessarily) in the form of semi-structured interviews where an interview schedule is used flexibly and the participant has an important stake in what is covered. Transcripts of interviews are analysed case by case through a systematic, qualitative analysis. This is then turned into a narrative account where the researcher's analytic interpretation is presented in detail and is supported with verbatim extracts from participants.

This book will examine each of the theoretical perspectives which are central to IPA: phenomenology, hermeneutics and idiography, in depth, showing the particular take IPA has on them. The following chapters take the reader through each of the steps required to put this approach into practice. The book will also provide detailed examples of studies which demonstrate what can be achieved by the careful examination of significant experiences in people's lives.

History of IPA

IPA has a short and a long history. Its first real mark came with the publication of Jonathan Smith's (1996) paper in *Psychology and Health* which argued for an approach to psychology which was able to capture the experiential and qualitative, and which could still dialogue with mainstream psychology. An important aim at this point was to stake a claim for a qualitative approach centred in psychology, rather than importing one from different disciplines. The point here was not that there was anything wrong with other subject areas but to revive a more pluralistic psychology as envisaged by William James. Thus the argument is that psychology was, could and should be both experimental and experiential and recognizes the important, if suppressed, role for the experiential within the intellectual history of psychology. It is also the case that while IPA appeared on the scene in the mid-1990s, it is clearly drawing on concepts and ideas which have much longer histories. So IPA has been influenced by important theoretical ideas and is an attempt to operationalize one way of working with those ideas. It isn't the only research approach trying to make manifest ideas from phenomenology and hermeneutics and it is also not a fixed thing itself. Although there are core features to IPA, this book will demonstrate the range of ways those core elements can be made to happen.

So IPA started in psychology and much of the early work was in health psychology. Since then it has been picked up particularly strongly in clinical and counselling psychology as well as in social and educational psychology. It is not surprising that the key constituency for IPA is what can broadly be described as applied psychology, or 'psychology in the real world'. We prefer to use slightly different terms and to think of IPA's core interest group as people concerned with the human predicament; this clearly takes us to a focus on people engaging with the world.

We welcome the fact that IPA is also beginning to be used in cognate disciplines in the human, health and social sciences and we encourage this expansion. Yes, we think it is important that IPA is seen as psychological – its core concerns are psychological, and psychology needs space for approaches concerned with the systematic examination of the experiential – however, IPA is psychological with a small p, as well as with a big P. Researchers in other disciplines are interested in psychological questions, even if they are not formally psychologists. So, we think, for example, that a researcher in occupational therapy or film studies can use IPA and can therefore speak to the psychological aspects of that other identity.

The geographical distribution of IPA follows a similar pattern of expansion. Most of the early work was in the UK, which interestingly has been a real crucible for qualitative psychology in the last 20 years. However, researchers using IPA can now be found around the world. Not surprisingly, more of this work is in the English-speaking world, but it is also being picked up in regions where English is not the first language.

How does the book work?

As we said earlier, we have in mind a number of different types of reader for this book. For the newcomer we attempt to give a detailed and step-by-step guide to conducting an IPA study. Doing an experiential qualitative study for the first time can seem daunting, and each stage draws on skills which are different from those taught on the quantitative programmes which tend to dominate training in psychology courses. However, we have also tried to make clear the danger of 'methodolatory' (the glorification of method) so that we hope the novice also sees these guidelines as recommendations for getting started, rather than as permanent prescriptions. Relatedly, within each methodological chapter, we point to a range of ways of thinking, so that we hope the more experienced IPA researcher will also find much of value. Our aim overall has been to show the developmental process of doing experiential qualitative psychology. One starts by cautiously adopting tried and tested strategies, but as confidence grows one becomes more aware of process and the development of skills and the formal procedures shrink into the background.

The underlying philosophy of IPA is just as important as matters of procedure. Researchers who familiarize themselves with it will be able to produce more consistent, sophisticated and nuanced analyses. They will also be able to draw on their understanding of the underlying philosophy to help them to solve unanticipated problems, and, as their confidence and experience grow, to develop their IPA work in ways which extend *beyond* the procedures described above. Therefore, we have attempted to present some complex philosophical ideas, again in an accessible manner. We believe the IPA researcher does need to know something of the philosophical theory which has influenced and informed IPA. At the same time the key thing is appreciating the spirit and sensibility of IPA. IPA is not trying to operationalize a specific philosophical idea, but rather draws widely, but selectively, from a range of ideas in philosophy.

We also believe one of the most helpful things for the newcomer is seeing what the results of IPA look like in practice. We present a set of studies where we have used IPA to examine a range of topics. These will help the reader to see what can be achieved using IPA and give researchers at different levels illustrations of quality work they can aspire to.

Being a book, there has to be a linear structure. And we suspect most people will find it useful to work through the chapters in the order presented. However, it is perfectly possible to read them in different sequences and we encourage people to decide for themselves how to navigate through the book. Thus some people will wish to begin with the practical chapters on how to do IPA and will choose to come back to the theory chapter later. Others may well decide to start by seeing what IPA looks like in practice and therefore will go first to some of the chapters showing completed studies in Section B, before returning to chapters in Section A, which show what it takes to produce one of those studies. We also hope readers will find themselves coming to the book a number of times as their needs and levels of experience change.

The chapters

Chapter 2 outlines the main theoretical underpinnings of IPA: phenomenology, hermeneutics, idiography. The philosophical literature here is pretty difficult, and the aim of this chapter is to present some of the core ideas in an accessible way. We think IPA researchers need to know something of the history of phenomenology and hermeneutics in order to be able to place IPA in an intellectual history. Therefore the chapter starts with a narrative to show the developments within phenomenological and hermeneutic thinking. The chapter then makes explicit how IPA draws on each of the main theoretical ideas.

Chapters 3–6, which comprise the rest of Section A, take the reader step by step through the stages involved in the process of conducting an IPA study: research design (Chapter 3), data collection (Chapter 4), analysis (Chapter 5), writing up (Chapter 6). As we have said above, the aim is not to be prescriptive but rather to have two ways of seeing in mind – offering an accessible guide to practice for the newcomer and offering other insights to help more experienced researchers.

Section B has four chapters which each show a completed piece of IPA research. The research examples come from our own research projects and all but one appear in print for the first time. We have been careful to select examples that we think are good and which we are proud of. The aim is to show the diversity of topics which can be examined with IPA and so we have studies on health and illness (Chapter 7), sex and sexuality (Chapter 8), psychological distress (Chapter 9), life transitions and identity (Chapter 10). The examples also show the different ways that IPA works: for example, as a case study, or with a larger sample; staying close to the material, or dialoguing with other theoretical frameworks.

Finally, in Section C there are two chapters concerned with important current issues for IPA. Chapter 11 considers ways of evaluating the validity of IPA research, and Chapter 12 considers the links between IPA and core concerns for psychology as a whole, for example, cognition, language and embodiment. As part of this, the chapter describes the relationship between IPA and other qualitative approaches and how IPA can connect with other approaches to psychology. Chapter 13 consists of a few concluding comments and looks to some future developments for IPA.

Most of the chapters are clearly multi-authored in the sense that usually one of us wrote a first draft for a chapter but then extensive redrafting incorporated text from the others and we consider the finished pieces to be ones which genuinely reflect a collective vision or voice. We have thus been conscious as we write the book that this vision is both singular and plural. The chapters reflect our long experience working with IPA and most of them also reflect the wide range of possibilities within an approach which has agreed principles at the core. However, the chapters in Section B work rather differently. They are drawn from our separate research studies and therefore have been written by us as individual authors, as is clearly signalled in the introduction to each of them. Just for the record, Chapters 7 and 10 are written by Jonathan, Chapter 8 by Paul, and Chapter 9 by Michael, though in each case we have had helpful comments from the other co-authors which have led to changes being made.

SECTION A

Doing IPA: Theory and Method

As indicated in Chapter 1, this section begins with a chapter on the theoretical foundations of IPA. This is followed by chapters providing detailed guidance to carrying out an IPA study. The chapters offer a range of levels of praxis, offering step by step guidance for the newcomer to IPA but also discussing a range of issues for the more experienced IPA researcher.

TWO

The theoretical foundations of IPA

Introduction

As we have seen in Chapter 1, interpretative phenomenological analysis is an approach to qualitative, experiential and psychological research which has been informed by concepts and debates from three key areas of the philosophy of knowledge: phenomenology, hermeneutics and idiography. This chapter will introduce each of them, and discuss their connections to IPA. In order to be clear and do justice to the existing ideas themselves, the first part of the chapter presents an introduction to these major intellectual movements in their own terms, and hopefully in a way which is reasonably accessible. Within each section, brief consideration will be given to the implications for research in psychology, and for IPA in particular. The latter part of the chapter will more explicitly and fully show how IPA draws on key concepts from the outlined approaches in order to fashion its own particular way of working.

Phenomenology

Phenomenology is a philosophical approach to the study of experience. There are many different emphases and interests amongst phenomenologists, but they have all tended to share a particular interest in thinking about what the experience of being human is *like*, in all of its various aspects, but especially in terms of the things which matter to us, and which constitute our lived world. Many phenomenologists have also been committed to thinking about how we might come to understand what our experiences of the world are like. For psychologists, one key value of phenomenological philosophy is that it provides us with a rich source of ideas about how to examine and comprehend lived experience.

We will be considering the work of four of the major phenomenological philosophers: Husserl, Heidegger, Merleau-Ponty, Sartre. Each can be seen as working in a way which is consistent with a core phenomenology but each also took the project on in a distinctive way. This then will illustrate phenomenology as a singular but also pluralist endeavour.

Husserl

The founding principle of phenomenological inquiry is that experience should be examined in the way that it occurs, and in its own terms. Husserl first argued for this as the basis of a programmatic system in philosophy but the principle has since been further developed, both in philosophy and in psychology.

For Husserl, phenomenology involves the careful examination of human experience. He was particularly interested in finding a means by which someone might come to accurately know their *own* experience of a given phenomenon, and would do so with a depth and rigour which might allow them to identify the *essential* qualities of that experience. If this could be done, then Husserl reasoned that these essential features of an experience would *transcend* the particular circumstances of their appearance, and might then illuminate a given experience for others too.

Famously, Husserl argued that we should 'go back to the things themselves.' The 'thing' he is referring to, then, is the experiential content of consciousness, and he is alluding to the various obstacles that can get in the way of its pursuit. Our predilection for order can mean that we can too quickly look to fit 'things' within our pre-existing categorization system. Instead, Husserl suggests that we should endeavour to focus on each and every particular thing in its own right.

Husserl's phenomenology involved stepping outside of our everyday experience, our *natural attitude* as he called it, in order to be able to examine that everyday experience. Instead, adopting a *phenomenological attitude* involves and requires a reflexive move, as we turn our gaze from, for example, objects in the world, and direct it inward, towards our perception of those objects. It is worth looking at an extended quote from Husserl (1927) which describes this neatly:

> Focusing our experiencing gaze on our own psychic life necessarily takes place as reflection, as a turning about of a glance which had previously been directed elsewhere. Every experience can be subject to such reflection, as can indeed every manner in which we occupy ourselves with any real or ideal objects – for instance, thinking, or in the modes of feeling and will, valuing and striving. So when we are fully engaged in conscious activity, we focus exclusively on the specific thing, thoughts, values, goals, or means involved, but not on the psychical experience as such, in which these things are known as such. Only reflection reveals this to us. Through reflection, instead of grasping

simply the matter straight-out – the values, goals, and instrumentalities – we grasp the corresponding subjective experiences in which we become 'conscious' of them, in which (in the broadest sense) they 'appear.' For this reason, they are called 'phenomena,' and their most general essential character is to exist as the 'consciousness-of' or 'appearance-of' the specific things, thoughts (judged states of affairs, grounds, conclusions), plans, decisions, hopes, and so forth. (para. 2)

Thus, in our everyday life we are busily engaged in activities in the world and we take for granted our experience of the world. In order to be phenomenological, we need to disengage from the activity and attend to the taken-for-granted experience of it. So for example, take an incident which might happen: a car drives past my window. Seeing the car passing by outside, thinking about who might be driving it, wishing we could have a car like it, later remembering the car going by, even wishing that a car would go by when it had not done so – these are all activities happening in the everyday, natural attitude. Once we stop to self consciously *reflect on* any of this seeing, thinking, remembering and wishing, we are being phenomenological. See Chapter 12 for more discussion of this reflective dimension.

For Husserl, phenomenological inquiry focuses on that which is experienced in the consciousness of the individual. He invokes the technical term *intentionality* to describe the relationship between the process occurring in consciousness, and the object of attention for that process. So in phenomenological terms, experience or consciousness is always consciousness *of* something – seeing is seeing of something, remembering is remembering of something, judging is judging of something. That something – the object of which we are conscious – may have been stimulated by a perception of a 'real' object in the world, or through an act of memory or imagination. Thus, there is an *intentional* relationship between the car and my awareness of it. Note that the term intentionality is being used in a different way to its everyday meaning in English. If I say that my memory has an intentional relation to a car, I mean that my memory is oriented towards the car; that is, I am remembering it. I do not mean that I am mentally striving for the car to come into existence.

In order to achieve the phenomenological attitude, Husserl developed a 'phenomenological method' which was intended to identify the core structures and features of human experience. Firstly, he suggested that we need to consider the consequences of our taken-for-granted ways of living in the familiar, everyday world of objects. We need to 'bracket', or put to one side, the taken-for-granted world in order to concentrate on our perception of that world. This idea of bracketing has mathematical roots. It relates to the idea of separating out, or treating separately, the contents of the brackets within equations: 'Putting it in brackets shuts out from the phenomenological field the world as it exists for the subject in simple absoluteness; its place, however, is taken by the world as given in *consciousness* (perceived, remembered, judged, thought, valued, etc.)' (Husserl, 1927: para. 3).

However, it is important to realize that bracketing does not mean that we are making the taken-for-granted world disappear:

> The specific experience of this house, this body, of a world as such, is and remains, however, according to its own essential content and thus inseparably, experience 'of this house,' this body, this world; this is so for every mode of consciousness which is directed towards an object. It is, after all, quite impossible to describe an intentional experience – even if illusionary, an invalid judgment, or the like – without at the same time describing the object of that consciousness *as such*. (Husserl, 1927: para. 3)

The method which Husserl described proceeds through a series of 'reductions.' Each reduction offers a different lens or prism, a different way of thinking and reasoning about the phenomenon at hand. Together, the sequence of reductions is intended to lead the inquirer away from the distraction and misdirection of their own assumptions and preconceptions, and back towards the essence of their experience of a given phenomenon.

As will be evident from the quotation above, Husserl intended that such an examination should include a description and reflection upon every salient particularity of a given phenomenon. However, the description of the phenomenological experience of, for example, this particular house, was for Husserl just the first step. What he really wanted to do was to get at the experience of 'houseness' more generally. While we have unique perceptual experiences of different individual houses, these experiences also have something in common. The task for Husserl therefore was to try and establish what is at the core of the subjective experience of a house, what is the 'essence' or 'eidos' or 'idea' of house.

The '*eidetic reduction*' therefore involves the techniques required in order to get at the essence – the set of invariant properties lying underneath the subjective perception of individual manifestations of that type of object. For Husserl, one such technique is 'free imaginative variation', where one carefully considers different possible instances of house. This will of course involve drawing on one's past experience of houses, but will also involve imagining new examples, and checking the boundaries – 'what is it that makes this a house and not a shop?' and so on. The aim of this process is to help one establish the essential features of *houseness* – that is, to establish its essence. This process is likely to attend to what houses mean to us in lived experience – the practical and emotional features of housing.

In his grandest vision, Husserl wanted to go even further, to try to look at the nature of consciousness *per se* – the thing that underlies and makes possible our consciousness of anything at all. Husserl called this the '*transcendental reduction*'. Thus, in one sense, what we have been describing until now are Husserl's attempts to get at the *content* of conscious experience – by focusing upon experience itself and describing it in terms of its particular and essential features. These first aspects of Husserl's work are the ones which have most influenced phenomenological psychology, including IPA. It will be evident that Husserl had further, more esoteric aims in mind, which exceed the aims of most phenomenological psychologists – notably the pursuit of an additional reduction, to bracket the *content* of consciousness, in order to gaze in wonder at consciousness itself.

There is disagreement between writers as to what Husserl's main project was, and whether this remained consistent over time. Indeed, in different writings by Husserl one finds different emphases, so that sometimes the eidetic reduction seemed the priority while at other times the main project seemed to be to tackle pure consciousness itself. Whether this transcendental phenomenology is even possible is a moot point and most subsequent phenomenologists have turned away from it.

Husserl had an interesting relationship with science. He was critical of science's privileged knowledge claims, reminding us that the *lifeworld* (the taken-for-granted, everyday life that we lead) provides the experiential grounding for what we might call the objective or scientific world:

> It is of course itself a highly important task, for the scientific opening-up of the life-world, to bring to recognition the primal validity of these self-evidences and indeed their higher dignity in the grounding of knowledge compared to that of the objective logical self-evidences ... From objective-logical self-evidence (mathematical 'insight,' natural-scientific, positive-scientific 'insight,' as it is being accomplished by the inquiring and grounding mathematician, etc.), the path leads back, here, to the primal self-evidence in which the life-world is ever pregiven. (1970: 128)

Thus Husserl saw science as a second-order knowledge system, which depends ultimately upon first-order personal experience. For Husserl, an extensive and rigorous phenomenological account of the world as it is experienced would be an essential precursor to any further scientific account. Equally, when conducting phenomenological inquiry, scientific constructs need to be bracketed, because they act as a screen from experience *per se*. For these reasons, Husserl was critical of the way in which psychology was beginning to identify itself as a natural rather than as a phenomenological science. However, Husserl was also a trained scientist. While critical of existing approaches to science, he also hoped that phenomenology could lay the firm conceptual foundations for a different and more authentic science – another very ambitious project.

Two final caveats. Firstly, remember that Husserl was a philosopher and not a psychologist. Most of his writing about the process of phenomenology is conceptual. For example, he doesn't describe in detail the steps involved in an eidetic reduction. While Husserl does provide concrete examples of what the results of the phenomenological method would look like, they are scattered through his writing and can be difficult to locate.

Secondly, as a philosopher, Husserl was mainly engaged in thinking about generic processes, and when it came to particularities he was mainly concerned with first-person processes – that is, what he had to do himself to conduct phenomenological inquiry on his own experience. Psychologists are more usually concerned with analysing other people's experiences. Husserl knew this and recognized it as important, but again it is underdeveloped in his own writing. Therefore his thinking has to be adapted when it comes to psychological inquiry. This point is picked up later in the chapter.

Husserl's work has helped IPA researchers to focus centrally on the process of reflection. He sets the agenda for the attentive and systematic examination of the content of consciousness, our lived experience, which is the very stuff of life. Bracketing, or the attempt at bracketing, has been taken up by many qualitative research approaches and is seen by IPA as offering an important part of the research process, as we will see later. While Husserl was concerned to find the essence of experience, IPA has the more modest ambition of attempting to capture particular experiences as experienced for particular people.

Heidegger

Heidegger began his philosophical career as a student of Husserl's. He acknowledged an intellectual debt to Husserl, but also emphasized his divergence from him. Heidegger's approach to phenomenology is often taken to mark the move away from the transcendental project, and to set out the beginnings of the hermeneutic and existential emphases in phenomenological philosophy. For this reason, we have written about Heidegger in both the *Phenomenology* and the *Hermeneutics* sections of this chapter.

It is important to note that Heidegger's move away from Husserl was not initially a move away from phenomenology. Rather, he thought that his work was actually more phenomenological than Husserl's! For Heidegger, Husserl's phenomenology was too theoretical, too abstract: 'The Being-question, unfolded in Being and Time, parted company with this philosophical position, and that on the basis of what to this day I still consider a more faithful adherence to the principle of phenomenology' (Heidegger, Preface in Richardson, 1963: xiv).

Heidegger questioned the possibility of any knowledge outside of an interpretative stance, whilst grounding this stance in the lived world – the world of things, people, relationships and language. Meaning is thus of fundamental importance here, because for phenomenologists, consciousness: 'makes possible the world as such, not in the sense that it makes possible the existence of the world, but in the sense that it makes possible a *significant* world' (Drummond, 2007: 61, our emphasis).

In his major work, *Being and Time* (1962/1927), Heidegger's subject is Dasein (literally, 'there-being'). This word, Dasein, is Heidegger's preferred term for the uniquely situated quality of 'human being'. In *Being and Time*, he is concerned with establishing the fundamental nature of Dasein, which he argued had been neglected in Western philosophy, either because it was taken for granted, or because it was inaccessible. Thus we might characterize Husserl as primarily concerned with what can be broadly classified as individual psychological processes, such as perception, awareness and consciousness. In contrast, Heidegger is more concerned with the ontological question of existence itself, and with the practical activities and relationships which we are caught up in, and through which the world appears to us, and is made meaningful. It is worth noting that Heidegger's writing style is also very different from Husserl's. Heidegger seems to be attempting his own poetics, inventing his own vocabulary, and eschewing almost entirely Husserl's more technical terminology.

So what is Heidegger's central interest? While he is concerned with the conceptual basis of existence, this is from a deliberately *worldly* perspective. The Heideggerian concept of 'worldliness' affords the embodied, intentional actor a range of physically-grounded (what is possible) and intersubjectively-grounded (what is meaningful) options. Thus much of the early part of *Being and Time* is taken up with an extended description of the world as one which is ready to be used by the individual, with objects 'ready to hand' for the person to exploit: 'Such entities are not thereby objects for knowing the world theoretically, they are simply what gets used, what gets produced, and so forth' (Heidegger, 1962/1927: 95). For Heidegger, Dasein is 'always already' *thrown* into this pre-existing world of people and objects, language and culture, and cannot be meaningfully detached from it.

Dasein also implies and necessitates a degree of reflexive awareness: 'Dasein is an entity which is in each case I myself: its being is in each case mine' (Heidegger, 1962/1927: 150). However, this selfhood also requires the existence of others. Even being alone is only further proof of the existential requirement for others:

> 'Dasein is essentially being-with … Even Dasein's being alone is being with in the world. The other can be missing only in and for a being with. Being alone is a deficient mode of being with; its very possibility is the proof of this. (Heidegger, 1962/1927:156–157)

Heidegger's view of the person as always and indelibly a worldly 'person-in-context,' and the phenomenological concept of *intersubjectivity*, are both central here. The term *intersubjectivity* refers to the shared, overlapping and relational nature of our engagement in the world. From Heidegger's perspective, we are mistaken if we believe that we can occasionally choose to move outwards from some inner world to take up a relationship with the various somatic and semantic objects that make up our world, because relatedness-*to*-the-world is a fundamental part of our constitution (see Larkin, Watts, & Clifton, 2006). Intersubjectivity is the concept which aims to describe this relatedness and to account for our ability to communicate with, and make sense of, each other.

The later part of *Being and Time* becomes increasingly existential in focus, as Heidegger engages in an extended contemplation of the significance of death; discussing how it gives a temporal dimension to our being-in-the-world, and how it is, unlike life, something which is to be faced essentially alone. Being itself only lasts for a finite time, and we do not know in advance how long that time will be. By the end of *Being and Time*, one gets a sense of how our being-in-the-world can be understood to be multi-modal. As well as a practical engagement with the world, it involves self-reflection and sociality, affective concern, and a temporal existential location.

The key ideas for IPA researchers to take from Heidegger at this stage are, firstly, that human beings can be conceived of as 'thrown into' a world of objects, relationships, and language; secondly, that our being-in-the-world is always perspectival, always temporal, and always 'in-relation-to' something – and consequently, that the interpretation of people's meaning-making activities is central to phenomenological inquiry in psychology. A crucial feature of *Being and Time* is Heidegger's reading of phenomenology through a hermeneutic lens – this is picked up further in the section on hermeneutics below.

Merleau-Ponty

As with Heidegger, when reading Merleau-Ponty, one has a sense of the continuities and discontinuities in the phenomenological project. Merleau-Ponty engages with, and owes an intellectual debt to, Husserl. He shares Husserl's and Heidegger's commitments to understanding our being-in-the-world, but he also echoes some of Heidegger's wish for a more contextualized phenomenology. Heidegger and Merleau-Ponty both emphasized the situated and interpretative quality of our knowledge about the world. Whereas Heidegger addressed this issue by emphasizing the *worldliness* of our existence, Merleau-Ponty developed it in a different direction, by describing the *embodied* nature of our relationship to that world and how that led to the primacy of our own individual situated perspective on the world.

In *Phenomenology of Perception* (1962), Merleau-Ponty gives a nice description of the primacy of the situated viewpoint – the one we can never escape:

> I am not the outcome or the meeting-point of numerous causal agencies which determine my bodily or psychological make-up. I cannot conceive myself as nothing but a bit of the world, a mere object of biological, psychological or sociological investigation. I cannot shut myself up within the realm of science. All my knowledge of the world, even my scientific knowledge, is gained from my own particular point of view, or from some experience of the world without which the symbols of science would be meaningless. (p. ix)

Thus Merleau-Ponty suggests that, as humans, we see ourselves as different from everything else in the world. This is because our sense of self is holistic and is engaged in looking at the world, rather than being subsumed within it. Merleau-Ponty also echoes Husserl's view of science, as offering second-order knowledge derived from a first-order experiential base. However, for Merleau-Ponty, empirical science failed to conceptualize the mechanisms of perception and judgement adequately. As a result, Merleau-Ponty focuses much of his work on the embodied nature of our relationship to the world, as *body-subjects*: 'The body no longer conceived as an object in the world, but as our means of communication with it' (1962: 106). For example, my hand, if it reaches out to touch the desk, represents the meeting point of the self and the world. It draws my self to the world in the act of touching.

Merleau-Ponty's concerns with subjectivity and embodiment come together when we think about how we see another. My perception of 'other' always develops from my own embodied perspective. This means that my relations to others begin from a position of difference:

> I perceive the other as a piece of behavior, for example, I perceive the grief or the anger of the other in his conduct, in his face or his hands, without recourse to any 'inner' experience of suffering or anger ... But then, the behavior of another, and even his words, are not that other. The grief and the anger of another have never quite the same significance for him as they have for me. For him these situations are lived through, for me they are displayed. (Merleau-Ponty, 1962: 414–415)

Thus, while we can observe and experience empathy for another, ultimately we can never share entirely the other's experience, because their experience belongs to their own embodied position in the world. The intentional quality and meaning of the 'mineness' and 'aboutness' of an experience are always personal to the body-subject.

For qualitative researchers in general, and IPA researchers in particular, Merleau-Ponty's view, that the body shapes the fundamental character of our knowing about the world, is critical. For Merleau-Ponty, practical activities and relations – the physical and perceptual affordances of the body-in-the-world – are thus more significant than abstract or logical ones (Anderson, 2003). While different phenomenologists will give different degrees of priority to the role of, for example, sensation and the physiological as opposed to more cerebral concerns, the place of the body as a central element in experience must be considered. The lived experience of being a body-in-the-world can never be entirely captured or absorbed, but equally, must not be ignored or overlooked.

Sartre

Sartre (1956/1943) extends the project of existential phenomenology. As with Heidegger, Sartre emphasized that we are caught up in projects in the world. While we have self-consciousness and seek after meaning, this is an action-oriented, meaning-making, self-consciousness which engages with the world we inhabit.

Sartre stresses the developmental, processual aspect of human being. His famous expression 'existence comes before essence' (1948: 26) indicates that we are always becoming ourselves, and that the self is not a pre-existing unity to be discovered, but rather an ongoing project to be unfurled. As Kierkegaard (1974: 79) puts it: 'An existing individual is constantly in the process of becoming'.

This concern with what we will be, rather than what we are, connects with another important concept for Sartre, *nothingness*. For Sartre, things that are absent are as important as those that are present in defining who we are and how we see the world. This is beautifully captured in a vignette in *Being and*

Nothingness. Sartre describes how he approaches a café for an appointment with Pierre. He enters the café, expecting to see Pierre. All that is there is mere background to the anticipated meeting. When Pierre is not there, Sartre's relation to the café is altered – things fight for attention, but quickly fall back – all is unsettled, and cannot become fixed and focused because the *raison d' être* of the café (for Sartre, on this occasion) is missing:

> I myself expected to see Pierre and my expectation has caused the absence of Pierre to happen as a real event concerning this café. It is an objective fact at present that I have discovered this absence, and it presents itself as a synthetic relation between Pierre and the setting in which I am looking for him. Pierre absent haunts this café and is the condition of its self-nihilating organization as ground. (Sartre, 1956/1943: 42)

If Pierre was there, the rest of the café would fit into place around him, and give texture to him. Instead, Pierre *not* being there, his nothingness, fixes the meaning of the café for Sartre at this point in time.

Of course, our projects in the world inevitably lead us to encounters with others. For Sartre this is often a tensile relationship. The world is not mine alone and furthermore my perception of the world is shaped largely by the presence of others and others have their own projects they are engaged in. This is illustrated in two more vivid passages, in the section called 'The Look' in *Being and Nothingness*. First, Sartre describes entering a park and being aware of someone else in the grounds. As a result, perceptually, all the features of the park shift into place around the other person, who takes centre stage. The presence of the other man means that Sartre cannot experience the park in its own terms and for himself.

The direction of perception can work the other way too. In the second passage in 'The Look', Sartre describes looking through a keyhole at events in another room and then becoming aware of someone else who is watching him, watching. His self-consciousness only becomes apparent on being aware of being the object of the gaze of the other. The consequent emotion, shame, only makes sense when seen within its interpersonal context.

Because human nature is, for Sartre, more about becoming than being, the individual has freedom to choose and is, in that sense, responsible for their actions. However, Sartre stresses that these are always complex issues, which need also to be seen within the context of the individual life, the biographical history and the social climate in which the individual acts.

For researchers in phenomenological psychology, the reiteration of Heidegger's emphasis on the wordliness of our experience is significant. Sartre extends this, developing the point in the context of personal and social relationships, so that we are better able to conceive of our experiences as contingent upon the presence – and absence – of our relationships to other people. What Sartre also offers is perhaps the clearest glimpse of what a phenomenological analysis of the human condition can look like. While IPA analyses will usually be of different topics than those which were presented so vividly by Sartre, his portraits show a penetrating analysis of people engaged in projects in the world and the embodied, interpersonal, affective and moral nature of those encounters.

Summary

Husserl, Heidegger, Merleau-Ponty and Sartre are leading figures in phenomenological philosophy, and, in describing some of their ideas here, we have been able to chart some of the main developments in phenomenology and to point out those which are likely to be most relevant to IPA researchers. Husserl's work establishes for us, first of all, the importance and relevance of a focus on experience and its perception. In developing Husserl's work further, Heidegger, Merleau-Ponty and Sartre each contribute to a view of the person as embedded and immersed in a world of objects and relationships, language and culture, projects and concerns. They move us away from the descriptive commitments and transcendental interests of Husserl, towards a more interpretative and worldly position with a focus on understanding the perspectival directedness of our involvement in the lived world – something which is personal to each of us, but which is a property of our relationships to the world and others, rather than to us as creatures in isolation.

Thus, through the work of all of these writers, we have come to see that the complex understanding of 'experience' invokes a lived process, an unfurling of perspectives and meanings, which are unique to the person's embodied and situated relationship to the world. In IPA research, our attempts to understand other people's relationship to the world are necessarily *interpretative*, and will focus upon their attempts to make *meanings* out of their activities and to the things happening to them. For this reason, we need to move on now to discuss a second body of writing, hermeneutics, which has focused upon the matter of interpretation itself.

Hermeneutics

The second major theoretical underpinning of IPA comes from hermeneutics. Hermeneutics is the theory of interpretation. It enters our story as a much older and entirely separate body of thought from phenomenology, but the reader will already have noted that the two strands are due to meet, in the work of hermeneutic phenomenologists – notably Heidegger.

Originally, hermeneutics represented an attempt to provide surer foundations for the interpretation of biblical texts. Subsequently, it developed as a philosophical underpinning for the interpretation of an increasingly wider range of texts, such as historical documents and literary works. The sorts of things which concern hermeneutic theorists are: what are the methods and purposes of interpretation itself? Is it possible to uncover the intentions or original meanings of an author? What is the relation between the context of a text's production (e.g. its historical genesis in the distant past) and the context of a text's interpretation (e.g. its relevance to life in the present day)?

In this section, we will discuss the ideas of three of the most important hermeneutic theorists: Schleiermacher, Heidegger and Gadamer. As with phenomenology, when we read these sources from our positions as psychologists or researchers, we need to remember that hermeneutics has been engaged with, and informed by, other concerns, and take care in drawing out its resonance for our current practices.

Schleiermacher

Schleiermacher, at the turn of the nineteenth century, was one of the first to write systematically about hermeneutics as a generic form. For him, interpretation involved what he called *grammatical* and *psychological* interpretation. The former is concerned with exact and objective textual meaning, while the latter refers to the individuality of the author or speaker:

> Every person is on the one hand a location in which a given language forms itself in an individual manner, on the other their discourse can only be understood via the totality of language. But then the person is also a spirit which continually develops, and their discourse is only one act of this spirit of connection with the other acts. (Schleiermacher, 1998: 8–9)

This sounds very contemporary. Schleiermacher is offering a holistic view of the interpretative process. A text is not only shaped by the conventions and expectations of a writer's own linguistic community, but also by the individual work that she does with that language. Thus Schleiermacher bridges the essentialist and discursive divide: he suggests that there is something unique about the techniques and intentions of a given writer, which will impress a very particular form of meaning upon the text which they produce. This meaning is available for the interpretations of a reader, but those interpretations must also be accommodated to the wider context in which the text was originally produced. This seems like a very helpful position for those of us who are interpreting qualitative research data in phenomenological psychology.

For Schleiermacher, interpretation is not a matter of following mechanical rules. Rather it is a craft or art, involving the combination of a range of skills, including intuition. Part of the aim of the interpretative process is to understand the writer, as well as the text, and Schleiermacher believes that if one has engaged in a detailed, comprehensive and holistic analysis, one can end up with 'an understanding of the utterer better than he understands himself' (Schleiermacher, 1998: 266).

Readers will notice that this opens up a very different position to the interpretative stances which are offered by post-modern literary theory (where the author is typically either irrelevant or inaccessible) and by the social constructionist strand of qualitative psychology (where analysis focuses on the effects of the language used by a person, rather than on the meanings of that language for the person herself). From an IPA perspective, we should not view this as a licence to claim that our analyses are more 'true' than the claims of our research participants, but it does allow us to see how our analyses might offer meaningful insights which exceed and subsume the *explicit* claims of our participants. How might such an interpretative position be justified? Schleiermacher views the relationship between the interpreter and author of a text as follows:

> Partly because it is in fact an analysis of his procedure which brings to consciousness what was unconscious to himself, partly because it also conceives of his relationship to language via the necessary duplication which he himself does not distinguish in it. In the same way he also does not distinguish what emerges from the essence of his individuality or his level of education from what coincidentally occurs as abnormality, and what he would not have produced if he had distinguished it. (1998: 266)

Thus, the interpretative analyst is able to offer a perspective on the text which the author is not. In the context of IPA research, some of this 'added value' is likely to be a product of systematic and detailed analysis of the text itself; some of it will come from connections which emerge through having oversight of a larger data set, and some of it may come from dialogue with psychological theory.

The possibility of such an interpretation depends on sharing some ground with the person being interpreted:

> [Interpretation] depends on the fact that every person, besides being an individual themself, has a receptivity for all other people. But this itself seems only to rest on the fact that everyone carries a minimum of everyone else within themself, and divination is consequently excited by comparison with oneself. (1998: 92–93)

Here we might read Schleiermacher as anticipating the intersubjective dimension of the phenomenological philosophy which was to follow.

Heidegger

As we have already seen, one of Heidegger's aims was to articulate the case for a hermeneutic phenomenology. Lived time and engagement with the world are primary features of Heidegger's account of Dasein, but he points out that our access to such things is always through interpretation.

In *Being and Time*, Heidegger (1962/1927) looked to an etymological definition of phenomenology and observed that the word is made up of two parts, derived from the Greek *phenomenon* and *logos*. *Phenomenon* can be translated as 'show' or 'appear'. Heidegger carefully dissects the various meanings which can appertain to appearance, in order to outline the way he interprets the 'appearance' of our being. In the verb form particularly, to say something appears suggests that it is entering a new state, as it is coming forth, presenting itself to us – and in contrast to a previous state, where it was not present.

Appearance has a dual quality for Heidegger – things have certain visible meanings for us (which may or may not be deceptive), but they can also have concealed or hidden meanings. This is central to his reading of what phenomenology *is* – a discipline which is concerned with understanding the thing as it shows itself, as it is brought to light:

> Manifestly it is something that proximally and for the most part does not show itself at all; it is something that lies hidden in contrast to that which proximally and for the most part does show itself but at the same time it is something that belongs to what this shows itself and it belongs to it so essentially as to constitute its meaning and its ground. (Heidegger, 1962/1927: 59)

Thus for Heidegger, phenomenology is concerned in part with examining something which may be latent, or disguised, as it emerges into the light. But it is also interested in examining the manifest thing as it appears at the surface because this is integrally connected with the deeper latent form – which it is both a part of, and apart from.

Logos can be variously translated as discourse, reason and judgement. Heidegger settles on 'to make manifest what one is "talking about" in one's discourse' (1962/1927: 56). Whatever the particularities, it seems fair to say that the difference between the two source words suggests that while *phenomenon* is primarily perceptual, *logos* is primarily analytical, and this is useful in illuminating the complementary activities which are involved in phenomenology. The primary aim is to examine 'the thing itself' as it appears to show itself to us. Heidegger writes about this as though this happens almost spontaneously. However, the analytical thinking required by the *logos* aspect then helps us to facilitate, and grasp, this showing. So the phenomenon appears, but the phenomenologist can facilitate this, and then help to make sense of that appearing.

It is this micro-analysis and synthesis which take Heidegger down the road of defining phenomenology as hermeneutic. As Moran (2000) points out:

> Phenomenology is seeking after a meaning which is perhaps hidden by the entity's mode of appearing. In that case the proper model for seeking meaning is the interpretation of a text and for this reason Heidegger links phenomenology with hermeneutics. How things appear or are covered up must be explicitly studied. The things themselves always present themselves in a manner which is at the same time self-concealing. (p. 229)

In a later part of *Being and Time*, Heidegger discusses interpretation explicitly, and this section has been used by commentators as the basis for arguing against a presuppositionless descriptive phenomenology, thus setting Heidegger in opposition to Husserl: 'Whenever something is interpreted as something, the interpretation will be founded essentially upon the ... fore-conception. An interpretation is never a pre-suppositionless apprehending of something presented to us' (Heidegger, 1962/1927: 191–192). Thus the reader, analyst or listener brings their fore-conception (prior experiences, assumptions, preconceptions) to the encounter, and cannot help but look at any new stimulus in the light of their own prior experience. However, it is important to look closely at what Heidegger (1962/1927) goes on to say:

> Our first, last, and constant task in interpreting is never to allow our ... fore-conception to be presented to us by fancies and popular conceptions, but rather to make the scientific theme secure by working out the fore-structures in terms of the things themselves. (p. 195)

The fore-structure is always there, and it is in danger of presenting an obstacle to interpretation. In interpretation, priority should be given to the new object, rather than to one's preconceptions. And note the sequence – here the suggestion seems to be that one makes sense of these fore-structures in terms of the things themselves. In other words, while the existence of fore-structures may precede our encounters with new things, understanding may actually work the other way, from the thing to the fore-structure. For example, when encountering a text, I don't necessarily know which part of my fore-structure is relevant. Having engaged with the text, I may be in a better position to know what my preconceptions were. This is an important and neglected way of considering what happens in interpretation.

From the perspective of IPA work, there are two key points here. Firstly, Heidegger's formulation of phenomenology as an explictly interpretative activity, and the connections which he makes to hermeneutics are clearly important – IPA *is* an interpretative phenomenological approach, after all. Secondly, the manner in which Heidegger unpacks the relationship between interpretative work and the fore-structure of our understanding should cause us to re-evaluate the role of bracketing in the interpretative of qualitative data. Indeed a consideration of Heidegger's complex and dynamic notion of fore-understanding helps us see a more enlivened form of bracketing as both a cyclical process and as something which can only be partially achieved. In fact this connects bracketing with reflexive practices in qualitative psychology more generally (see Finlay & Gough, 2003).

Gadamer

Like previous writers on hermeneutics Gadamer (1990/1960), in his primary work *Truth and Method*, is concerned with the analysis of historical and literary texts. Gadamer tends to emphasize the importance of history and the effect of tradition on the interpretative process. He engages in a detailed intellectual dialogue with both Schleiermacher and Heidegger.

First, Gadamer picks up on Heidegger's hermeneutics, and the relation between the fore-structure and the new object. His analysis echoes our reading of Heidegger above, where we pointed to the complex relationship between the interpreter and the interpreted:

> It is necessary to keep one's gazes fixed on the things throughout all the constant distractions that originate in the interpreter himself. A person who is trying to understand a text is always projecting. He projects a meaning for the text as a whole as soon as some initial meaning emerges in the text ... Working out this fore-projection which is constantly revised in terms of what emerges as he penetrates into the meaning, is understanding what is there. (Gadamer, 1990/1960: 267)

This is very much in line with our reading of Heidegger above. Rather than putting one's preconceptions up front before doing interpretation, one may only really get to know what the preconceptions are once the interpretation is underway. Indeed the process is even more multi-faceted and dynamic:

> Every revision of the fore-projection is capable of projecting before itself a new projection of meaning; rival projects can emerge side by side until it becomes clearer what the unity of meaning is; interpretation begins with fore-conceptions that are replaced by more suitable ones. This constant process of new projection constitutes the movement of understanding and interpretation. (1990/1960: 267)

Thus the phenomenon, the thing itself, influences the interpretation which in turn can influence the fore-structure, which can then itself influence the interpretation. One can hold a number of conceptions and these are compared, contrasted and modified as part of the sense-making process.

In more everyday terms, when we read a text, our reading and understanding are forms of engaging in a dialogue between something that is old (a fore-understanding) and something which is new (the text itself):

> A person trying to understand something will not resign himself from the start to relying on his own accidental fore-meanings, ignoring as consistently and stubbornly as possible the actual meaning of the text until the latter becomes so persistently audible that it breaks through what the interpreter imagines it to be. Rather a person trying to understand a text is prepared for it to tell him something ... But this kind of sensitivity involves neither neutrality with respect to content not the extinction of one's self but the foregrounding and appropriation of one's own fore-meanings and prejudices. The important thing is to be aware of one's own bias, so that the text can present itself in all its otherness and thus assert its own truth against one's own fore-meanings. (1990/1960: 269)

This passage emphasizes that the aim is to allow the new stimulus to speak in its own voice, and that one's preconceptions can hinder this process. However, our preconceptions are inevitably present. Hence the dialogue between what we bring to the text, and what the text brings to us. Sometimes we can identify our preconceptions in advance; sometimes they will emerge during the process of engaging with the new object presented. Either way, this requires a spirit of openness:

> Only the person who knows how to ask questions is able to persist in his questioning which involves being able to preserve his orientation towards openness ... It requires that one does not try to argue the other person down but that one really considers the weight of the other's opinion ... Dialectic consists not in trying to discover the weakness of what is said, but in bringing out its real strength. (1990/1960: 367)

This is helpful when it comes to thinking about the interview process. We will pick this up again later in this chapter and in Chapter 4.

Gadamer also engages in an intellectual dialogue with Schleiermacher – though here of course the dialogue spans a longer historical time than that with Heidegger. Gadamer has a mixed reaction to Schleiermacher's claim that the interpreter can know the author better than he/she knows themselves. Gadamer agrees that the author does not automatically have interpretative authority over the meaning of a text. However, Gadamer makes a distinction between understanding the meaning of the text and understanding the person, and he argues that the former is the priority: 'Understanding means primarily to understand the content of what is being said and only secondarily to isolate and understand another's meaning as such' (1990/1960: 294). Gadamer is also sceptical of the possibility of recreating the intention of the author because of the historical gap. Thus, interpretation is a dialogue between past and present: 'The essential nature of the historical spirit consists not in the restoration of the past but in thoughtful meditation with contemporary life' (1990/1960: 168–169). The aim should not be to relive the past but rather to learn anew from it, in the light of the present. This represents a very interesting debate which we will pick up again later in the chapter. For now we will state that we think Gadamer is astute about what is involved in making sense of texts which originated in the historical past. Interpretation will focus on the meaning of the text and that meaning will be strongly influenced by the moment at which the interpretation is made. Of course, with qualitative psychology research projects, we are much more usually engaged with conversations conducted in real time and texts produced contemporaneously. Under these circumstances, we think that Schleiermacher, rather than sounding old-fashioned beside Gadamer's modern voice, actually sounds remarkably fresh and insightful. Thus, as we will see later in the chapter, we think IPA can learn from both Schleiermacher and Gadamer.

The hermeneutic circle

The hermeneutic circle is perhaps the most resonant idea in hermeneutic theory and is picked up by most hermeneutic writers, rather than being identified with one in particular. It is concerned with the dynamic relationship between the part and the whole, at a series of levels. To understand any given part, you look to the whole; to understand the whole, you look to the parts. This has been criticized from a logical perspective, because of its inherent circularity. In analytical terms, however, it describes the processes of interpretation very effectively and speaks to a dynamic, non-linear, style of thinking.

The concept of the hermeneutic circle operates at a number of levels. 'The part' and 'the whole' can thus be understood to describe a number of relationships. For example:

The part	The whole
The single word	The sentence in which the word is embedded
The single extract	The complete text
The particular text	The complete oeuvre
The interview	The research project
The single episode	The complete life

So, for example, the meaning of the word only becomes clear when seen in the context of the whole sentence. At the same time, the meaning of the sentence depends upon the cumulative meanings of the individual words. We have already seen facets of the hermeneutic circle at work above. Indeed, the interpretation of this piece of text is seen within the context of the reader's history of textual interpretation (what you have previously read), and that history is changed by the encounter with this new piece of text.

The hermeneutic circle provides a useful way of thinking about 'method' for IPA researchers. Approaches to qualitative analysis tend to be described in linear, step by step fashions, and IPA is no exception. But it is a key tenet of IPA that the process of analysis is iterative – we may move back and forth through a range of different ways of thinking about the data, rather than completing each step, one after the other. As one moves back and forth through this process, it may help to think of one's relationship to the data as shifting according the hermeneutic circle, too. The idea is that our entry into the meaning of a text can be made at a number of different levels, all of which relate to one another, and many of which will offer different perspectives on the part–whole coherence of the text.

Summary

Hermeneutics is an important part of intellectual history and offers important theoretical insights for IPA. IPA is an interpretative phenomenological approach and therefore Heidegger's explicit ascription of phenomenology as a hermeneutic enterprise is significant. Following Heidegger, IPA is concerned with examining how a phenomenon appears, and the analyst is implicated in facilitating and making sense of this appearance. Heidegger and Gadamer give insightful and dynamic descriptions of the relationship between the fore-understanding and the new phenomenon being attended to. These help to thicken our understanding of the research process. There are a number of ways in which IPA is instantiating the hermeneutic circle and this will become apparent at a number of points in the book. Finally, Schleiermacher was originally writing with historical texts in mind. His ideas come alive again when applied to contemporary texts as in IPA research – this will be picked up again later in the chapter.

Idiography

The third major influence upon IPA is idiography. Idiography is concerned with the particular. This is in contrast to most psychology, which is 'nomothetic', and concerned with making claims at the group or population level, and with establishing general laws of human behaviour. IPA's commitment to the particular operates at two levels. Firstly, there is a commitment to the particular, in the sense of *detail*, and therefore the depth of analysis. As a consequence, analysis must be thorough and systematic. Secondly, IPA is committed to understanding how particular experiential phenomena (an event, process or relationship) have been understood from the perspective of particular people, in a particular context. As a consequence, IPA utilizes small, purposively-selected and carefully-situated samples, and may often make very effective use of single case analyses. Idiography can also refer to the commitment to the single case in its own right, or to a process which moves from the examination of the single case to more general claims. Thus, idiography does not eschew generalizations, but rather prescribes a different way of establishing those generalizations (Harré, 1979). It locates them in the particular, and hence develops them more cautiously.

This emphasis on the particular (and the focus on grasping the meaning of something for a given person) cannot be conflated exactly with a focus on the individual – even though this may appear to provide a convenient shorthand for what idiography does. As we have seen earlier, the phenomenological view of experience is complex. On the one hand, experience is uniquely embodied, situated and perspectival. It is therefore amenable to an idiographic approach. On the other hand, it is also a worldly and relational phenomenon, which offers us a concept of the person which is not quite so discrete and contained as the typical understanding of an 'individual'. Dasein is not the assemblage of dispersed and disparate *personae* commonly posited by social constructionism (e.g. see Gergen, 1991) – but it is thoroughly immersed and embedded in a world of things and relationships. Because Dasein's experience is understood to be an *in-relation-to* phenomenon, it is not really a *property* of the individual per se. However, a given person *can* offer us a personally unique perspective on their relationship to, or involvement in, various phenomena of interest.

The problem with nomothetics*

A number of writers have pointed to problems associated with nomothetic inquiry. A nomothetic approach is one where data are collected, transformed and analysed in a manner which prevents the retrieval or analysis of the individuals who provided the data in the first place. This is typically achieved by measurement (transforming psychological phenomena into numbers), aggregation and inferential statistics.

For example, Lamiell (1987) is particularly critical of so-called 'individual differences' research. This work typically attempts to produce typologies of personality. He argues that it is flawed, as well as being a misnomer:

> The empirical findings generated by individual differences research cannot be interpreted at the level of the individual, and consequently cannot possibly inform in an incisive manner a theory of 'individual' behaviour/psychological functioning. Moreover, and for this very reason, individual differences research cannot possibly be suited to the task of establishing general laws or nomothetic principles concerning individual behaviour/psychological functioning. That is, the empirical findings generated by such research cannot logically establish that something is the case for *each of many* individuals. (1987: 90–91).

The nomothetic domain can only be actuarial and probabilistic, dealing with group averages rather than particular cases. Such analyses produce what Kastenbaum describes as, 'indeterministic statistical zones that construct people who never were and never could be' (quoted in Datan, Rodeheaver, & Hughes, 1987: 156).

The case for the case

There is an alternative to nomothetical analysis, and a supportive literature on the value of single case studies, in particular. Platt (1988) argues that the case study is justified when it describes something intrinsically interesting. Yin (1989) makes the related point that a case study is intended to demonstrate existence, not incidence. Thus, at one level, single case studies simply show us that (or how) something *is*, and can unfold this in an insightful manner. Platt goes on to show how a single case can also point to flaws in existing theoretical claims for a population, and may then point out ways to revise the theory. Similarly, Campbell (1975) points to Becker's belief that a good case study usually either disconfirms our expectations, or reveals things that were not expected. Thus, the additional value of the case study is that it provides a means of troubling our assumptions, preconceptions and theories.

These statements point to the scientific credibility of the case study's painstaking attention to detail. As Sloman (1976) argues, science includes the

* The next two sections draw on material which first appeared in Smith, Harré, & Van Langenhove (1995).

study even of unique occurences, which therefore, 'justifies elaborate and detailed investigation and analysis of particular cases: a task usually shirked because of the search for statistically significant correlations. Social scientists have much to learn from historians and students of literature' (p. 17). Support for this comes from a perhaps surprising quarter. Francis Galton, who was a pioneer in the development of statistics, wrote:

> Acquaintance with particulars is the beginning of all knowledge – scientific or otherwise ... starting too soon with analysis and classification, we run the risk of tearing mental life into fragments and beginning with false cleavages that misrepresent the salient organizations and natural integrations in personal life. (Galton, 1883, in Allport, 1951: 56)

Bromley (1986) explicitly legitimates a role for the case study within mainstream psychology: 'The notion that a case-study, even an extended case-study can only be exploratory, whereas a social experiment or survey can provide definitive results, is incorrect' (p. 15). A further important point is that single cases can themselves be drawn together for further analysis. A number of approaches have been developed for moving from the single case to more general claims. Here we consider two examples, analytic induction, and the quasi-judicial approach.

Analytic induction is a method for attempting to derive theoretical explanations from a set of cases (Hammersley, 1989; Robson, 1993). It involves proposing an initial tentative hypothesis which is then tested against each of one's cases in turn. With each case, one revises the hypothesis to fit the case. Thus analytic induction is an iterative procedure, allowing one to reflect on and modify one's thinking in the light of the next piece of evidence assessed. While the ideal of analytic induction would be to produce a final theoretical statement which was true of all cases, usually it is not possible to be so definitive, and a successful outcome will be a revised hypothesis which accounts for most of the data, for most of the cases examined.

Alternatively, Bromley (1985) advocates a *quasi-judicial* approach to the conduct and assessment of case studies. Here there is a parallel with the gradual development of case law, as single cases are written up and considered in relation to each other. This will produce, 'highly circumscribed accounts of persons in situations, giving rise to low level generalizations within relatively narrow areas of scientific and professional interest' (1985: 8).

We have been arguing for a role for the case study, and an idiographic level of analysis. We must recognize that the particular and the general are not so distinct, however. In a quote which echoes the hermeneutic circle, Goethe states: 'The particular eternally underlies the general; the general eternally has to comply with the particular' (quoted in Hermans, 1988: 785). Thus Warnock (1987) makes the important point that delving deeper into the particular also takes us closer to the universal. We are thus better positioned to think about how we and other people might deal with the particular situation being explored, how at the deepest level we share a great deal with a person whose personal circumstances may, at face value, seem entirely separate and different from our own. Thus in some ways the detail of the individual also brings us closer to significant aspects of the general.

Summary

Idiography is an argument for a focus on the particular, which also leads to a re-evaluation of the importance of the single case study. As we will see in Chapter 5, IPA adopts analytic procedures for moving from single cases to more general statements, but which still allow one to retrieve particular claims for any of the individuals involved. We believe this approach has an important role to play in psychology, and that there is considerable ground for the development of phenomenologically-informed models for the synthesis of multiple analyses from small studies and single cases.

IPA and the theory

IPA is concerned with the detailed examination of human lived experience. And it aims to conduct this examination in a way which as far as possible enables that experience to be expressed in its own terms, rather than according to predefined category systems. This is what makes IPA phenomenological and connects it to the core ideas unifying the phenomenological philosophers we have discussed. IPA concurs with Heidegger that phenomenological inquiry is from the outset an interpretative process. IPA also pursues an idiographic commitment, situating participants in their particular contexts, exploring their personal perspectives, and starting with a detailed examination of each case before moving to more general claims. Thus IPA is connected to each of the intellectual currents outlined in this chapter. Here we will describe in turn the particular relationship IPA has with each of the ideas we have presented.

Reflecting upon personal experience

When reading the philosophical literature on phenomenology, where the writing is often very difficult, it is easy to forget that at its heart, the topic and approach of phenomenology does, or should, connect with our everyday experience. While philosophy has made an enormous contribution to understanding the process of examining experience it is important to realize that philosophy does not own phenomenology. As Halling (2008) helpfully states: 'In everyday life each of us is something of a phenomenologist insofar as we genuinely listen to the stories that people tell us and insofar as we pay attention to and reflect on our own perceptions' (p. 145).

Thus, what the philosopher is doing is formalizing a rigorous description of an approach and ability which is elementally a human one. And remember when Husserl says we should go back to the thing itself, the thing is lived experience, not the philosophical account of lived experience. The philosophical account can be insightful and illuminating but it should be there to serve the stuff of lived experience rather than the other way round. Of course, our propensity for this sort of thinking will vary. Doing phenomenological psychology will generally involve a more sustained and systematic analysis than is part of everyday human activity, but the connection is an important one. We are stressing this at this point to show that phenomenology is a live dynamic activity, nor just a scholarly collection of ideas. We hope to emphasize that we, as researchers and readers, should feel inspired by the philosophical writers to take the project on, and to keep phenomenology alive in our research studies.

Like Husserl, we see phenomenological research as systematically and attentively reflecting on everyday lived experience, and with Husserl we see that that everyday experience can be either first-order activity or second-order mental and affective responses to that activity – remembering, regretting, desiring, and so forth. Thus in IPA we are concerned with examining subjective experience, but that is always the subjective experience of 'something'.

Of course experience is a very broad term. So what type of experience is IPA particularly interested in? As we have seen in Chapter 1, IPA is usually concerned with experience which is of particular moment or significance to the person. So, for example, IPA studies have looked at how people decide whether to take a genetic test, how HIV-positive gay men think about sexual relationships, and how ex-offenders describe the process of 'going straight'. Thus, with IPA, we are concerned with where ordinary everyday experience becomes 'an experience' of importance as the person reflects on the significance of what has happened and engages in considerable 'hot cognition' in trying to make sense of it.

Experience is itself tantalizing and elusive. In a sense, pure experience is never accessible; we witness it after the event. Therefore, when we speak of doing research which aims to get at experience, what we really mean is we are trying to do research which is 'experience close'. Indeed, because IPA has a model of the person as a sense-making creature, the meaning which is bestowed by the participant on experience, as it becomes an experience, can be said to represent the experience itself.

And of course there is another way in which IPA research is separated from experience per se. Human and health science researchers are not usually concerned with examining their own experiences but rather with attending to the experiences of others. Thus, the challenge for phenomenological psychology is to translate the insights of phenomenological philosophy into a practical but coherent approach to the collection and analysis of third-person data. The steps outlined in the book represent our way of trying to realize such a project.

While phenomenology has a core concern with the exploration of human lived experience, as Ricoeur has pointed out (see Moran, 2000), phenomenology is not a single thing, and each subsequent phenomenological philosopher added something particular to the original scheme of Husserl. Thus while Husserl's phenomenology can be described as relatively intrapsychic, Merleau Ponty's is more centrally concerned with embodiment, and Heidegger and Sartre's accounts are more focused upon existential questions – both with practical and worldly, as well as moral and ethical issues. One can see these different emphases as either in competition with each other, or as complementary. We take the latter view, seeing their collective contributions as leading to a mature, multi-faceted and holistic phenomenology.

Thus rather than trying to operationalize or privilege one particular phenomenology or phenomenological theorist, IPA is influenced by the core emphases of the approach, and by a number of further elements drawn from the different positions. In that sense, IPA can be seen as operating within, and attempting to further, the intellectual current of phenomenology, in the context of psychology. Thus IPA is concerned with human lived experience, and posits that experience can be understood via an examination of the meanings which people impress upon it. These meanings, in turn, may illuminate the embodied, cognitive-affective and existential domains of psychology. People are physical and psychological entities. They do things in the world, they reflect on what they do, and those actions have meaningful, existential consequences.

A brief example might help here. One of us (Jonathan) conducted a study with Mike Osborn (see Osborn & Smith, 1998; Smith & Osborn, 2008) on the experience of chronic back pain. The participants' experience was embodied, and they reflected cognitively on this embodiment. They were also concerned with how they lived their lives – with the practical everyday arrangements and with the choices they had to make – and these are existential issues. And they were worried about how they might be having detrimental effects on other people – and described in some depth the difficult and unpleasant emotional experiences which accompanied their physical pain. Thus the participants' and the researchers' concerns were embodied, cognitive, affective and existential, in focus. This study is typical of IPA. When people are having major experiences and facing big issues, the multidimensional aspect of their response to that experience comes to the fore and so a holistic phenomenological analysis is particularly apposite.

The hermeneutic turn

IPA is also strongly influenced by the hermeneutic version of phenomenology. We see no conflict here. Just as phenomenology can be seen as the joint product of a number of related but distinct philosophers, so phenomenology can also be seen as either distinct from or connecting to hermeneutics. We take the latter position and consider Heidegger and Gadamer, for example, to be forging a hermeneutic phenomenology.

For IPA, analysis always involves interpretation. We think Heidegger's notion of *appearing* captures this well. There is a phenomenon ready to shine forth, but detective work is required by the researcher to facilitate the coming forth, and then to make sense of it once it has happened. We are also very much in accord with Heidegger and Gadamer's view of this process as outlined in the section on hermeneutics earlier in the chapter, and offer this as a helpful commentary on what happens *during* analysis. Making sense of what is being said or written involves close interpretative engagement on the part of the listener or reader. However, one will not necessarily be aware of all one's preconceptions in advance of the reading, and so reflective practices, and a cyclical approach to bracketing, are required.

We would position this view of the dynamics of preconceptions within a model of the hermeneutic circle of the research process. Here the 'whole' is the researcher's ongoing biography, and the 'part' is the encounter with a new participant, as part of a new research project. In the passage below, (taken from Smith (2007)) Jonathan has described how this can help our understanding of the research process:

> I start where I am at one point on the circle, caught up in my concerns, influenced by my preconceptions, shaped by my experience and expertise. In moving from this position, I attempt to either bracket, or at least acknowledge my preconceptions, before I go round to an encounter with a research participant at the other side of the circle. Whatever my previous concerns or positions, I have moved from a point where I am the focus, to one where the participant is the focus as I attend closely to the participant's story, facilitate the participant uncovering his/her experience. This requires an intense attentiveness to, and engagement with, the participant as he/she speaks. Of course this is only a simplified version of what is a complex dynamic process ... see Dahlberg, Drew and Nystrom (2001) for more on the qualities of openness required here.
>
> Having concluded the conversation, I continue the journey round the circle, back to where I started. So I return home to analyze the material I collected from the perspective I started from, influenced by my prior conceptions and experience. However, I am also irretrievably changed because of the encounter with the new, my participant and her/his account. Then I engage in movement round a virtual mini-circle where, in my home location, I mentally take on again a conversation with my participant, as I rehear his/her story, ask questions of it, try to make sense of it. Indeed the various actions inherent in the hermeneutic circle between part and whole ... take place in this cognitive space at home base. (p. 6)

Here we would emphasize the importance of the positive process of engaging with the participant more than the process of bracketing prior concerns, in the sense that the skilful attention to the former inevitably facilitates the latter. See Chapters 4 and 5 where we consider in greater detail the processes involved.

IPA involves a 'double hermeneutic' (Smith & Osborn, 2003). The researcher is making sense of the participant, who is making sense of x. And this usefully illustrates the dual role of the researcher as both like and unlike the participant. In one sense, the researcher is like the participant, is a human being drawing on everyday human resources in order to make sense of the world. On the other hand, the researcher is not the participant, she/he only has access to the participant's experience through what the participant reports about it, and is also seeing this through the researcher's own, experientially-informed lens. So, in that sense, the participant's meaning-making is first-order, while the researcher's sense-making is second-order.

There is another way in which IPA operates a double hermeneutic. Ricoeur (1970) distinguishes between two broad interpretative positions, a hermeneutics of empathy, and a hermeneutics of suspicion. The former approach attempts to reconstruct the original experience in its own terms; the latter uses theoretical perspectives from outside (e.g. as with psychoanalysis) to shed light on the phenomenon. Smith (2004) and Larkin et al. (2006) have suggested that IPA can take a centre-ground position here, where interpretative work can be judged to be appropriate so long as it serves to 'draw out' or 'disclose' the meaning of the experience.

Here we suggest that this centre-ground position combines a hermeneutics of empathy with a hermeneutics of 'questioning'. Thus the IPA researcher is, in part, wanting to adopt an 'insider's perspective' (Conrad, 1987), see what it is like from the participant's view, and stand in their shoes. On the other hand, the IPA researcher is also wanting to stand alongside the participant, to take a look at them from a different angle, ask questions and puzzle over things they are saying. Here the analysis may move away from representing what the participant would say themselves, and become more reliant on the interpretative work of the researcher. Successful IPA research combines both stances – it is empathic *and* questioning, and the simple word 'understanding' captures this neatly. We are attempting to understand, both in the sense of 'trying to see what it is like for someone' and in the sense of 'analysing, illuminating, and making sense of something'.

Let's look at this another way. IPA is always interpretative, but there are different levels of interpretation. Typically, an analysis will move through those levels to a deeper analysis, as it progresses. Critically for IPA however, those interpretations must always be grounded in the meeting of researcher and text. For example, Smith (2004) outlines a series of levels of interpretation of a very small piece of text, taken from an interview with a woman talking about the experience of chronic back pain. The first level engaged with the main emerging substantive theme – a nested set of social comparisons which pointed to how the woman was losing out in comparison with a whole set of other selves, that is, her past self, her ought self, other selves she met, and so forth. The second level involved a close look at the metaphors the woman used, and how these added weight to her particular sense of loss, as it compared to others. The third level took a detailed reading of the temporal construction of her account and argued that the way the woman moved between describing herself in the present tense and the past tense reflected a battle for the 'real self' that she was engaged in. Each analysis became more interpretative but each was based on a reading from within the text itself. These interpretations, all of which were compatible with IPA, were then contrasted with one which was not, a psychoanalytic reading based on importing an interpretation from outside the text and also based on the employment of phallic symbols.

So for IPA, a successful interpretation is one which is principally based on a reading from *within* the terms of the text which the participant has produced. It is not usually based on importing a reading from without. In this sense our questioning hermeneutics is clearly different from Ricoeur's hermeneutics of suspicion. This is discussed again in more detail in Chapter 5.

Finally, we would like to revisit the Schleiermacher-Gadamer debate. Gadamer argued that when reading a text we are trying to make sense of the text rather than the author. He suggests that, as a result, our sense-making will be strongly influenced by the time at which we are doing the reading, and that this will get in the way of being able to recreate an original meaning of the text. This is clearly pertinent to the sort of texts that were the main concern of Schleiermacher and Gadamer. These are usually self-consciously constructed, for an expressive or functional purpose. They have usually been written in a previous historical age, and they may involve a foreign language or a quite specific vocabulary or genre. However, if one changes the territory, and considers the material faced by IPA researchers, then we think Schleiermacher has much to say. The texts examined by IPA researchers are usually contemporary or have been produced in the recent past and in response to a request by the researcher rather than a purpose driven by the author. Under these circumstances we think that the process of analysis is geared to learning both about the person providing the account and the subject matter of that account, and therefore, that Schleiermacher usefully speaks to us across the centuries. For more on the relationship between hermeneutics and human sciences, and a worked example of the application of hermeneutic ideas in qualitative psychology, see Smith (2007).

Thus IPA requires a combination of phenomenological and hermeneutic insights. It is phenomenological in attempting to get as close as possible to the personal experience of the participant, but recognizes that this inevitably becomes an interpretative endeavour for both participant and researcher. Without the phenomenology, there would be nothing to interpret; without the hermeneutics, the phenomenon would not be seen.

Focusing on the particular

IPA has an idiographic sensibility. We see the value of IPA studies, first and foremost, as offering detailed, nuanced analyses of *particular* instances of lived experience. A good case study, with an insightful analysis of data from a sensitively conducted interview, on a topic which is of considerable importance to the participant, is making a significant contribution to psychology. In our view, only through painstakingly detailed cases of this sort can we produce psychological research which matches and does justice to the complexity of human psychology itself.

We have been increasingly advocating the case study in IPA (e.g. Smith, 2004) and hope to see increasing numbers of case studies conducted. However, most IPA is, and is likely to continue to be, idiographic in focus, but with a sample size larger than one. Such studies have important and powerful contributions to make. The analytic process here begins with the detailed examination of each case, but then cautiously moves to an examination of similarities and differences across the cases, so producing fine-grained accounts of patterns of meaning for participants reflecting upon a shared experience. In a good IPA study, it should be possible to parse the account both for shared themes, and for the distinctive voices and variations on those themes.

This concern with the particular, with nuance and with variation means that IPA is working at quite an early stage in relation to Husserl's ambitious programme for phenomenology. For Husserl it was important to move from the individual instances to establish the eidetic structure or essence of experience. This is of course a noble aim. For IPA, however, the prior task of detailed analyses of particular cases of actual life and lived experience remains the priority at this time. Of course we do not see this as the end of the story. It will be possible with time to establish larger corpuses of cases and this may lead to the ability to consider the essential features of particular phenomena.

In the meantime the detailed idiographic analyses which IPA offers can make a significant contribution. Through connecting the findings to the extant psychological literature, the IPA writer is helping the reader to see how the case can shed light on the existing nomothetic research. Again we see echoes of part and whole relationships.

And the reader can in turn continue this process of theoretical transferability as they examine the case from the perspective of their own experiential knowledge base, and begin to think of the implications for their own work. As Warnock has suggested, the insightful case study may take us into the universal because it touches on what it is to be human at its most essential. The specifics are unique, but they are hung on what is shared and communal. This in turn echoes the original insight of Schleiermacher, 'that everyone carries a minimum of everyone else within themself' (1998: 92–93).

Concluding thoughts

In this chapter we have introduced the ideas of some of the leading writers in phenomenology, hermeneutics and idiography. We have done this in sufficient detail so that the IPA researcher can understand the theoretical underpinnings of the approach. We have emphasized the plural vision of the thinking and articulated IPA's take on the theoretical ideas offered. In the next set of chapters we move to considering how to put the ideas into practice as we offer guidance on how to conduct a piece of research using IPA.

Further Reading

The philosophical phenomenology literature can be pretty tough going. Moran (2000) offers a highly readable, useful and thorough introduction and Moran and Mooney (2002) provide a useful collection of readings from the main phenomenological philosophers. Perhaps the most readable and concise primary source for Husserl's position can be found in the translation of the piece he wrote for the *Encyclopaedia Britannica* (1927).

Dahlberg et al. (2008) and Van Manen (1990) offer accessible and more detailed overviews of much of the theoretical terrain covered in this chapter, and Langdridge (2007) also introduces the main ideas of phenomenology in a psychological context. Ashworth (2008) offers a very helpful account of the origins of qualitative psychology which includes a consideration of some of the concepts in this chapter. An engaging introduction to phenomenology research in psychology and the human sciences is provided by Becker (1992). Von Eckartsberg (1986) gives a useful overview of different approaches to phenomenological psychology and interesting examples of each.

A key text on hermeneutics is by Palmer (1969). A more recent entrée is offered by Vandevelde (2005). Packer and Addison (1989) present an edited collection of psychological work connected to hermeneutics. Josselson (2004) provides a detailed discussion of the relationship between empathic and critical hermeneutics. Smith (2007) introduces some key concepts in hermeneutics and illustrates their value by examining a small piece of empirical work. Larkin et al. (2006) provide further exposition on Heidegger's relevance to IPA, and to the place of interpretation in analytic work.

Useful accounts of the rationale and methods for an idiographic psychology can be found in Allport (1951, 1965), De Waele and Harré (1979) and Smith, Harré and Van Langenhove (1995).

Acknowledgement note

We would like to thank Dermot Moran and Peter Ashworth for extremely useful and insightful comments on an earlier version of this chapter.

THREE

Planning an IPA research study

Introduction

As we have seen in the preceding chapter, IPA is concerned with understanding personal lived experience and thus with exploring persons' relatedness to, or involvement in, a particular event or process (phenomenon). In choosing IPA for a research project, we commit ourselves to exploring, describing, interpreting and situating the means by which our participants make sense of their experiences. Thus, IPA researchers need first of all to access rich and detailed personal accounts. These accounts will be elicited from persons who are able and willing to offer us a view of the phenomena under investigation. In the following sections we will explore some of the key processes involved in designing a study to explore the concerns and lifeworlds of research participants.

IPA is an approach to doing research. As a consequence of taking this approach, certain methods for collecting and analysing data are likely to be preferred. This chapter, and the remaining chapters in Section A, are about these methods. The reader and researcher must be wary of 'methodologism' (Salmon, 2002) or 'methodolatry' (Chamberlain, 2000). These cautionary terms remind us that, from the perspective of most qualitative researchers, methods are understood *not* to have 'stand-alone integrity'. They do not, by themselves, produce meaningful outcomes. They are not, in and of themselves, guarantees of quality. As researchers, we must be creative in our application of these methods. Successful data collection strategies require organization, flexibility and sensitivity. Successful analyses require the systemic application of ideas, and methodical rigour; but they also require imagination, playfulness, and a combination of reflective, critical and conceptual thinking. As outlined in the previous chapter, the researcher who is engaging in a phenomenological inquiry is central to the IPA research focus.

We can think of methods as providing us with a partial map of the territory which we wish to cross. Each available method should, at least, show us where we are hoping to get to (by virtue of its commitment to a particular epistemological position). Most methods will also describe some of the routes which we can take to get there. Some methods will describe these routes in more detail than others. Some may actively encourage travellers to stray from the beaten path; others may be more prescriptive. But in all cases, there are many ways to get where you are going, and it is up to you to choose and justify the best route for your purposes.

In the remainder of this first section of the book we aim to *describe* what has been done, drawing on our own IPA research, and on other published examples. This description should provide a useful starting point for new researchers (it should identify a few 'well-worn routes across the map', to extend the metaphor). This should not necessarily constrain what *can* be done: constraints are largely put in place by the commitments of the *approach*, rather than the conventions of methodological practice. Throughout we also aim to offer suggestions for variation and complexity within IPA, as the section develops (these are the roads less-travelled, so to speak).

Starting out

First-time qualitative researchers may find themselves with a topic in mind, and an idea that qualitative research may be the way to investigate it. It is sensible to read some methods literature, of course, and it may also be especially helpful to read some research papers. On the one hand, this allows you to see, more clearly than in any methods paper, what it is that you are getting yourself into. On the other hand, it also allows you to identify those features of other people's approaches which most strongly resonate with your own concerns, and your own preferences with regard to style and voice. Qualitative research tends to be a rather *writerly* activity; this requires a willingess to use the first-person, to take up positions and develop arguments. We should therefore be mindful, even at the outset of starting a project, of a third hermeneutic level; the imagined reader of our eventual write-up. The reader is trying to make sense of the researcher making sense of the participant making sense of X! It also requires that one can reflect upon issues associated with subjectivity in this kind of work. It can help to foreshadow these issues at an early stage in project development, and to start thinking about how you will write up your work (in what style, with what voice), and what it will look like (the structure and presentation of the analysis). Of course, your ideas may well change as the project develops, but at least you will have a place to start.

Others may start out with a commitment to qualitative research, or to IPA in particular, and the desire to apply it in a particular setting. In this case, it is important to think carefully about narrowing down the topic, and formulating the research question, so that this is consistent with the aims and scope of your preferred way of working. During this process, it is also worth reflecting on *why* this is your preferred way of working.

Choosing a topic

Choose a topic which interests you. Qualitative research is time-consuming, labour-intensive, and both imaginatively and emotionally demanding. If you're going to expend all this effort, it's a good idea to care about the outcome. In fact, caring about the outcome is often important for other reasons, too: research in the qualitative tradition has often been characterized and motivated by the author's commitment to facilitating change (Kidder & Fine, 1997), and by their willingness to reflect upon the consequences of this commitment (Finlay, 2002). At the same time, try to identify a potential participant group – one that you can access, for a start (see later in this chapter). It is also worth thinking about the extent to which you can relate to, or imagine, the likely experiences, concerns and claims of your participant group. IPA does not require that you have 'insider' status (Styles, 1979), though there is certainly a rich tradition of qualitative research carried out from that position (e.g. see Lieblich, 1996). IPA *will* require that you can imagine what that status might entail, however, and it *does* require you to negotiate access to insider accounts via suitable participants. It makes sense then to reflect upon your previous knowledge of, and experience with, your proposed participants. As we have already suggested in Chapter 2, it is not the case that there is such a thing as 'too much' or 'too little' in the way of previous knowledge, but simply that you ought to be frank with yourself and, where appropriate, with your research team, about the likely consequences of your preconceptions (the 'fore-structure' of your knowledge). Moreover, as we stated in the previous chapter, you may not be able to access all your preconceptions at the start of the project but it is useful none the less to reflect on what you can access.

You might widen your knowledge with a literature review. In IPA, primary research questions, and the subsequent interview questions which may devolve from them, are not usually theory-driven (see later in this chapter for more on this). But a literature review should help you to identify a gap which your research question can then address, and it should also help you to learn something about your participants. The IPA approach to data collection is committed to a degree of open-mindedness, so you will have to try to suspend (or 'bracket off') your preconceptions when it comes to designing and conducting your interviews or other data collection events. As far as we can, we aim to enable participants to express their concerns and make their claims on their own terms. It doesn't hurt to have some idea of what form these claims are likely to take – indeed it may be important when thinking about applying for ethical approval – but one should not presume that this will be the case.

As such, this kind of literature review can be quite short, and may be more evaluative than most. Your aim, as usual, is to introduce readers to the field, but you will also need to inform them about some of the strengths and weaknesses within the key contributions to that field – and to offer an argument which shows why your study can make a useful contribution. This will help you to be explicit about what particular aspect of the topic you are interested in, and how you are going to go about examining it.

Choosing IPA

It makes sense to choose an approach to data analysis before you begin formulating research questions, devising data collection methods, negotiating access to participants, or collecting data. The approach that you take will influence your strategies at each of these early stages in the research process. A number of introductory texts provide some basis for comparing the more established qualitative methods (e.g. Smith, 2008; Willig, 2008). This is not so much a matter of choosing 'the tool for the job' (as it might be when selecting a quantitative method of analysis), but a question of identifying 'what the job *is*'. Each major approach (the various versions of narrative, phenomenological, discursive and grounded methods) will offer a different view of what might constitute 'data,' what might be inferred from it, and what an analysis might seek to achieve.

We will offer a brief exploration here, of what is likely to be assumed within an IPA approach (while referring the reader back to Chapter 2 for further detail), but first it seems reasonable to situate IPA in relation to other methods (while referring the reader forward to Chapter 12 for a further development of this). There are a vast number of 'identified' methods of qualitative data analysis. We can choose from several distinctive *versions* of these methods in the four main approaches (phenomenology, grounded theory, discourse analysis and narrative analysis). We have already had an extended discussion of phenomenology in the previous chapter.

For the purposes of context, a brief summary of the other approaches may be useful here – and it makes sense to begin with grounded theory. This is because grounded theory was one of the first formally-identified *methods* for qualitative researchers. At its inception (Glaser & Strauss, 1967) grounded theory was developed in order to offer social researchers a clear, systematic and sequential guide to qualitative fieldwork and analysis. Grounded theory generally sets out to generate a theoretical-level account of a particular phenomenon. This often requires work of considerable scale, in comparison to other qualitative approaches, and a very particular approach to sampling. The topic for a grounded theory study need not be psychological, and it has no formal psychological focus – but it can, and often does, engage with psychological phenomena.

There are several versions of this approach (some with a more idealist focus, and some a more realist one), but constructivist grounded theory (e.g. Charmaz, 2006) is now probably the most widely used in psychology.

Compared with other strands of grounded theory, the constructivist version appears to offer greater flexibility of process and a clearer epistemological position. Grounded theory is likely to be attractive to you if you have the time and space to deal with a lot of data, if your focus is not necessarily (or primarily) psychological, if you are keen to have a relatively structured protocol to follow, and if you wish to move to quite a high level conceptual account.

Discursive approaches are again various, but can be loosely categorized according to their primary interest in either power (after Foucault) or interaction (after Garfinkel and Sacks), and their shared basis in social constructionism. In the case of Foucauldian discourse analysis, 'discourse' is understood to be a body of knowledge (a way of understanding), and these bodies of knowledge are held to be constitutive (that is they shape and constrain ways of understanding a topic or experiencing). Thus, Foucauldian discourse analysis explores the regulatory and constructive function of language and practices (Parker, 1992). This is likely to be an attractive approach if your topic is ripe for a deconstructive critique. The other major strand of discourse analysis has developed broadly within the ethnomethodological tradition, and is often called discursive psychology. Here, 'discourse' is understood to refer to a communicative interaction, and thus discursive psychology is concerned with the use of available cultural resources to achieve interactive ends (Potter & Wetherell, 1987). This is likely to be an attractive approach if you are interested in *how* people make use of these resources and how language functions in specific contexts (i.e. the focus is performative).

Approaches to narrative analysis span an even wider range. The field of narrative psychology has also developed from social constructionism (see Bruner, 1990) but it has overlapped and integrated with several aspects of phenomenological and discursive psychology during its development (see Chapter 12 for more details of the relationship between narrative analysis and IPA). Some narrative researchers are interested in the *content* of people's stories about various events (e.g. Crossley, 2000), and as such they obviously make contact with the interests of some grounded theorists and phenomenologists. Some narrative researchers are interested in the *structure* of people's stories (e.g. Gergen & Gergen, 1998), and aim to explore the constraints and opportunities which these structures place upon human experience – and we can see that this has some commonalities with the project of discourse analysis. Others still are interested in the relationship between stories which are 'out there' in the cultural realm (as a 'medium for understanding something' – a bit like a discourse) and the stories we tell about our own experiences (e.g. see Andrews, Sclater, Squire, & Treacher, 2000), and these seems to sit somewhere in between IPA and discursive psychology.

So, the field is confusing! It may help to step back from these 'methods,' and consider what they have in common, and what distinguishes them from conventional approaches. Quantitative research tends to try to explain associations between events. That is, it focuses on *what happens.* In psychology, where thoughts and emotions and meanings are part of the topic in hand, it is often difficult to *observe* what happens *directly,* and so psychologists have generally been forced to observe 'what happens' at one remove, by inferring mental events from observations of *behaviour*. Qualitative research has a different subject, and it tends to focus on meaning, sense-making and communicative action. That is, it looks at how people *make sense* of what happens; what the meaning of that happening is. Within this broad territory, a range of alternatives is available. For the purposes of making a crude distinction, we might consider it as presented in Box 3.1. Here we see a series of questions around the experience of anger. How the particular question is formulated leads to a suggestion for what is probably the appropriate qualitative approach to use. This is not a definitive

---

Box 3.1 Different questions, different qualitative approaches

Research question	Key features	Suitable approach
What are the main experiential features of being angry?	Focus on the common structure of 'anger' as an experience.	Phenomenology
How do people who have complained about their medical treatment make sense of being angry?	Focus on personal meaning and sense-making in a particular context, for people who share a particular experience.	Interpretative phenomenological analysis
What sorts of story structures do people use to describe events which made them angry?	Focus on how narrative relates to sense-making (e.g. via genre or structure).	Narrative psychology
What factors influence how people manage being angry?	Willingness to develop an explanatory level account (factors, impacts, influences, etc.).	Grounded theory
How do people talk about 'being angry' in close relationships?	Focus on interaction over and above content, and caution about inferring anything about anger itself.	Discursive psychology
How is 'anger' constructed in incident reports from a residential home for older people?	Willingness to use a range of data sources, and the focus on how things 'must be understood' according to the conventions of a particular setting.	Foucauldian discourse analysis

list, it is suggestive; we could think of many other formulations of the question which would be compatible with each approach and it would be possible to think of questions which would cut across the approaches. Box 3.1 is intended to help the reader with their thinking about the right research method for the question they want to ask.

Your prime reason for choosing IPA over any other qualitative approach should be because it is consistent with the epistemological position of your research question. Implicit in the formulation of any research question is an assumption about what the data can tell us. Thus epistemology is a conceptual issue with a practical impact upon the research that we do. This becomes evident as soon as we have a data transcript in front of us: there are infinite things we could infer, about action, meaning, purpose, etc. How are we to direct our gaze? What are we to code *for*?

In IPA we are assuming that our data (provided that they permit us access to a reasonably rich and reflective level of personal account) can tell us something about people's involvement in and orientation towards the world, and/or about how they make sense of this. Typically, this requires us to identify, describe and understand two related aspects of a participant's account: the key 'objects of concern' in the participant's world, and the 'experiential claims' made by the participant in order to develop a phenomenological account. Within IPA, analyses have different 'flavours', because researchers direct their attention towards different features of the participants' world, on the one hand, and because different features of that world are made salient *by participants*, on the other hand. For the purposes of generating a plausible and persuasive analytic account, it helps to keep track of these choices from the start, and we'll come back to this issue in Chapter 11. We will also return to the relationship of IPA and other qualitative approaches in Chapter 12.

Aims and research questions

The aims set by IPA researchers tend to focus upon people's *experiences* and/or *understandings* of particular phenomena. For example, the topic of an investigation may be outlined as the 'understandings and experiences of health care professionals who treat young people with anorexia nervosa' (Jarman, Smith, & Walsh, 1997). Other common focal points for IPA researchers are the *perceptions* and *views* of participants (as alternatives to 'understandings'). These trends reflect both the phenomenological and interpretative aspects of IPA.

The orientation of researchers *towards* these objects of interest (experiences, understandings) is generally open and often explicitly process-oriented. For example, 'exploring' has been used more commonly than any other verb to state the IPA researchers' actions and intentions in relation to their chosen objects of interest. 'Investigating', 'examining' and 'eliciting' are the next most common alternatives. Again, these are consistent with IPA's inductive procedures, and its focus on the interpretation of meaning.

Primary research questions

Research questions will be grounded in an epistemological position. Implicit in the formulation of a question is an assumption about what the data can tell us. We have seen already that in IPA we are assuming that data can tell us something about people's involvement in and orientation towards the world, and/or about how they make sense of this. Primary research questions in IPA are directed towards phenomenological material: they focus upon people's understandings of their experiences. Such questions should be 'open' not 'closed', and they should be exploratory not explanatory. They may well reflect process rather than outcome, and they will focus on the meaning, or rather the concrete causes or consequences, of events.

Researchers new to qualitative research often come up with questions which are causal and/or closed. The question needs to be directed towards 'meaning' (rather than 'difference' or 'causality', as a hypothesis would be). Thus we ask questions about people's understandings, experiences and sense-making activities, and we situate these questions *within* specific contexts, rather than between them. Primary research questions should also avoid imposing too many *a priori* theoretical constructs upon the phenomena. For example, we might ask 'How do people in situation y understand process x?' which is better than 'What are attitudes to x amongst type-of-people y?' See Box 3.2 which shows the research questions which can be inferred as having motivated some IPA studies.

Box 3.2   Examples of research questions addressed in IPA studies

- How do gay men think about sex and sexuality? (Flowers, Smith, Sheeran, & Beail, 1997)
- How does a woman's sense of identity change during the transition to motherhood? (Smith, 1999a)
- How do people in the early stage of Alzheimer's disease perceive and manage the impact on their sense of self? (Clare, 2003)
- How do homeless people describe the impact on their identity? (Riggs & Coyle, 2002)
- How do people diagnosed with MS think about the experience of exercise? (Borkoles, Nicholls, Bell, Butterly, & Polman 2008)

IPA research is always concerned with the detailed examination of lived experience. Therefore one should not expect one's research question to be on too grand a scale or too ambitious in its reach. Look ahead to the principal outcome of the research – the written report (e.g. dissertation or thesis) – and bear in mind that you will want to be able to evaluate the extent to which you have achieved what you set out to achieve. Salmon (2002) has pointed out that there can be a problem with these very open kinds of research questions: how do we know when we have answered them? Thus, you may find it useful to identify a series of objectives, steps which, once achieved, will allow you to show that your question has been answered. For example, '*Describe the key features of anger as it is understood by persons seeking help from this service*' might be one useful objective for assessing the outcome, and containing the scope, of a project which aims to '*Explore the meaning of anger for men receiving anger management counselling*'.

Of course IPA questions and answers are necessarily open and it may be that your study deviates from what your original question is. Having a realizable goal can still be useful as it helps indicate the extent to which the inductive analysis has emerged from the material examined. Thus in effect you can replace one realizable goal with another as you see where your write-up is now moving.

Secondary, or theory-driven, research questions

Second-tier research questions may be used to explore theory-driven questions. Quite often it is useful to have a few more refined or theory-driven questions, but to treat these as 'secondary' – because they can only be answered at the more interpretative stage, and because, given the open nature of qualitative data collection, you can't be certain that you *will* be able to answer them. Often such analyses use the data as a lever to evaluate existing theories and models (Flowers et al., 1997). We can do this by comparing the fit between 'understandings utilized by participants' (sex as a relational expression of intimacy and commitment) and 'constructs in the literature' (sex as a health behaviour) but this does need to be done cautiously, and at the interpretative end of the analysis, because a second-order research question infers something about the meaning of the account which is quite external to the account itself. For example, we might have a primary research question which is very open (such as 'how do people make sense of their treatment decisions?'). More pointed questions (such as, 'to what extent can accounts of the decision-making process be explained by theory y?') can be secondary. These questions are not hypotheses – they may engage with a theory, but they do not *test* it. Such analyses do need to be grounded in a more phenomenological account, which should usually be established *first*.

Finding a sample

Sampling must be theoretically consistent with the qualitative paradigm in general, and with IPA's orientation in particular. This means that samples are selected purposively (rather than through probability methods) because they can offer a research project insight into a particular experience. Most frequently, potential participants are contacted via: *referral*, from various kinds of gatekeepers; *opportunities*, as a result of one's own contacts; or *snowballing* (which amounts to referral by participants).

Participants are selected on the basis that they can grant us access to a particular perspective on the phenomena under study. That is, they 'represent' a perspective, rather than a population. Because IPA is an idiographic approach, concerned with understanding particular phenomena in particular contexts, IPA studies are conducted on small sample sizes. The detailed case-by-case analysis of individual transcripts takes a long time, and the aim of the study is to write in detail about the perceptions and understandings of these participants. This follows from a critique of nomothetic psychology as only allowing actuarial or group level claims (see Chapter 2) and not being able to say anything substantive and specific about the particular individuals who, in fact, provided the data for the study in the first place.

IPA researchers usually try to find a fairly homogeneous sample, for whom the research question will be meaningful. The extent of this 'homogeneity' varies from study to study. Making this decision is partly a practical problem (Which people are in this situation? How easily can they be contacted?), and partly an interpretative problem (In what other ways do these people vary from one another? How much of that variation can be contained within an analysis of this phenomenon?). In some cases, the topic under investigation may itself be very rare, and thus define the boundaries of the relevant sample. Sometimes it may be necessary, or useful, to divide the sample, so that the phenomenon (e.g. 'relationship break-up', or 'psychotherapy') can be understood from more than one perspective (e.g. both partners, or therapist and client). This kind of analysis is more demanding, however.

Let's think about what this purposive homogeneous sampling might mean in practice. If you were conducting a study on individuals' personal expectations of a new president or prime minister and you were going to interview six participants for an IPA study, it would not make sense to try and make the participants representative of the UK or US population – there is not a large enough number of participants to be able to do that sensibly. Instead one says, for example, 'let's look at the expectation of first time female working-class voters from an urban centre in the north east of England'. You may then find six working-class women, between 18 and 21 years of age, who live in Newcastle. And the analysis will be a detailed examination of the expectations of this particular group. This is not to privilege this group as the only one that is interesting. One could, if one had the time or inclination, do a follow-up study looking at working-class young men in Newcastle or working-class women in rural north east England and so on. And indeed as more IPA is conducted, it will make sense for researchers to conduct studies where sampling is defined in relation to a previous study on the topic. And so it will be possible to gradually build a picture for larger populations.

It is also important that this purposive homogeneous sampling is not seen as treating the members of the sample as an identikit. Quite the contrary, by making the groups as uniform as possible according to obvious social factors or other theoretical factors relevant to the study, one can then examine in detail psychological variability within the group, by analysing the pattern of convergence and divergence which arises.

How homogeneity is defined depends on the study. For the example above, the potential population was very large and so it was necessary to factor in a number of obvious socio-demographic factors. Sometimes the total population will be smaller and so one can be more selective about which factors to consider for homogeneity and which are likely to be most important. The study itself will also have a bearing on selection factors. For example, in a study of the first experience of therapy for depression, one may wish to select a group which is reasonably homogeneous in terms of how long the participants have had depression, how severe it is, how long they have been in therapy, and whether they have had previous treatment of some sort.

Our advice to a newcomer to IPA is to try to obtain a group which is pretty homogeneous, along the lines specified above. However, sometimes people wish to make a comparison within their study and this needs to be done with particular care. For example, it would be possible in a single IPA study to compare the experience of therapy of people who have been depressed for a short time (e.g. less than three months) with those who have been depressed for a longer time (around 18 months). In this case however it would be even more important to make sure the groups are homogeneous in other ways and that they are well matched by other criteria. So, for example, it would be a flaw in the study if participants in the first group (depressed less than three months) were mainly women and those in the second group (depressed around 18 months) were mainly men. Equally it would be problematic if the severity of depression of participants in the first group was significantly different to that in the second group. If you are really committed to conducting a comparison study in this way then: a) you will need to include more participants than in a single group study (e.g. you might have five in each group); and b) it is usually only possible within an IPA design to compare on one dimension, otherwise the numbers needed become much larger.

A final word on the practicalities of sampling. It is a good idea to construct a well designed study in the first place and to think carefully about one's ideal sample in terms of homogeneity. Of course one then needs to be pragmatic. Review recruitment as it is occurring and if it is difficult to recruit participants from a particular group one may need to expand one's inclusion criteria or to change path and approach a different group.

The logic behind sample-specificity is related to the inductive logic of IPA and has consequences for the applicability of findings. Cases and accounts are held to be local, and so analyses are cautious and are built cumulatively. They must therefore be dealt with in detail, and in context. The logic is similar to that employed by anthropologists conducting ethnographic research in one particular community. The anthropologist reports in detail about the view from within a particular cultural frame, but does not claim to be able to say something about all cultures. Subsequent studies may add to this, so that very gradually more general claims can be made, with each founded on the detailed examination of a set of case studies.

It is also possible to think in terms of theoretical transferability rather than empirical generalizability. In this case, the reader makes links between the analysis in an IPA study, their own personal and professional experience, and the claims in the extant literature. The analyst should provide a rich, transparent and contextualized analysis of the accounts of the participants. This should enable readers to evaluate its transferability to persons in contexts which are more, or less, similar. Further points which situate the sample in relation to the extant literature will help the reader to make that assessment. The effectiveness of the IPA study is judged by the light it sheds within this broader context.

Sample size

There is no right answer to the question of the sample size. It partly depends on: the degree of commitment to the case study level of analysis and reporting; the richness of the individual cases; and the organizational constraints one is operating under. We suspect there is a historical process at work here too. Initially qualitative researchers have been cautious in their designs, and, predicting criticism from their quantitative colleagues, they have opted for quite large sample sizes. As the approach has matured, as more studies are published, as researchers become more experienced, sample sizes are typically coming down. This is because the primary concern of IPA is with a detailed account of individual experience. The issue is quality, not quantity, and given the complexity of most human phenomena, IPA studies usually benefit from a concentrated focus on a small number of cases.

Single case studies can be especially powerful, but note that they may require some previous experience of qualitative data analysis. Potentially, the value of a detailed case study is two-fold. Obviously one learns a great deal about a particular person and their response to a specific situation. There is also space to explore connections *within* a participant's account. See Chapter 4 for more on this.

As a rough guide, we would suggest that between three and six participants can be a reasonable sample size for a student project using IPA. Indeed many studies by experienced IPA researchers now have numbers in this range. This should provide sufficient cases for the development of meaningful points of similarity and difference between participants, but not so many that one is in danger of being overwhelmed by the amount of data generated. In effect, it is more problematic to try to meet IPA's commitments with a sample which is 'too large', than with one that is 'too small'.

Our own practice is now to treat $n = 3$ as the default size for an undergraduate or Masters-level IPA study. Three is a very useful number. It allows one to conduct a detailed analysis of each case – in effect, to develop three separate case studies – but it then also allows for the development of a subsequent micro-analysis of similarities and differences across cases. For example, how is case A different to case B? How are cases A and B different from C? How are all three cases similar?

It is more difficult to give a number for PhD studies which are obviously on a different scale. There is time to analyse more cases in a PhD, but it is not especially helpful to think of satisfying the extra demands primarily through increasing numbers. There is also a great deal of flexibility in terms of what a PhD looks like. Without prescribing this or even recommending it especially, we often think of a PhD as being made up of three self-contained but related studies. In that case it would be possible, for example, for the first study to be a single case study, the second to offer a detailed examination of three cases, and the third to examine a larger sample of eight participants from a different location or to draw on one of the bolder designs suggested below. Much depends on the research question and the quality of the data obtained.

Professional doctorates present other forms of demands. Typically, numbers of interviews (rather than participants) of between four and ten are adopted in such circumstances, and that range seems about right. Note we have said number of interviews rather than participants, as we have in mind, for example, a study with four participants interviewed twice. It is important not to see the higher numbers as being indicative of 'better' work, however. Successful analysis requires time, reflection and dialogue, and larger datasets tend to inhibit all of these things, especially amongst less experienced qualitative researchers.

Bolder designs

Most studies have adopted straightforward designs: recruiting small, homogeneous groups of participants, and collecting data from them once. It is possible to be more adventurous, but of course, this does make more demands on the analyst. Obviously, one option is to interview participants more than once. Certain longitudinal and 'before-and-after' phenomena can benefit from this treatment (e.g. Smith, 1994a, 1999a). There is also the possibility of using a first interview as a prompt for further discussion with a participant at a subsequent interview (e.g. see Smith, 1994b). Flowers (2008) considers some of the issues which arise with multiple interviews with the same participant.

In multi-perspectival studies (e.g. Clare 2002), the exploration of one phenomenon from multiple perspectives can help the IPA analyst to develop a more detailed and multifaceted account of that phenomenon. For example, Larkin and Griffiths (2004) explore the experience of risk from the point of view of both Ecstasy-users and bungee-jumpers. This is one kind of 'triangulation' (see Elliott, Fischer, & Rennie, 1999). On the other hand, case study approaches which focus on one 'unit' (one participant or one couple) have also been used to generate rich and *particular* accounts, with the aim of either 'problematising existing concepts or helping to develop ways of looking at new areas of study' (Smith, Flowers, & Osborn, 1997: 87).

Ethical practice

Ethical research practice is a dynamic process which needs to be monitored throughout data collection and analysis. While it is certainly important to meet the ethical 'start-up criteria' of professional bodies such as the BPS, and to pass the scrutiny of institutional ethics committees, qualitative research also requires sustained reflection and review.

An important starting-point for any project is avoidance of harm: there is rarely *any* case to be made for deliberately violating this principle in qualitative research. However, one must always evaluate the extent to which simply *talking about* sensitive issues might constitute 'harm' for any particular participant group.

In qualitative research in general, and in IPA in particular, informed consent must be gained not only for participation in data collection (you will need to think about how best to explain to your participants what to expect from an interview or focus group), but also for the likely outcomes of data analysis (and particularly, the inclusion of verbatim extracts in published reports). With regard to the data collection, it is normal practice to let the participant know the type of topics to be covered. Under certain circumstances the researcher may even decide to show the potential participant the interview schedule prior to giving consent. We believe it is good practice to revisit the issue of consent within the interview itself, with specific oral consent being sought for unanticipated emerging sensitive issues. Raw, unedited data transcripts should only be seen by the research team: any data for wider use must be edited for anonymity. Note that anonymity is all that qualitative researchers can offer. To say that something is 'confidential' is to say that no one else will see it, and this is not the case. The counterpoint to this is 'representation'. Many participants may be pleased to have their experiences represented, and their voices heard, within a professional or academic forum, but this should not be achieved at the cost of anonymity. With regard to publication and presentation of the analyses, if the material or context is especially sensitive, sometimes researchers may decide to give participants the option of reviewing those data extracts from their own interviews which will be chosen to appear in any public-domain document.

It is conventional to see both qualitative and quantitative researchers offering participants 'the right to withdraw at any time'. Rarely is this the intended message. Generally, we are really offering participants the right to withdraw 'at any time during data collection'. Sometimes in qualitative research we can, and should, extend this, by offering the right to withdraw *up to the point* at which either data analysis begins, or publication takes place. Certainly, it is impossible for participants to withdraw once publication has occurred. It is in our interest to be accurate about such offers. A time-limited right to withdraw (up to one month after the interview), combined with opportunities to review the transcript for accuracy (and sometimes to withdraw any particular comments which the participant does not want to appear in the public domain), can be a more honest strategy.

The management of data collection events, such as interviews and focus groups, requires sensitivity and care (see the next chapter for more details). It is important to work with supervisors and peers to anticipate any safety issues (for the researcher and the participant). It is also important to think about how to provide participants with access to appropriate support. If there is any chance that the interview may be upsetting for some of your participants, then you will need to provide all of them with access to this support.

There is no exhaustive list of ethical solutions to the problems thrown up by qualitative research. More detailed accounts are available, however (e.g. Cieurzo & Keitel, 1999; Hopf, 2004). In our experience, each new project comes with new issues to be considered. Often it is the case that the issues increase in complexity as a greater range of perspectives are included in the research – for example, when multi-perspectival designs are used. The principle of protecting anonymity can cause many complications, but with sufficient forethought and planning it can usually be upheld by taking practical steps to inform, protect and gain consent from participants.

It is sometimes possible in IPA work for participants to be more actively enlisted in the research process. This may be in the role of co-analysts, or via participant validation. They may also be trained to conduct interviews, or asked to help to review or generate questions for an interview schedule.

Planning for time

Setting aside things like writing proposals, getting ethical clearance, developing and reviewing materials, gaining access, organizing data collection, and so on, there are some obvious time constraints to consider. Transcription at a level appropriate for IPA (see Chapter 4) generally takes around seven hours for every hour of recorded sound. Qualitative analysis itself is very time consuming, and sufficient time must be built into a project to allow the analysis to be carried out systematically and comprehensively – but also to allow space for reflection, consultation with others, and further development. This is a personal process, and people work in very different ways, so it is difficult for us to give more than a rough estimate. However, if we are thinking about a full-time student, new to IPA, in our experience a first transcript can take

anything from between one week and several weeks to analyse. Subsequ[...]
transcripts may be analysed more quickly, but the task will continue to requir[...]
days, rather than hours, for each transcript. The process of comparing across
cases will then take in the order of a week. And usually at least two weeks will
also be required to write a first draft of the analysis. This means that the analysis
stage for an IPA study of three cases may take at least two months of full-time
work. For a part-time student, obviously, the time needed will be longer
according to what 'part-time' really means! We are giving these figures here,
crude though they are, to indicate just how time-consuming it can be to carry
out good qualitative work, and to stress the importance of budgeting enough
time for this work when planning the study.

Final thoughts

The underlying qualities required of the IPA researcher are: open-mindedness;
flexibility; patience; empathy; and the willingness to enter into, and respond
to, the participant's world. Investigations beginning from an IPA perspective
should follow these principles wherever possible. At the same time, the
researcher also needs determination and persistence and curiosity. This is a
demanding set of qualities and researchers new to IPA may well take time to
pick up the skills and be working effectively. Here good supervision can be
very helpful. It is also important to remember that there is no such thing as a
'perfect' data collection event, and no version of events which is 'the truth'.
We simply aim to understand our participants' perspectives as best we can.

Qualitative research requires that one is willing to engage with complexity.
Complexity is a polite, mature and rather scientific-sounding word. The experienced qualitative researcher, and the perceptive reader, will realize that it
stands in for a certain amount of unpredictability, chaos and mess. All of the
advice above and to follow is intended to help IPA researchers to plan for, and
engage with, the messy chaos of the lived world. Sadly, it will not enable them
to contain or constrain it. Before beginning any qualitative research project, it
is wise to consider that you will not be entirely in control of the process which
follows, and that occasionally you are likely to feel out of your depth. This is
where preparation pays off, and where supervision becomes important. Neither
will offer you control, but both will help you to cope with your lack of it!

FOUR

Collecting data

Choosing a suitable method to collect data

In the previous chapter we noted that many of the established approaches to qualitative research tend to have certain requirements, limitations or preferences for methods of data collection. IPA is no exception. In terms of devising a data collection method, IPA is best suited to one which will invite participants to offer a rich, detailed, first-person account of their experiences. In-depth interviews and diaries may be the best means of accessing such accounts. These facilitate the elicitation of stories, thoughts and feelings about the target phenomenon. They are also consonant with an intimate focus on one person's experience and therefore are optimal for most IPA studies. They are not the only way to collect data of course and under certain circumstances other approaches such as focus groups or participant observation (where the activity being observed includes discussion of experience) may work.

IPA also requires 'rich' data. This is clearly a subjective judgement, but when we say that 'rich data' are required, we mean to suggest that participants should have been granted an opportunity to tell their stories, to speak freely and reflectively, and to develop their ideas and express their concerns at some length. With each of the data collection methods mentioned above, these things have the greatest opportunity to happen. By contrast, in a highly structured interview, or within the limits of the kinds of questions which may be included at the end of a questionnaire, these things are much less likely to occur. Indeed, because of wide exposure to market research and to popular questionnaires in magazines, most people have learned to give personal information in bite-sized, box-ticking packages and may need encouragement and guidance in engaging in fuller, deeper disclosure.

Beyond these constraints, there is great room for imaginative work in collecting data for IPA. This is an approach which benefits from detailed engagement with a small sample, from accessing the chosen phenomenon from more than one perspective, or at more than one time-point, and from the creative and reflective efforts of participants. Any overall design or particular data collection strategy which capitalizes on these features is likely to be an effective one.

In IPA, as we have seen, we are aiming to design data collection events which elicit detailed stories, thoughts and feelings from the participant. Semi-structured, one-to-one interviews have tended to be the preferred means for collecting such data (see Reid, Flowers, & Larkin, 2005, for a review). One-to-one interviews are easily managed, allowing a rapport to be developed and giving participants the space to think, speak and be heard. They are therefore well-suited to in-depth and personal discussion. They also fit most closely the model of the relationship between researcher and participant outlined in Chapter 2.

Other methods have been used, and some of these, such as postal questionnaires (Coyle & Rafalin, 2000), and electronic e-mail dialogue (Turner, Barlow, & Ilbery, 2002), can be seen to share some of the advantages of interviewing. Focus groups (Flowers, Knussen, & Duncan, 2001; Roose & John, 2003) and observational methods (Larkin & Griffiths, 2002) have also been used for IPA work, but require some recognition of the problems involved in applying experiential analyses to more complex social activities. Surprisingly, there has been little published IPA work to date utilizing diaries (exceptions are Smith, 1999a, 1999b, and see Chapter 10). More recently there have also been developments within IPA, in terms of computer-mediated data collection and the use of synchronous and asynchronous interviews (e.g. see Flowers, 2008).

Interviewing allows the researcher and participant to engage in a dialogue whereby initial questions are modified in the light of participants' responses, and the investigator is able to enquire after any other interesting areas which arise. In this chapter we will concentrate on interviewing and also briefly discuss focus groups. For a discussion of other data collection methods, either used in or consonant with IPA, see the sources above, plus Smith (1993) and Plummer (2001). Note that we do not assume that some kind of direct, unproblematic or 'true' account is accessed in such interviews – but we do set out from a commitment to understand our participant's perspective, and to take their claims and concerns seriously. Obviously we should also attend to contextual factors which may influence what the participant tells us in the interview.

In-depth interviews

A qualitative research interview is often described as 'a conversation with a purpose'. This purpose is informed, implicitly at least, by a research question. The 'conversation' here is also rather artificial; the aim of an interview is largely to facilitate an interaction which permits participants to tell their own stories, in their own words. Thus, for the most part, the participant talks, and the interviewer listens.

The plan for IPA interviews is an attempt to come at the research question 'sideways'. Often, research questions are pitched at the abstract level and so it is not usually helpful or effective to ask them directly of the participant. Instead, we aim to set up the interview as an event which facilitates the discussion of relevant topics, and which will allow the research question to be answered subsequently, via analysis.

IPA researchers usually use an interview schedule to help them with this. A schedule is a way of preparing for the likely content of an interview. In it, the researcher typically sets out the questions as she would like to ask them (in an ideal world), and in the order which she expects might be most appropriate for the participant. These things can and do change once an interview is underway, but the preparation of a schedule allows the researcher to set a loose agenda (topics which she would like to discuss with the participant), to anticipate potential sensitive issues (and to inform the participant in advance), and to frame her questions in suitably open forms. A schedule is not always necessary, however – some forms of qualitative research interviewing are even less structured than this, and more participant-led. Even if one has prepared an interview schedule, it is important to note that, while this will shape the interview, it will not guarantee its content or quality. A good interview is essential to IPA analysis. Unless one has engaged deeply with the participant and their concerns, unless one has listened attentively and probed in order to learn more about their lifeworld, then the data will be too thin for analysis.

As an interaction, both interviewer and interviewee are active participants within the research process. The initial focus of the participant's talking may well be determined by questions asked by the researcher. It is generally assumed, however, that the interview will in part be led by the participant's concerns, and that the interviewer will follow up matters arising, even if they are not on the schedule, so long as they might be relevant to the research question. In our experience, it is wise to be generous when making such judgements. These unexpected turns are often the most valuable aspects of interviewing: on the one hand they tell us something we did not even anticipate needing to know; on the other, because they arise unprompted, they may well be of particular importance to the participant. The participant is the experiential expert on the topic in hand and therefore they should be given much leeway in taking the interview to 'the thing itself'.

If the aim of the interview is to enter the participant's lifeworld or allow the participant to recount their life experience, one may well ask the question, why do you need a schedule? Although an investigator conducting an in-depth interview is likely to see it as a co-determined interaction in its own right, it is still usually important when working in this way to produce an interview schedule in advance. This is because the process of developing a schedule requires us to think explicitly about what we expect the interview to cover. More specifically, it enables us to plan for any difficulties that might be encountered.

These difficulties might include the phrasing of complex questions, or the introduction of potentially sensitive topics, and thinking through possible referral mechanisms to therapeutic support such as specific agencies, counselling or help-lines. It also helps us prepare for more reserved participants who might be less forthcoming, and may prefer a slightly more structured approach. Without prior thought to possible questions, such an interview is likely to make the interviewer anxious, and a less effective interview may ensue. A poor interview is often characterized by a rapid pace, closed questions, and more frequent, leading and judgemental contributions from the interviewer – communicative strategies which people also often resort to when they are wrong-footed by an interaction. An interviewer's anxiety is also likely to be picked up by the participant, making him or her feel even less comfortable.

So by constructing a schedule, the researcher is thinking of virtual maps for the interview, which can be drawn upon if, during the interview itself, things become difficult or stuck. As a consequence of this preparation, the researcher is generally able to be a more engaged and attentive listener, and a more flexible and responsive interviewer.

This is particularly the case for the novice IPA researcher. Most people new to IPA have had little qualitative research training or experience. However they will, if they are psychologists, have had a great deal of training in quantitative methods. This means there is a large number of new skills which need to be learned quickly. Many students, while excited at the prospect, are understandably nervous. Constructing a schedule is a very useful way of beginning to think qualitatively, outside the stress of a real interview – particularly because it can be refined and rehearsed with supervisors and peers.

Most of what follows is written with the novice interviewer in mind. We therefore give quite a lot of detailed guidance on constructing a schedule, and then separately on conducting the interview. However, if you already have experience of IPA, you may wish to consider a less structured approach – we will discuss this more, later in the chapter.

Constructing a schedule for a semi-structured interview

The aim of developing a schedule is to facilitate a comfortable interaction with the participant which will, in turn, enable them to provide a detailed account of the experience under investigation. Questions should be prepared so that they are open and expansive; the participant should be encouraged to talk at length. Verbal input from the interviewer can be minimal. Interviews typically move between sequences which are primarily narrative or descriptive, and those where the participant is more analytic or evaluative. It is a good idea to aim for the interview to start with a question which allows the participant to recount a fairly descriptive episode or experience. This way the participant quickly becomes comfortable talking. Invitations to be more analytical can be introduced as the participant begins to ease into the interview.

In phrasing particular questions, it is important to choose formulations which are open (rather than closed), and which do not make too many assumptions about the participant's experiences or concerns, or lead them towards particular answers. Box 4.1 illustrates some suitable kinds of questions for research interviews and Box 4.2 shows some kinds of questions to avoid.

Box 4.1   Some kinds of questions for in-depth interviews

- *Descriptive* – Please could you tell me what you do in your job?
- *Narrative* – Can you tell me about how you came to get the job?
- *Structural* – So what are all the stages involved in the process of dispatching orders?
- *Contrast* – What are the main differences between a good day and a bad day at work?
- *Evaluative* – How do you feel after a bad day at work?
- *Circular* – What do you think your boss thinks about how you do your job?
- *Comparative* – How do you think your life would be if you worked somewhere else?
- *Prompts* – Can you tell me a bit more about that?
- *Probes* – What do you mean by 'unfair'?

Box 4.2   Some kinds of questions to try to avoid

- *Over-empathic* – I can imagine that your job is quite boring – is that right?
- *Manipulative* – You've described your job as quite repetitive. Is it even worse than that?
- *Leading* – So I don't suppose you'd say that your job is rewarding?
- *Closed* – So you've been working here for five years then?

How many questions? For adult, articulate participants, a schedule with between six and ten open questions, along with possible prompts, will tend to occupy between 45 and 90 minutes of conversation, depending on the topic. Note that it is common to come up with too many questions when producing the first draft of any schedule and so, during redrafting, some questions may be dropped.

What follows is a suggested sequence for producing an interview schedule. This process should be seen as iterative: you may find that your ideas develop and change, both during the process, and then again after a pilot or first interview.

1. Do not simply ask your participants your research questions. To design an interview schedule, you will need to look at your research questions, and then try to come up with a set of interview questions which, when answered by your participants, will provide *you* with an opportunity to answer your research questions. To begin with, identify the broad area which you hope to hear about from your participants; this will be why you selected them in the first place.

2. Having determined the overall area to be tackled in the interview, think about the range of topic areas that you want your interview to cover. So, for example, a study on the personal experience of therapy for phobia might have three topic areas: finding the therapist, experience of the therapy, how therapy fits in with the participant's life.

3. Put the topics in the most appropriate sequence. There are a number of decisions to make here. It can help to identify a 'logical' order for the topics (e.g. perhaps in terms of temporal sequence). It can help to identify any sensitive issues, or very specific topics, and to construct the interview so as to work gradually towards them ('funnelling'). It can also help to try to come up with a few good 'first topics' – these are typically scene-setting issues, which can be raised by inviting the participant to tell you about 'what happened when [something happened]' – before you settle on the one you will use. Sometimes you may need to think more creatively about how to get the interview started: it can be useful to ask participants to draw something for example, or to respond to an image or vignette. With the research project above, it would probably be good to start with the process of finding the therapist to enable the participant to relax into the interview before asking questions about the experience of therapy itself.

4. Think about how you might phrase appropriate, open questions relating to each topic. Sometimes the question that you want to ask may sound very abstract – by the time you have eliminated everything which is leading or loaded, there is often only an abstraction left! For example, 'Can you tell me about how you have been since the stroke?' is an attempt to enquire after the participant's experiences, without presuming to limit those experiences to *only one of* a range of possible events/thoughts/feelings/actions. To prepare for this you can construct prompts. As a rule, prompts should be open too. Sometimes, however, it may be necessary to offer participants a range of more concrete options, in order for them to know what sort of question you are asking. You really only need to prepare prompts for those more complex or abstract questions which are likely to need them.

5. Discuss the list of questions with someone else – a potential participant, co-researcher or supervisor – and re-draft them as appropriate. You may well have too many. You may well find that the questions on your initial schedule are actually too direct; a light touch is usually better. Also, despite the preceding advice, it is hard to get out of the habit of asking questions which will give you simple answers, and harder still to 'bracket off' one's assumptions about the content of those answers. You may well discover that you still have some leading or closed questions within your schedule, and that you need to rethink these, too. Remember you are trying, as far as possible, to allow the participant to tell you what it is like to live in their personal world. You are not trying to find out what they think about your views of their personal world.

Box 4.3 illustrates a schedule developed for a project by Pnina Shinebourne (Shinebourne and Smith, in press) exploring the experience of women in rehabilitation for addiction problems. The schedule starts with a question about the present as this seems a straightforward way to begin and is likely to be something that the participant can talk about at some length. Questions about identity have been placed later in the schedule on the assumption that for most people these things will be easier to talk about after the less abstract topics earlier on. The word *problem* does not appear until late in the schedule in order to present as neutral a tone as possible early on. However, the study is with participants who have elected for rehabilitation and have acknowledged they have a 'problem' with drugs or drink and so the use of this word here is appropriate. Prompts have been prepared in case a participant finds it difficult to respond, and to offer a range of possible routes.

Conducting semi-structured, in-depth interviews

Preparing for the interview

In-depth interviews generally last for a considerable amount of time (usually an hour or more). It is a good idea to let your participants know what to expect – in terms of the time commitment, and to make sure that they understand what an interview is. Consider some of the more usual senses in which the word is used (job interviews, interviews as assessments, interviews as medical consultations, interviews as police interrogations) and the need for clarity is evident. Therefore the participant needs some guidance or socialization into what to expect. You can give the participant information on the style of interviewing as part of the recruitment and informed consent procedures. And you may even choose to give your participants a copy of the proposed schedule ahead of the interview. The main principles can be briefly summarized again at the beginning of the interview.

It is also a good idea to ask your participant where they would like the interview to take place. The site of the interview is important: a comfortably familiar setting (for the participant) is preferable, but this must also be safe (for all parties) and reasonably quiet, and free from interruptions. Generally, you will want to interview the participant on their own. Of course, there are situations where this would neither be practical nor sensible (e.g. if your participants are young children, then you will usually need to ensure that they are accompanied by an adult who is authorized to act in their interests).

It is important to learn your schedule in advance. It is distracting for the participant to see you referring to it. It is also distracting for you: if you are trying to recall where you are and where you should be next, you are unlikely to be giving your full attention to the participant. Doing pilot interviews with friends or colleagues a few times should be enough to help you learn the schedule.

The principles of interviewing

Interviewing represents a quite different phase in the data collection from constructing the schedule and it requires different skills. As we said above, constructing a schedule is very useful in helping prepare for possible interviews, thinking through how the interview might go and how you might respond to the participants' responses. However, now you have to deal with the reality of this particular interview with this particular participant.

Good interview techniques vary, depending on both your research question and your analysis method. The kinds of interview technique which elicit 'natural interactions' may not be the same ones which prompt experiential details, or interesting narratives, or frames of understanding, for example. As we have implied in the previous section, the kinds of technique favoured by IPA researchers are not likely to be preferred by all other methods. Thus, some of the advice in this chapter is rather general, whilst other aspects may be pertinent to IPA.

A lot of it is about learning in practice. If you are clear and confident about your interviewing style, the participant will learn that you don't have a pre-set agenda, and that you are interested in what they have to say about the topic in as much detail as they care to give. It is useful to tell your participants at the beginning of the interview that you are interested in them and their experiences; be clear that there are no right or wrong answers. It may be helpful to state that the interview is rather like a one-sided conversation. You may wish to explain that you will say very little, and might also state that some of your questions may seem self-evident, but that this is because you are trying to get to grips with how your interviewee understands things. Remember, you are like a naïve but curious listener trying to get to know the person in front of them. In addition, it is important to state that the participant can take their time in thinking and talking (and also to reassure them in the interview itself). If you speak slowly and clearly, allowing yourself time to phrase questions well, it can set the tone for the participant to do likewise.

During the interview phase of the research project, you are leaving your research world and coming round the hermeneutic circle to the participant's world. We described this process in some detail in Chapter 2. Here the participant has experiential expertise and is the sole focus for your attention. By focusing on attending closely to your participant's words, you are more likely to park or bracket your own pre-existing concerns, hunches and theoretical hobby horses. It is not that you should not be curious and questioning; it is that your questioning at this phase of the project should all be generated by attentive listening to what your participant has to say. There is time and space to bring in more of your own interpretations and ideas as you pass back around the hermeneutic circle to your home base after you leave the interview.

Conducting the interview

The most important thing at the beginning of the interview is to establish a rapport with the participant. They need to be comfortable with you, to know what you want and to trust you. Unless you succeed in establishing this rapport, you are unlikely to obtain good data from your participant. Once both of you are comfortable begin with the first question on your schedule. Give your participant time to give as full an answer as possible and if they seem uncertain or restrained use your prompts to help them. The most important thing in this opening phase is to help the participant get used to talking. Try not to jump in too quickly unless you feel the participant is needing assistance and only intervene to help keep the conversation going. Once the participant is used to talking and realizes that is what you want them to do you can begin to concentrate on the topic of the conversation.

In conducting the interview it is important to use the schedule in a flexible manner. The schedule is a guide, which can incorporate ideas about how best to phrase the questions, and how best to move from general issues to more particular ones. But it is not a rigid structure, and the role of the interviewer as an *active* listener (or more accurately, through listening, as an active co-participant) will often suggest times when it is preferable to abandon the structure and to follow the concerns of the participant. Indeed, remember that in one sense the participant is the experiential expert on the topic, so that in some instances it may be that the interview moves completely away from the schedule and instead follows a course set by the participant.

Similarly, it is important to probe the participant to find out more about the interesting or important things they say. This requires listening attentively and probing spontaneously at certain points (e.g. 'How did that make you feel? or 'Can you tell more about that?') An alternative if the participant is in full flow is to make a short note of key words/topics the participant refers to which you want to follow up. As the participant comes naturally to the end of a turn, you can then say that you would like to ask some more questions about some things they have just said. This sort of tactic employed early in the interview is also indicating to the participant the level of depth and detail you are interested in, and will encourage her/him to talk at this level so that you may well find you are needing to probe less as the interview proceeds.

In our experience, getting the relationship between the schedule and the interview right is one of the hardest things for students to acquire. The novice interviewer, confronted for the first time by a research participant, may feel safer going through the questions which were constructed carefully beforehand, and which were considered to be the right questions to ask. Similarly, for psychology students more used to the control, structure and predictability inherent in survey or experimental work, opening up to the unpredictability of in-depth interviewing can be difficult. However, it is vital to realize that this style of interviewing is an integral part of the inductive principles of phenomenological research. It is precisely because we want to find out about the participant's lifeworld – rather than learn more about our own – that we need to throw ourselves into the unknown. Good research interviewing requires us to accept, and indeed relish, the fact that the course and content of an interview cannot be laid down in advance.

As we have seen, the interview does not have to follow the sequence on the schedule, nor does every question have to be asked, or to be asked in exactly the same way of each participant. Thus the interviewer may decide that it would be appropriate to ask a question earlier than it appears on the schedule, because it follows on from what the participant has just said. Similarly the phrasing of a question will partly depend on how the interviewer feels the participant is responding.

It is important to take your time in an interview and to listen to what you are being told by your participant. The participant should be given time to finish answering a question before the interviewer picks up a new thread. Often the most interesting questions require time for reflection, and richer, fuller answers will be cut short if the interviewer jumps in too quickly. Similarly, it is important to ask one question at a time. Multiple questions can be difficult for the participant to unpick. This can also present difficulties in analysis: you may find yourself trying to work out from a transcript *which* question the participant is answering.

Resist the urge to interpret what you are being told while the interview is still underway. It is often tempting to test out interpretations, connections and other insights of your own during the interview, particularly if you are some way into a sequence of data collection. Obviously, it is reasonable to check that you have understood your participant (and so you might ask them to confirm this), but remember that anything more is analysis, and is generally best left to subsequent stages. For more on multiple interviews and the timing of analysis, see Flowers (2008).

Monitor the effect of the interview on the participant. It may be that the participant feels uncomfortable with a particular line of questioning and this may be expressed in their non-verbal behaviour, or in how they reply. You need to be ready to respond to this, either by backing away from that issue, by rephrasing the question more cautiously, or sometimes by deciding that it would be inappropriate to continue altogether. As an interviewer it is important to remember that you have ethical responsibilities towards the participant.

It is a very good idea to transcribe the first interview in any new sequence of interviews before you go on to conduct any others. Use the transcript to review both your schedule and your interviewing strategies, preferably with a supervisor or co-researcher. Focus on what you would have ideally asked the participant after each of their utterances and compare this to what you did ask them.

Some issues to think about

Research interviews must be viewed as interactions, and as partial in their scope. They provide us with a snapshot of a person's attempts to make sense of their experiences. We can improve the quality of these snapshots by taking care to prepare for them, and by managing the conditions with sensitivity. We do this in order that we are able to take their claims and concerns seriously. The understandings accessed in interviews are not held to be 'the truth' – but they are seen to be 'meaning-full', and in IPA we do recognize them as originating from the situated concerns of our participants. Used effectively, and sensitively, semi-structured interviews can facilitate rapport and empathy, and permit great flexibility of coverage. As a result, they do tend to produce rich and interesting data.

Disclosure from the interviewer needs to be handled carefully. There are many reasons why one might choose to be open with participants about one's own experiences or perspectives (not least ethical reasons). But in interviews such as these, where the aim is to enter into the participant's lifeworld, such disclosure probably belongs outside of the interview per se. On the one hand, such dynamics can facilitate a sense of rapport and the comparative dynamics can facilitate more detailed personal disclosure. On the other hand, however, personal disclosure of shared experience (e.g. being diabetic) can set up competitive, or comparative, dynamics and even lead to a kind of response bias (for example, a self-presentation of being a 'good diabetic'). Therefore, disclosure might usefully be part of an informal debriefing or may happen towards the end of the interview after the participant has been free to express themselves on their own terms. However, some discursive and feminist approaches to qualitative research do advocate more dialogical (or 'active') interviewing styles (e.g. see Burman, 1994; Gubrium & Holstein, 2002).

Doing this sort of interviewing is demanding. New students almost invariably tell us that it is harder than they expected. Thus it is a truism of semi-structured interviewing, as with most aspects of IPA, that it seems deceptively easy to do, but is hard to do well. Potential problems for the interviewer include the challenge of remembering issues to return to, the effort to remain focused and attentive, feelings of being overly intrusive, and feelings of being over excited about the issue and accidentally leading the participant. It is important to remember that it is never possible to achieve a perfect interview technique and that you will always miss things out, but also to acknowledge that your technique will improve with practice.

You will need to find a comfortable 'research persona' for yourself. This is not always as easy it sounds, even if you are used to dealing with people in a professional context. Research interviewing generally requires that we put aside certain common interactional habits (such as: sharing our experience and knowledge; exercising our therapeutic capacity, academic authority or clinical judgement; demonstrating the full extent of our empathy; or steering participants towards new and more positive appraisals of their problems). In their place we have to do a lot of highly engaged listening and some well-timed, and sensitive, questioning.

One striking facet of such interactions is the silences: in a 'normal' conversation, one would often take such silences as a cue to speak about one's own experiences or beliefs. In an interview these silences have to be waited out a little longer: participants often pick up the topic again. Implicitly, your silence signals that you are waiting for more detail. Even if they do not, it is better to read the silence as an opportunity to ask a new question, than to talk, as one usually would, about one's own perspective on the matters under discussion. If you are new to research interviewing, you might find it useful to try out the exercises which we have provided at the end of this chapter, in order to get a 'feel' for the dynamics and positions which this complex process tends to evoke.

Rhythm

The interview is a complex phenomenon. We have already discussed how, because it is the participant's own account of their experience that we are dealing with, there may be topic shifts away from those on the interview schedule. One will then be able afterwards to parse the interview for the topics as they come up during the interview.

However, it is also important to think of another major feature which affects the interview process – the rhythm or dynamic of the interaction. At the beginning of the interview there will be condensed meanings, narratives and understandings. As the interview progresses and the participant warms to the exercise and relaxes into it there is likely to be a move from the descriptive to the affective, from the general to the specific, from the superficial to the disclosing. And this will be happening in parallel to, but at least partly independent of, the unfolding topic sequence. This means the interviewer has to be alert to the interview dynamics and ready to revisit an early topic at a later point if the interviewer feels the participant is now ready to go deeper into it.

Some of this can be predicted by putting more sensitive topics later in the interview schedule. But what one cannot predict is what will be easy or sensitive for any particular participant. In addition, what is said in the interview may itself influence the participant so they realize during the course of it that they now have more to say on a topic covered earlier.

In the early stages of the interview the interviewer typically repeatedly asks for more detail and further information relating to what has just been said. As the interview progresses the participant learns that this dynamic shapes the interview dialogue and the interviewer no longer has to ask repeatedly 'Could you tell me more about that?' Throughout the interview there is a key set of questions which may be used repeatedly. These are shown in Box 4.4. The pattern of questioning is to pick up on key words and phrases the participant uses and to ask for more detail. Again, however, as the interview progresses and the participant warms to what is needed, the interviewer may need to ask even these minimalist questions less and less.

Box 4.4   Going deeper

- Why?
- How?
- Can you tell me more about that?
- Tell me what you were thinking?
- How did you feel?

As the interview progresses the interview technique should facilitate a general shift from talking about things at the generic to the specific level. In other words, there should be a move away from discussing topics at a summary level to specific accounts of particular experiences and the associated thoughts and feelings. It is the latter that provide the best kind of interview data for IPA. Whilst interviewing it is important to think not only about what it seems natural to ask questions about, but to also make a conscious effort to address things that, at face value, you think you already understand. In this way, we attempt to expose the 'obvious' (see the example in Box 4.5) and to reveal the 'strange' in the familiar.

Box 4.5   Exposing the obvious within an interview

P: It's a big thing [*being diagnosed*] to get your head around if you've never really thought of it as an option before.

I: Sorry if this is a stupid sounding question, but why is it a big thing?

P: Well it shouldn't be a big thing, it was it was my perception of it and the way that I thought of HIV and the, you know: it'll never happen to me and that kind of thing, that that um … or I would never be so stupid as to to get HIV, I would never have unprotected sex – all these things, and then I realized that I'd done these things with this person.

Participants sometimes seem to prefer to give an account which is generic and impersonal, rather than personal and detailed. Alternatively, they may talk about the issues in terms of other people (partners, friends) rather than about themselves. Both of these can be difficult for an analysis with a phenomenological focus. If this occurs, you can remind your participants that you are interested in them and their experiences and understandings – not other people's. It is important, of course, not to pressure people to talk about things which they do not want to talk about, but it can be helpful to give people permission to talk about themselves (they may not realize that this is appropriate, or they may feel that they are speaking 'on behalf of' a family, group or community). Encouraging participants to tell you stories about what happened to *them* (as we suggested for the earlier part of interviews, above) can be a good way of bringing people back to the personal meaning of events.

Unstructured interviews

As was said earlier, as an interviewer becomes more experienced, they may choose to conduct even less structured interviews for certain projects. In this form of interviewing, the interviewer has a single core interview question which they will ask at the beginning of each interview (see Box 4.6). How the interview unfolds will then depend entirely on how the participant answers this first question.

This approach to interviewing is an attempt to implement IPA's inductive epistemology to the fullest extent. The resulting interaction is defined even more by the participant and is not structured around *a priori* issues or researcher-led assumptions or topics. This approach also facilitates an appreciation of the participants' priorities and a sense of the relative importance of what the participants talk about and bring to the focus of the interview. The interviewer is attempting to avoid directing the interview in any way, except as an on-going extensive exploration from the general to the specific in terms of what a participant brings to the interview. Adopting an unstructured approach also limits the potential danger of analysis merely reflecting the key topics identified within the interview schedule. It capitalizes upon IPA's ability to explore unanticipated and unexpected findings.

The participant's response to your initial question is likely to reflect an overall summary of what they wish to talk about within the interview, or a list of their priorities. At this stage it can sometimes be helpful to respond by stating that you have heard the key things they have said and telling them that you would like to go back to each in turn. Not only does this give the participant a sense of being actively listened to, it also shares the burden of remembering which subjects to return to. Repeating the participant's response to the core question can be thought of as setting a participant-led agenda, or structure.

Thinking of the rhythm of this type of interview, a participant's response to the core question is likely to generate a series of parallel, 'horizontal' topics (presented in an order of what is most important to the participant), usually at a summary level. Following this, the shared task of the interviewer and interviewee is one of selecting a topic to pursue vertically downwards (moving from the general to the specific). Then returning to the initial set and pursuing the next topic vertically, and so on. This does represent a simplification of the interview dynamics; the actual flow of an interview is messier, but the general pattern often emerges.

In a research project that explored relationships amongst HIV-positive gay men, the core question chosen was 'What do relationships mean to you?'. The participants gave general lists of key issues. These tended to be condensed summary issues. As can be seen in the extract in Box 4.7 the interviewer attempts to give their affirmation but also summarizes, reflects and then shares the task of returning to each issue in turn with the participant.

This type of unstructured interview can work very well. However, as we suggested earlier, we would not recommend it for the newcomer to IPA for whom we think the semi-structured style of working from a schedule is better. Later on you can try unstructured interviewing.

A note on focus groups

We have largely concentrated on interviewing here. Focus groups are another popular choice for collecting data in qualitative research. They may be less obviously suitable for IPA researchers, but they have certainly been employed in published IPA work (e.g. Flowers, Duncan & Frankis, 2000; Flowers et al., 2001). Occasionally this has involved something of a focus group/interview hybrid. For example, MacLeod, Craufurd, & Booth (2002) interviewed 'family units' presenting at a consultation.

Focus groups allow multiple voices to be heard at one sitting, drawing a larger sample into a smaller number of data collection events. The presence of multiple voices, and the interactional complexity of such events does make it more difficult to infer and develop the *phenomenological* aspects of IPA, however – and does tend to give rise to research questions which are often better suited to more explicitly discursive approaches. Thus we would strike a cautious note here, before advising the prospective IPA researcher to adopt focus groups (see Palmer, Larkin, De Visser, & Fadden, in press, for some more detailed advice on this topic). Consider carefully what your research question is, and what you are likely to observe from a focus group. It can be quite difficult to use such events to elicit experiential narratives. It is more likely to be the case that a group discussion will give rise to direct evaluations and positionings ('attitudes' and 'opinions'), third-person stories, and these may need to be dealt with slightly differently:

> My advice to someone committed to conducting focus groups within an IPA perspective is to 'parse' transcripts at least twice, once for group patterns and dynamics and subsequently, for idiographic accounts. If the researcher is convinced that participants are able to discuss their own personal experiences in sufficient detail and intimacy, despite the presence of the group, then the data may be suitable for IPA. (Smith, 2004: 50–51)

Of course, in order to read for more interactive features, one may require a different level of transcription (see below), and, in practice, the enabling of personal and experiential accounts will depend upon the skill of the facilitator, the topic under discussion, the data collection materials, and the relationships between, and characteristics of, the participants.

The starting-point for your decision, as usual, should be your research question. If your research question has an immediate and applied perspective, and a requirement to hear the concerns of larger numbers of participants, then focus groups may be helpful. For example, you might ask, 'What could be done to improve the service that we provide to *group X?*'. You might want to know more about the experiences and concerns of *group* X, in order to help you to develop this. Then you would need to make sure that you have access to the people who can help you to answer this question. This might include a range of stakeholders, not just *group* X themselves. You would also need to think about how the focus groups should be composed. In some cases, it may be more sensitive to run a few separate, homogeneous focus groups (for example, one for families, one for service-users, one for service-providers). In other cases, it may be more productive to run groups of mixed composition.

As with interviewing, it is important to consider how best to inform potential participants about what they are agreeing to do. There are important questions to ask yourself: Do your participants know what a focus group is? Do they understand who else will be there, and what will be discussed? Are they clear about consenting to the public disclosure of their experiences (confidentiality between participants is not guaranteed)? Do they know what will happen to the things that they say? Have you thought about who will see the final report, if you intend to write up the work? Make each of these issues clear in advance, and seek advice from a colleague if you are unsure about the implications of any of them.

Planning the focus group requires consideration of three further questions: What do you want your participants to do? How will you manage the situation? And, how will you capture the data? The first of these can be summarized as a choice among the following options:

- Answer questions, asked by you or another team member.
- Discuss pre-prepared scenarios (e.g. a case study).
- Evaluate source materials (e.g. a draft of an information pack that you are planning to produce).
- Work as a group to solve practical or moral dilemmas (e.g. resource management decisions).

Again, prepare the materials and the wording of your prompts and questions carefully. They should be open-ended, and they should offer relatively 'neutral' opportunities for all participants in the group to engage with the issue under discussion. Once you have decided what you want your participants to do, it is sensible to work out how you intend to run the group. There are three main tasks involved in running a focus group. It is possible to combine these roles, but one way to manage all of them, whilst reducing your own anxiety, is to ask a colleague to help you, and divide roles between you. These roles are:

- Facilitating the discussion – dealing with the pre-prepared structure of the session (asking questions, introducing scenarios, making a map of the interview room, seating and microphone positions, etc.).
- Monitoring the discussion – listening to what is being said, and who is saying it (prompting for more information, following up interesting points, bringing in quieter participants).
- Maintaining a reasonable and ethical environment – making sure that the discussion does not become a confrontation.

In terms of participant numbers per group, four to five is a good size for a focus group. You need sufficient people to generate a discussion, but not so many as to make it difficult to manage. If you are the only researcher present, four to five will keep you very busy. If you have a colleague helping you, then you may find that you can handle two or three more. As with interviewing, a range of further sources is available on focus groups (e.g. Bohnsack, 2000; Wilkinson, 2003). A very useful further introduction to the principles behind both interviews *and* focus groups is provided by Wilkinson, Joffe and Yardley (2004).

Contextualizing the interview: additional data

It can sometimes be useful to collect extra data to help contextualize the interview material. For example, participant observation can be helpful for understanding particular local contexts and activities, and the sampling of media representations can be a way of further exploring the available cultural resources for making sense of the topic in hand. In some settings, you might be able to draw upon case notes or files (provided that access has been approved) as a means of contextualizing the interview. At the very least, it will be possible to make some notes after the interview, as a means of reflecting upon your impressions of your interaction with the participant (e.g. see Hollway & Jefferson, 2005). All these additional data sources can be useful resources for the subsequent contextualization and development of your analysis.

Transcription

IPA also requires a verbatim record of the data collection event. If the event is a writing activity (such as a diary) then the written material will probably need to be transferred to a line-numbered transcript. If the event is an interaction, then it should be recorded, either on audio or video media. For individual interviews the norm is just an audio-recording. Obviously, participants must consent to the making and use of such recording, though in our experience they rarely object. Recordings should be stored according to the requirements of data protection legislation.

Because analysis in IPA aims primarily to interpret the meaning of the *content* of the participant's account, it does not require a particularly detailed transcription of the prosodic aspects of the recordings. That is, it does not require a record of the exact length of pauses, or of all non-verbal utterance as favoured by conversation analysis.

As a rule of thumb, it is pointless to transcribe information which will not be analysed (O'Connell & Kowal, 1995). It is also important to recognize that there is a whole range of features of social interactions which *might* be selected for transcription, and that transcription is itself a form of interpretative activity. It is crucial, therefore, to consider your requirements. IPA requires a semantic record of the interview: that means a transcript showing all the words that are spoken by everyone who is present. Usually these words are spelt conventionally, unless the words used are themselves 'non-conventional'. Generally the transcript includes a note (rather than a coded 'representation') of notable non-verbal utterances (such as laughter), significant pauses, and hesitations (represented in the example below by bracketed text in capitals). The transcripts should have wide margins for ease of coding and space should be left between each turn in the conversation. See Box 4.8 for an example of a short piece of transcript.

Box 4.8   Transcript example from Larkin (2001)

P: So I filled in the form, and it came back and I scored 49 [*pause*] Thought, that's quite good, 49, not a pass but you know, not bad at all – can't be an alcoholic.

I: Yeah

P: And then they told me it was out of 50 [*both laugh*] So – for some unknown reason, all the questionnaires here are marked out of 50 – so I scored 49 out of 50 and thought, 'Fuck. They've got a point'. You know, they'd diagnosed me as an alcoholic, and I had a very high reading. So [*pause*] I still didn't believe them and there's still a certain amount of – there's x per cent of doubt in my mind.

Some of the existing computer software produced to assist with the organization and coding of qualitative data will allow the analyst to code directly to text, images or digital recordings. If one is familiar with the software, this option can save some time at the earlier stages of data analysis. It does present challenges in terms of surveying the analysis in its later stages, and in choosing how to present and write-up the final analysis. Bear in mind, too, that you will want to listen to, or watch, the recordings as you familiarize yourself with the data: don't destroy them until your analysis is complete!

Practical exercises

Finally here we provide some exercises in constructing questions and conducting interviews which you might like to try out if you are new to IPA. These exercises will help you to reflect upon and evaluate your work.

What's wrong with this schedule?

Write down what you think is wrong with each of the questions in the schedule which follows. Don't look at the list of problems which comes after it until you have had a go yourself.

Schedule questions
1. Did you join the Army because you had been in the cadets at school?
2. Does Army-life run in your family at all?
3. Can you tell me why you decided to join up, whether you think it was a way out of a particular social background or not, what you hoped to get from the Army?
4. A life in the Army must be very tough. Was it a shock to your system?
5. What is the most frightening thing about being in the Army?
6. Please can you tell me about your career intentions?
7. With those prospects in mind, would you say you regret your decision to join the Army?

Now look at the list of problems we give below. Compare your list of problems with the ones we would point to:

Problems with the questions
1. Closed and leading; invites rationalization in first question, best to defer till later.
2. Closed and leading.
3. Too many questions at once; including patronizing assumption.
4. Over-empathic, closed, presumptuous, leading.
5. Unbalanced, presumptuous, leading.
6. Poorly contextualized – doesn't follow from previous questions; assumes 'career'.
7. Unbalanced, presumptuous, leading.

How would you improve these? Have a go at drafting some alternative questions. Now compare your suggestions with the alternative versions below which contain suggestions from our students. Neither version is 'perfect', but you can hopefully see that both are an improvement. They use different styles but both seem to have similar understandings of the topic at hand.

Alternative version A
1. What were you doing before you joined the Army?
2. How did you come to join the Army?
3. What did you expect Army life to be like?
4. Could you describe one of your more typical days in the Army for me?
5. For you, what is the best thing about Army life?
6. For you, what is the worst thing about Army life?
7. To what extent has the Army lived up to your original expectations?
8. What are your plans for the future?
9. Do you think that you made the right decision?

Alternative version B
1. Please could you tell me about how you came to join the Army?
   (*Prompt*: Can you tell me about what you did before? How did you arrive at your decision?)
2. What did you expect Army life to be like?
   (*Prompt*: What was the source of those expectations? (e.g. previous experiences of other organizations? Family associations? Films and TV?))
3. Please could you tell about the job that you currently do in the Army?
   (*Prompt*: Rank, unit? What sorts of things are involved? Describe a typical day?)
4. Could you tell me about your off-duty life since you joined the Army?
   (*Prompt*: Who do you socialize with, and what kinds of things do you do?)
5. How do your family feel about your life in the Army?
6. Could you tell me about your best experience in the Army?
7. Could you tell me about your worst experience in the Army?
8. To what extent has the Army been what you expected it to be?
9. What are your plans for the future?

Evaluating your interviewing technique

This is an exercise which works best in groups of three or four. Try out one of the interview schedules below on each other. Take turns to be the interviewer, the participant and the evaluator/timekeeper (this can be two separate roles if there are four of you).

The timekeeper in each turn should keep track of time (allow ten minutes only) and the evaluator should also make notes on the performance of the interviewer (use the checklist below). You don't need to try and get through the whole schedule in ten minutes – just stop when your time is up, complete the feedback exercise (should take another five minutes), and then swap around.

Sample schedule A: Best present
1. Can you tell me about the best present ever given to you? (*Prompts*: What, who from, when, why was it given to you?).
2. Can you tell me a little bit more about how you felt about the present itself? (*Prompts*: What did it mean to you? Why was it so special?)
3. Can you tell me about your relationship with the person who gave you the present? (*Prompts*: Do you think that the present indicated that person's feelings for you? Did it change your feelings about that person? What is your relationship with that person now?)

Sample schedule B: Best holiday

1. Can you describe your best holiday for me? (*Prompts*: Where? Who with? When? What did you do?)
2. Why do you think this was your best holiday? (*Prompts*: What made it so special?)
3. Do you think that this holiday changed you, or the pattern of your life, in any way? (*Prompts*: Did you learn anything from it? Did you make any major changes on your return? Would your life have been different if you had *not* gone on this holiday?)

Evaluator's notes:

- Does the interviewer give the participant enough time to fully answer the question?
- Does the interviewer use the schedule in a sufficiently flexible manner?
- Does the interviewer listen to what the participant says and follow it up?
- Are these follow-ups open or leading?
- Does the interviewer empathize with the participant in an appropriate manner?
- Does the interviewer present him/herself to the participant in a manner which is appropriate for a researcher?

At the end of the interview, the evaluator should ask the participant for his/her response to the interviewer's technique as well.

Interviewer's notes:

Once you have had feedback from the evaluator and participant, try answering these questions:

- What was the most effective part of your interview technique? Why?
- How could your performance as an interviewer have been improved?
- What was the most difficult thing about conducting the interview?
- In your own research, what will you need to work on to be an effective interviewer?

Finally, once all three of you have had a turn, discuss the content of the interviews:

- What have you learned about your research question from each participant's answers?
- What *kinds of knowledge* have you had access to?

What would you do next?

Another way of improving your technique is to transcribe your first interview. Only highlight one piece of a participant's talk at a time (cover your response and subsequent dialogue with a bit of paper, or use the scroll on a computer screen to isolate one piece of text). Give yourself the opportunity, with the luxury of time and the absence of the participant, to think of your ideal question. Then compare this with the question you actually asked. As your interview technique improves your ideal questions should look more like the questions you actually asked.

Completely unstructured

As we said earlier, one of the most difficult things for students to learn is how to feel comfortable moving away from their interview schedule, to go with the flow of the interview itself. Therefore for students to experience how important this is, it is a useful exercise to practise an interview with no schedule at all.

Pair off in twos. Select one of the following core questions. Student A should use it as your first interview question and then continue the interview for ten minutes. Then swap roles. At the end of the second interview, discuss, say for another ten minutes, what you have learnt about in-depth interviewing.

Topics:

1. Tell me what it is like to be a student.
2. Tell me about your favourite kind of music.
3. Tell me about your favourite holiday.

FIVE

Analysis

Introduction

This chapter illustrates the analytic process in IPA in considerable detail – but it is not intended to provide a definitive account. The existing literature on analysis in IPA has not prescribed a single 'method' for working with data. Indeed, many methods chapters and published papers have been characterized by a healthy flexibility in matters of analytic development. As with many other approaches in qualitative psychology, the essence of IPA lies in its analytic *focus*. In IPA's case, that focus directs our analytic attention towards our participants' attempts to make sense of their experiences.

As a result, IPA can be characterized by a set of common processes (e.g. moving from the particular to the shared, and from the descriptive to the interpretative) and principles (e.g. a commitment to an understanding of the participant's point of view, and a psychological focus on personal meaning-making in particular contexts) which are applied flexibly, according to the analytic task (see Reid, Flowers & Larkin, 2005). Typically, analysis has been described as an iterative and inductive cycle (Smith, 2007), which proceeds by drawing upon the following strategies:

- The close, line-by-line analysis of the experiential claims, concerns, and understandings of each participant (e.g. see Larkin, Watts & Clifton, 2006).
- The identification of the emergent patterns (i.e. themes) within this experiential material, emphasizing both convergence and divergence, commonality and nuance (e.g. see Eatough & Smith, 2008), usually first for single cases, and then subsequently across multiple cases.
- The development of a 'dialogue' between the researchers, their coded data, and their psychological knowledge, about what it might mean for participants to have these concerns, in this context (e.g. see Larkin et al., 2006; Smith, 2004), leading in turn to the development of a more interpretative account.
- The development of a structure, frame or gestalt which illustrates the relationships between themes.

- The organization of all of this material in a format which allows for analysed data to be traced right through the process, from initial comments on the transcript, through initial clustering and thematic development, into the final structure of themes.
- The use of supervision, collaboration, or audit to help test and develop the coherence and plausibility of the interpretation.
- The development of a full narrative, evidenced by a detailed commentary on data extracts, which takes the reader through this interpretation, usually theme-by-theme, and is often supported by some form of visual guide (a simple structure, diagram or table).
- Reflection on one's own perceptions, conceptions and processes (e.g. see Smith, 2007).

Within this repertoire of strategies, there is considerable room for manoeuvre. The route through them will not be a linear one, and the experience will be challenging. At the outset, it is important to bear in mind that 'doing' such analysis is inevitably a complex process. It may be an experience which is collaborative, personal, intuitive, difficult, creative, intense, and conceptually-demanding. Our own commitment to IPA stems from the fact that it can often be a uniquely interesting, insightful, and rewarding process.

There is no clear right or wrong way of conducting this sort of analysis, and we encourage IPA researchers to be innovative in the ways that they approach it. However, we are also aware that readers encountering IPA for the first time will need more than general principles. This chapter sets out to provide a heuristic framework for analysis, which draws on many of the processes, principles and strategies typically employed by IPA researchers. It draws them together in a structure which is intended to be flexible, but which is nonetheless sufficiently clear to enable first-time IPA researchers to find their way through the process. We also hope that it will provide more experienced analysts with some food for thought. In the latter part of the chapter we discuss levels of interpretation and how to take the analysis deeper and we also discuss working with larger samples.

In this chapter, we have maintained a practical focus on processes and strategies for analysing data, and for organizing and developing that analysis. But more experienced researchers may wish to move back and forth between this chapter and the material in Chapter 2, as a prompt for further developing the focus of these processes and strategies, within the conceptual framework of IPA.

The processes outlined below are designed to encourage a reflective engagement with the participant's account. Inevitably, the analysis is a joint product of the participant and the analyst. Although the primary concern of IPA is the lived experience of the participant and the meaning which the participant makes of that lived experience, the end result is always an account of how the analyst thinks the participant is thinking – this is the double hermeneutic described in Chapter 2. Thus the truth claims of an IPA analysis are always tentative and analysis is subjective. At the same time that subjectivity is dialogical, systematic and rigorous in its application and the results of it are available for the reader to check subsequently.

There is inevitably some tension in writing about analysis. In reality, analysis is an iterative process of fluid description and engagement with the transcript. It involves flexible thinking, processes of reduction, expansion, revision, creativity and innovation. Overall, the analytic process is multi-directional; there is a constant shift between different analytic processes. As such, analysis is open to change and it is only 'fixed' through the act of writing up. This dynamism is at the heart of good qualitative analysis and is what makes it both exhilarating but also demanding. It is also what allows for the possibility of a creative insightful and novel outcome. One important element of this involves moving between the part and the whole of the hermeneutic circle as is outlined in Chapter 2. This little bit of text is looked at in the context of the whole transcript; the whole interview is thought of from the perspective of the unfolding utterances being looked at.

All of this can seem daunting to the novice qualitative researcher. Therefore, to make the process more manageable for those new to IPA, we present a step by step, somewhat unidirectional guide to conducting IPA analysis. In this way we hope to minimize the potential for the novice analyst's anxiety and confusion and reduce the risk of feeling overwhelmed by the process of analysis. These steps are not analogous to steps in a recipe – each offers a different vantage point on, or way of thinking about, the data that we are interested in. However, one of the main roles in supervizing IPA studies involves fostering a sense of manageability in the analytic process and it is this sense of 'order' which these steps hope to engender. We have found that this set of steps, or something like it, has worked for students we are supervizing, gives them a sense of confidence and competence, and is likely to facilitate the development of an analysis which is 'good enough'. And in our view this is important while we are still in the early stages of introducing qualitative research within psychology. So we would advise the novice embarking on an IPA study for the first time to begin by working closely with the suggested set of steps, and then to adapt them when and where they feel comfortable to do so, and the data require it. And remember – the process of analysis gets easier with experience. The first analysis attempted will probably seem the most difficult.

For those more experienced? Someone said to us recently that it was only now that he had completed an IPA study by following the steps suggested in an IPA chapter that he realized that IPA wasn't about following a set of steps! What he meant was that you need to follow guidelines when you are doing IPA for the first time. At this stage confidence is gained by having a set of procedures mapped out quite closely. But the process of following the steps also helps you to realize what underlies those steps. Thus, once one has mastered those steps and seen the finished product, one is more able to recognize that IPA is an approach and sensibility, as much a way of thinking about and seeing, as of doing something. And so for your next study you may develop a way of working which is true to the principles of IPA and yet moves considerably away from the steps given here. This is the spirit in which we present these 'steps to analysis'.

We start with a description of the process of analysis for a single case. Given IPA's idiographic commitment, we almost always work in this way – analysing the first case in detail, moving to the second case and doing the same, then moving to the third case, and so on. It can be helpful to start with the interview that you found to be most detailed, complex and engaging.

Step 1: Reading and re-reading

The first step of an IPA analysis involves immersing oneself in some of the original data. In most IPA studies this would be in the form of the first written transcript and this stage of the process would involve reading and re-reading the data. If the transcript is from an interview, it is helpful to listen to the audio-recording at least once while first reading the transcript. Imagining the voice of the participant during subsequent readings of the transcript assists with a more complete analysis.

This first stage is conducted to ensure that the participant becomes the focus of analysis. Because most people are used to reading and summarizing complex information often in very short periods of time, this part of the process is about slowing down our habitual propensity for 'quick and dirty' reduction and synopsis. Part of this might actually involve recording some of your most own powerful recollections of the interview experience itself, or some of your own initial, and most striking, observations about the transcript in a notebook, in order to help you to bracket them off for a while. Sometimes the process of beginning analysis is accompanied by a feeling of being over-whelmed by ideas and possible connections – it can help to reduce the level of this 'noise' by recording it somewhere, thus allowing your focus to remain with the data. You can always come back to these notes later, safe in the knowledge that your first impressions have been captured.

To begin the process of entering the participant's world it is important to enter a phase of active engagement with the data. Repeated reading also allows a model of the overall interview structure to develop, and permits the analyst to gain an understanding of how narratives can bind certain sections of an interview together. Chronological accounts, for example, may provide an overall structure for the interview. Yet, embedded within these 'life stories' there may be a pattern of shifting from generic explanations to the specificities of particular events (e.g. someone explaining their experiences of being in a wheelchair may move from their overall life history to talking about specific thoughts and feelings concerning recent events which occurred in the days preceding the interview). This reading also facilitates an appreciation of how rapport and trust may build across an interview and thus highlight the location of richer and more detailed sections, or indeed contradictions and paradoxes. As discussed in the previous chapter, the general flow, or rhythm, of an interview tends to shape the tone of a transcript from the broad and general (in the beginning) to the specific micro-details of events (towards the middle of the interview), to some kind of synthesis or 'wrapping up' at the end of the interview.

Step 2: Initial noting

This initial level of analysis is the most detailed and time consuming. This step examines semantic content and language use on a very exploratory level. The analyst maintains an open mind and notes anything of interest within the transcript. This process ensures a growing familiarity with the transcript, and, moreover, it begins to identify specific ways by which the participant talks about, understands and thinks about an issue. In fact Steps 1 and 2 merge as you will, in practice, start writing notes on the transcript as you start reading, and further exploratory notes or comments can be added with subsequent readings.

This is close to being a free textual analysis. There are no rules about what is commented upon and there is no requirement, for example, to divide the text into meaning units and assign a comment to each unit. Your aim is to produce a comprehensive and detailed set of notes and comments on the data. Some parts of the interview will be richer than others and so will warrant more commentary. It is important to conduct a close analysis in order to avoid the sort of superficial reading which we engage in so often (leading to commenting only on what we expect to see in the text). The analyst should be concerned as much with the process of engaging with the transcript as with the outcome (i.e. legible comments to be used for the next step of analysis). At the centre of the account you develop through initial notes, there is likely to be a descriptive core of comments, which have a clear phenomenological focus, and stay close to the participant's explicit meaning. This is likely to describe the things which matter to them (key objects of concern such as relationships, processes, places, events, values and principles) and the meaning of those things for the participant (what those relationships, processes, places, etc. are *like* for the participant). Developing from this, and alongside it, you will find that more interpretative noting helps you to understand how and why your participant has these concerns. This involves looking at the language that they use, thinking about the context of their concerns (their lived world), and identifying more abstract concepts which can help you to make sense of the patterns of meaning in their account.

We illustrate this process here in Box 5.1, which contains a short extract from an interview with Jack (name changed), a gay man, talking about his experiences of living with HIV. Jack was diagnosed in his early twenties and was in his mid-twenties at the time of interview. The extract is used to illustrate the multiple ways in which exploratory commenting can be conducted. These are broken down into three discrete processes with different focuses, for the sake of illustration:

- *Descriptive* comments focused on describing the content of what the participant has said, the subject of the talk within the transcript (normal text).
- *Linguistic* comments focused upon exploring the specific use of language by the participant (italic).
- *Conceptual* comments focused on engaging at a more interrogative and conceptual level (underlined).

These ways of exploratory commenting are not intended to be exhaustive or prescriptive but are presented as useful analytic tools which the analyst may wish to employ. In conducting this first and most detailed level of analysis, these discrete ways of doing exploratory commenting should be combined on the same transcript because the links and connections between them are critical to attempting to immerse yourself in the participant's lifeworld and engaging in deep data analysis. You may find it useful to use different coloured pens for the three task areas.

Overall, as you move through the transcript, you are likely to comment on similarities and differences, echoes, amplifications and contradictions in what the person is saying. It is important to engage in analytic dialogue with each line of transcript, asking questions of what the word, phrase, sentence means to you, and attempting to check what it means for the participant.

In practice we find the best way to do analysis is with a hard copy of the transcript with wide margins. We use one margin to document the initial comments, leaving the other margin for the next stage – emergent themes (see Box 5.2, pp. 93–95). Conventionally, we have written of this process as moving from the left margin (comments/notes) to the right margin (themes). Firstly, this is just a convention, it doesn't have to be followed in that way and, second, we recently realized that that order had actually come about because Jonathan is left handed and so most naturally moves from left to right! Given that most people are right handed, we are now presenting the sequence the other way round, moving from right margin (initial comments) to left margin (emergent themes).

Descriptive comments

One basic element of exploratory commenting is analysing the transcript to describe content. In general, key words, phrases or explanations which the respondent used are recorded. These understandings of things which matter to the participant (the key objects, events, experiences in the participant's lifeworld) are often highlighted by descriptions, assumptions, sound bites, acronyms, idiosyncratic figures of speech, and emotional responses (for the participant, or for the analyst). This level of initial notes is very much about taking things at face value, about highlighting the objects which structure the participant's thoughts and experiences. As we have seen in Chapter 2, this involves thinking about the participant's experiences in terms of their relationship to the

Box 5.1 Initial comments

	Original Transcript	Exploratory comments
	I: Are you alright to tell me more about that?	
	R: More about that um … don't know if it was, hm … I think that was really because I had, I just I just didn't know who … in lots of ways I didn't know who I was, at that time, in the early days of being diagnosed and coming to terms with it, I couldn't stop thinking about it and um … I had to go through a process of finding out or finding myself again, um, and whilst I was around people that knew me well well, I found it really really well, I found it really really exhausting because, well well maybe they couldn't tell but I I was sure, I was paranoid that that they would know that something was wrong, so I was constantly trying to to be as near to how I imagined myself to being without HIV so … that in itself made it even more impossible, because the more you try to stop thinking about something, then the harder it becomes, you know so …	*Is there an underlying difficulty in articulating something this emotive and complex (repetition of 'I' and 'to')? Clear sense of struggling to articulate some very strong and confusing difficult feelings. Use of 'just' emphasizes his struggle to explain.*

Major issue of questioning self. <u>Who is Jack?</u> Many ways in which self-questioning occurred. <u>Who are you if you're not yourself?</u> Diagnosis and self-questioning are clearly linked? Impact of diagnosis

Critical sense of time frame <u>(these experiences are embedded within time, has he come to terms with it now?)</u>
<u>Maybe ideas like stages or vulnerable periods?</u>

Overwhelmed with thinking about HIV

<u>If something was found what was lost? Who does the finding in finding themselves?</u>
Impact of diagnosis <u>Does diagnosis mean you lose yourself?</u>
Importance of people who knew him <u>What does this say for the importance of social context? Is the self social?</u>

Emphasizing the enormity of the task with repetition of 'really'
Found it exhausting
Hesitant repetitions (well, well and I, I)
<u>Is paranoia an over concern with others' view of self?</u>

<u>'Wrong', the old self was 'right'? Performance. Working to manage people's perceptions of himself.
Some sense of performing, some pivotal loss of authenticity implicit within this, how can you perform yourself? Who is doing the performance? How can a medical procedure lead to this radical sense of being lost?</u>

Tails off
Things were impossible
Internal thinking about himself
<u>Intra-psychic process implied, thinking about thinking, major change in sense of his own mind.</u>
Impact of diagnosis <u>Does diagnosis make you think about thinking? Think about self?</u> |

(Cont'd)

I: And then, these these are your close friends are you thinking about?

R: Close friends, family, anybody, even new people that I'd meet; I just felt that I couldn't, I suppose I felt quite quite worthless because I didn't have the, [sighs] I felt like I'd lost something I couldn't um ... I just found everything so tiring, I couldn't, I didn't have anything to give, I didn't feel that I had anything worthwhile to kind of contribute or you know, the, I don't know, I was just kind of like shell shocked I supposed, you know. [sorry] So ... I don't know if that's answered the ...

I: Are you up, do you see the kind of style of questions that? [yeah, yeah] And again you just, you said some amazing things about a sense of loss, a sense of being worthless or nothing being worthwhile. But ... and are you alright with talking [yeah yeah] [unclear] but what what would you say that you had lost?

Everyone he knew
Begins with sense of people who knew the 'old' Jack but then includes 'new' people. Centrality of others and their thinking about him (all in absence of knowing his status too). It's all in his mind if he hasn't disclosed.
He felt worthless *Repetition of 'I' and 'quite', emphasizing meaning*

Sighs (sharing grief?) He had lost something

He felt everything was tiring
Impact of diagnosis Something is happening which is almost catastrophic, the effects of diagnosis are very broad and much more than medical.
Nothing was worthwhile
It seems strange to think of himself in a relational social way, this isn't about health but about what other people think of him? Deep impact of loss, grief, worth. In the past did he give a lot? What contribution is he talking about?
'Shell shock', first world war, horror, shock. Tremendous sense of difficulty. Impact of diagnosis

Tails off

I check he's OK. A very emotional moment.

R: Ju just er ... what had I lost? Um ... I'd lost the feeling that I had all the time in the world kind of, that I'd um ... I'd realized that at some point I was going to die, whether that was going to be 15, 20 how ever many years, I'd realized that that could happen and er ... I think that's what I'd lost. Um ... but also I'd lost my self esteem and my self respect as well because, I'm not sure why um, well because of the relation-ship that I was in but also because of the diagnosis defi-nitely um ... it was big big part of it.

Questions self, as if trying to get past the magnitude of his feelings and into the reality? Is he lost in thought and emotion at my questions?
A sense of emerging clarity in what had been lost. Language is clearer, easier and safer to say.

Impact of diagnosis Loss of future, sense of mortality. Life expectation, dramatically reduced
Idea of middle age and old age taken away? A new sense of the certainty of uncertainty in terms of mortality?
Clear awareness of much of the loss being in his own thinking about himself. His own beliefs about his worth.
Deep implications of questioning his self.

Lost self esteem Lost self respect

Is he confused about what he went through and its cause?
Cause was partly his relationship (where he became infected) Cause was also diagnosis

Diagnosis major impact
Realizes multiple causes to this, the relationship and the diagnosis. Holistic and major impact of diagnosis.

important things which make up their world. These descriptive exploratory comments could be as simple as 'story of negative experience', or indeed 'wheelchair' (i.e. just identifying something that matters). As your analysis develops, you are likely to be able to develop richer accounts of the meaning of these objects. For example, 'wheelchair' may become 'wheelchair meaning sustained independence vs wheelchair meaning visibly unwell'. From the interview with Jack we see how the comment 'Major issues of questioning self' is generated from the development of comments in the sequence of text around 'in lots of ways I didn't know who I was, at that time'.

Linguistic comments

Another key element of exploratory noting is concerned with language use. The analyst focuses upon how the transcript reflects the ways in which the content and meaning were presented. At times the language use and the content seem clearly interrelated and this is worth highlighting in the process of writing initial notes. Among things the analyst can attend to are: pronoun use, pauses, laughter, functional aspects of language, repetition, tone, degree of fluency (articulate or hesitant). Metaphor can be a particularly powerful component of the analysis here because it is a linguistic device which links descriptive notes (such as 'wheelchair') to conceptual notes (such as 'independence vs illness'). Jack's use of 'shell shock' as a metaphor for describing the impact of his HIV diagnosis is a good example of this. It's an explicit claim which he makes, but it opens out the potential for discussion of a range of more conceptual meanings – horror, trauma and shock on a massive scale, for example.

Conceptual comments

The third level of annotation, illustrated in Box 5.1, is more interpretative. It deals with the transcript data at a conceptual level. Conceptual coding may often take an interrogative form. This is particularly the case during the earlier stages of analysis, when one does not yet have a detailed overview of the data, and where each interesting feature of a participant's account may prompt further questions. Try not to worry about this. Ultimately, some questions may lead nowhere. Others may lead you back to the data, where re-analysing the data, or reflecting on what the codes might mean, may well furnish you with some tentative answers. Other questions still will lead you to work at a more abstract level.

As the comments underlined in Box 5.1 would suggest, this often represents a move away from the explicit claims of the participant. Conceptual annotating will usually involve a shift in your focus, towards the participant's overarching understanding of the matters that they are discussing. This stage asks a lot of the analyst. It takes time – for discussion, reflection, trial-and-error, and refinement of your ideas. An example of this sort of conceptual development might be the movement away from focusing on the particular meanings of specific instances of difficulties with relationships (with friends, partners, or employers), which have stemmed from Jack's HIV status, and moving towards an account of the increasing feeling of isolation which may be common to them all.

There is often an element of personal reflection to conceptual coding, too. The interpretations which you develop at this stage will inevitably draw on your own experiential and/or professional knowledge. You might usefully think of this as a Gadamerian dialogue (of the kind discussed in Chapter 2), between your own pre-understandings, and your newly emerging understandings of the participant's world. At times, it may be helpful to draw upon your own perceptions and understandings, in order to sound out the meaning of key events and processes for your participants.

So, for example, where the text has been annotated with 'Major issue of questioning self,' in Box 5.1, we may consider times when we have asked ourselves questions about who we are. Is it within the realm of our own experience to have doubted this, and to have said something like, 'In lots of ways I didn't know who I was'? If we have experienced anything like this, then we might usefully dwell upon it for a moment, and think about the life events that led us there. If this is beyond our experience, then we might ask what it tells us about the magnitude of such an expression, for the participant. In these ways, conceptual annotation is often not about finding answers or pinning down understandings; it is about the opening up of a range of provisional meanings.

On another level, the analyst may think logically about the construction of such an expression. Thus, a reasonable question to ask is 'Who was the participant if they weren't 'themselves?'. This may lead the analyst to think about the role of agency and identity, to think about the multiplicity of 'selves' that such a tiny but powerful expression implies. Similarly, broader interrogation may lead to questioning the relationship between diagnosis and this potential sense of fragmentation of self.

Other notes, for example, refer to a critical sense of time frame. For example, the phrase 'at that time, in the early days of being diagnosed and coming to terms with it', is annotated with '(these experiences are embedded within time, has he come to terms with it now?) Maybe ideas like stages or vulnerable periods?'

Thus, by beginning with the face value of the participant's words, the analyst can see that there are clear differences for the participant between 'the early days' and the present, or maybe even an imagined future. The analyst can question the implication that the participant has now 'come to terms with it', and indeed wonder how this may have been achieved. At times this kind of exploratory comment may feel like stretching the interpretation pretty far. However, these provisional conceptual questions can really add depth and sophistication to the analytic process. As long as the interpretation is stimulated by, and tied to, the text, it is legitimate. And as long as everything is documented, the stronger interpretative claims can be checked later at various points in the analytic procedure. This more questioning and abstract style of thinking is critical in moving the analysis beyond the superficial and purely descriptive. As we stated in Chapter 2, IPA is avowedly interpretative, and the interpretation may well move away from the original text of the participant. What is important is that the interpretation was inspired by, and arose from, attending to the participant's words, rather than being imported from outside.

The potential for this type of reflexive engagement will differ from analyst to analyst and from project to project. Although we suggest here that the analyst uses themselves and their own thoughts, feelings and experiences as a touchstone, this is complex. It is important to remember that the analysis is primarily about the participant, not oneself. One is using oneself to help make sense of the participant, not the other way around. If you start becoming more fascinated by yourself than the participant, then stop, take a break – and try again!

Deconstruction

It may be helpful, occasionally, to employ strategies of de-contextualization to bring into detailed focus the participant's words and meanings. For example, one possibility is to fracture the narrative flow of the interview by taking a paragraph and reading it backwards, a sentence at a time, to get a feel for the use of particular words. In this way, you are attempting to avoid focusing upon simplistic readings of what you think the participant is saying, or following traditional explanatory scripts, and so getting closer to what the participant is actually saying. Paradoxically such de-contextualization helps to develop an appreciation of the embedded nature of much of the participant's report and can emphasize the importance of context within the interview as a whole, thus helping one to see the interrelationships between one experience and another.

Overview of writing initial notes

The example from Jack's interview provides a sense of both the complexity and open-ended nature of exploratory commenting. The approach presented here is not meant to be prescriptive or exhaustive; many other ways of doing initial noting are also possible. Critically, the *process* of engaging with the data is almost as important as the actual physical task of writing on the transcript itself. We have presented the different elements of writing initial notes as occurring in parallel. Alternatively you can first try working on a section of the transcript with descriptive comments, and then go back and examine it with a linguistic focus. Finally, you could annotate the section with conceptual comments.

Here are two other ways of doing exploratory noting which could be used alongside the strategy we have already explored:

- Going through the transcript and underlining text which seems important. Then for each piece of underlined text, attempt to write in the margin an account of why you think it was underlined and therefore important.
- Free associating from the participant's text, writing down whatever comes into your mind when reading certain sentences and words.

These differing approaches share the fluid process of engaging with the text in detail, exploring different avenues of meaning which arise, and pushing the analyses to a more interpretative level.

Step 3: Developing emergent themes

Although the interview transcript retains its central place in terms of data, it will be clear that through comprehensive exploratory commenting, the data set will have grown substantially. Not only does the analyst have, by now, a very familiar model of the interview itself, but also has an additional level of potentially important, yet still provisional, notes. It is this larger data set that forms the focus of the next stage of analysis – developing emergent themes.

In looking for emergent themes, the task of managing the data changes as the analyst simultaneously attempts to reduce the volume of detail (the transcript and the initial notes) whilst maintaining complexity, in terms of mapping the interrelationships, connections and patterns between exploratory notes. This involves an analytic shift to working primarily with the initial notes rather than the transcript itself. However, if exploratory commenting has been done comprehensively it will be very closely tied to the original transcript.

Analysing exploratory comments to identify emergent themes involves a focus, at the local level, on discrete chunks of transcript. However, it also involves a recall of what was learned through the whole process of initial noting. Because the process of identifying emergent themes involves breaking up the narrative flow of the interview, the analyst may at first feel uncomfortable about seeming to fragment the participant's experiences through this re-organization of the data. This process represents one manifestation of the hermeneutic circle. The original whole of the interview becomes a set of parts as you conduct your analysis, but these then come together in another new whole at the end of the analysis in the write-up. Relatedly, since the data collection and exploratory comments were very much participant-led or participant-oriented, you may find it difficult to give yourself a more central role in organizing and interpreting the analysis at this stage. Remember, however, the importance of both the I and the P in IPA. At each stage the analysis does indeed take you further away from the participant and includes more of you. However, 'the you' is closely involved with the lived experiences of the participant – and the resulting analysis will be a product of both of your collaborative efforts.

The main task in turning notes into themes involves an attempt to produce a concise and pithy statement of what was important in the various comments attached to a piece of transcript. Themes are usually expressed as phrases which speak to the psychological essence of the piece and contain enough particularity to be grounded and enough abstraction to be conceptual. The focus is on capturing what is crucial at this point in the text but inevitably you will also be influenced by the whole text. Remember again the hermeneutic circle where the part is interpreted in relation to the whole; the whole is interpreted in relation to the part. See Box 5.2 which presents the emergent themes for the piece of transcript in Box 5.1.

As we can see, the themes reflect not only the participant's original words and thoughts but also the analyst's interpretation. They reflect a synergistic process of description and interpretation. Whilst initial notes feel very loose, open and contingent, emergent themes should feel like they have captured and reflect an understanding.

For example, the first emergent theme, *the questioning self*, captures the initial exploratory notes relating to language use and Jack's inability to articulate his struggle to come to terms with his diagnosis, a struggle still perhaps apparent within the interview as Jack attempted to articulate what is going on at this particular time in his life. Similarly, the theme title relates directly to the very content of Jack's talk; his own struggle to understand the changes in himself and his identity following diagnosis. Moreover, within the theme title, the use of 'self' reflects the analyst's interest in what can be called the 'psychological' construct of self. It is not something which Jack explicitly alludes to, but at the same time it is intimately connected to what he does say. Thus the theme brings together a range of understandings relating directly to both participant and analyst.

Along the same lines, *lost self* suggests the disassociation of self implicit in Jack's talk. *Time period* reflects a more abstract, or conceptual way of understanding Jack's talk, relating to the notion of temporality and echoing theoretical models which are often based around 'stages' – note that at this stage it is non-committal about the meaning of time for Jack. It merely notes that time is important, and so this is a good example of a theme which might develop further still through later stages of the analysis. Similarly, note that *coping as a process* and *excessive thinking (rumination)* are theme titles that relate to concepts evident within the psychological literature.

Step 4: Searching for connections across emergent themes

So far you have established a set of themes within the transcript and the themes are ordered chronologically, that is, in the order they came up. The

Box 5.2 Developing emergent themes

Emergent themes	Original Transcript	Exploratory comments
	I: Are you alright to tell me more about that?	
	R: More about that um … don't know if it was, hm … I think that was really because I had, I just I just didn't know who … in lots of ways I didn't know who I was, at that time, in the early days of being diagnosed and coming to terms with it, I couldn't stop thinking about it and um … I had to go through a process of finding out or finding myself again, um, and whilst I was around people that knew me well well, I found it really really exhausting because, well well maybe they couldn't tell but I was sure, I was paranoid that that they would know that something was wrong, so I was constantly trying to to be as near to how I imagined myself to being without HIV so … that in itself made it even more impossible, because the more you try to stop thinking about something, then the harder it becomes, you know so …	*Is there an underlying difficulty in articulating something this emotive and complex (repetition of 'I' and 'to')? Clear sense of struggling to articulate some very strong and confusing difficult feelings. Use of 'just' emphasizes his struggle to explain.*
The questioning self Lost self Time period		Major issue of questioning self. Who is Jack? Many ways in which self-questioning occurred. Who are you if you're not yourself? Diagnosis and self-questioning are clearly linked? Impact of diagnosis
Coping as a process Excessive thinking		Critical sense of time frame (these experiences are embedded within time, has he come to terms with it now?) Maybe ideas like stages or vulnerable periods?
		Overwhelmed with thinking about HIV
Finding the self (process)		If something was found what was lost? Who does the finding in finding themselves?
		Impact of diagnosis Does diagnosis mean you lose yourself?
Relationships as problematic		Importance of people who knew him What does this say for the importance of social context? Is the self social?
Work of managing the self		*Emphasizing the enormity of the task with repetition of 'really'*
		Found it exhausting
		Hesitant repetitions (well, well and I, I)
		Is paranoia an over concern with others' view of self?
The self as performance Diagnosis transforms the self Denial as protecting old self Disclosure as making diagnosis and new self real?		'Wrong', the old self was 'right?' Performance. Working to manage people's perceptions of himself. Some sense of performing, some pivotal loss of authenticity implicit within this, how can you perform yourself? Who is doing the performance? How can a medical procedure lead to this radical sense of being lost?
		Tails off
		Things were impossible
Excessive thinking (Rumination)		Internal thinking about himself
		Intra-psychic process implied, thinking about thinking, major change in sense of his own mind. Impact of diagnosis Does diagnosis make you think about thinking? Think about self?

(Cont'd)

Social relationships as problematic	I: And then, these these are your close friends are you thinking about?	Everyone he knew
		Begins with sense of people who knew the 'old' Jack but then includes 'new' people. Centrality of others and their thinking about him (all in absence of knowing his status too). It's all in his mind if he hasn't disclosed.
	R: Close friends, family, anybody, even new people that I'd meet; I just felt that I couldn't, I suppose I felt quite quite worthless because I didn't have the,	He felt worthless *Repetition of 'I' and 'quite', emphasizing meaning*
Mourning and grief (of self?) Loss – of self?	[sighs] I felt like I'd lost something I couldn't um ... I just found	*Sighs (sharing grief?)* He had lost something
Social relationships as problematic	everything so tiring, I couldn't, I didn't have anything to give, I didn't feel that I had anything worthwhile to kind of contribute or you know, the, I don't know,	He felt everything was tiring Impact of diagnosis Something is happening which is almost catastrophic, the effects of diagnosis are very broad and much more than medical.
Depression?		Nothing was worthwhile It seems strange to think of himself in a relational social way, this isn't about health but about what other people think of him? Deep impact of loss, grief, worth. In the past did he give a lot? What contribution is he talking about?
Shock, depression	I was just kind of like shell shocked I supposed, you know. [sorry] So ...I don't know if that's answered the ...	'Shell shock', first world war, horror, shock. Tremendous sense of difficulty. Impact of diagnosis
	I: Are you up, do you see the kind of style of questions that? [yeah, yeah] And again you just, you said some amazing things about a sense of loss, a sense of being worthless or nothing being worthwhile. But ... and are you alright with talking [yeah yeah] [unclear] but what what would you say that you had lost?	*Tails off* *I check he's OK. A very emotional moment.*

Grief and mourning of expected self	R: Ju just er ... what had I lost? Um ... I'd lost the feeling that I had all the time in the world kind of, that I'd um ... I'd realized that at some point I was going to die, whether that was going to be 15, 20 how ever many years, I'd realized that that could happen and er .... I think that's what I'd lost. Um ... but also I'd lost my self esteem and my self respect as well because, I'm not sure why um, well because of the relation-ship that I was in but also because of the diagnosis defi-nitely um ... it was big big part of it.	*Questions self, as if trying to get past the magnitude of his feelings and into the reality?Is he lost in thought and emotion at my questions?*
		A sense of emerging clarity in what had been lost. Language is clearer, easier and safer to say.
Loss of future/expected self		Impact of diagnosis loss of future, <u>sense of mortality. Life expectation, dramatically reduced</u>
		<u>Idea of middle age and old age taken away? A new sense of the certainty of uncertainty in terms of mortality?</u>
Ruminative thinking		<u>Clear awareness of much of the loss being in his own thinking about himself. His own beliefs about his worth.</u>
		<u>Deep implications of questioning his self.</u>
Loss of self esteem		Lost self esteem Lost self respect
Diagnosis as transforming the self		Is he confused about what he went through and its cause?
		Cause was partly his relationship (where he became infected) Cause was also diagnosis
		Diagnosis major impact
		<u>Realizes multiple causes to this, the relationship and the diagnosis. Holistic and major impact of diagnosis.</u>

next step involves the development of a charting, or mapping, of how the analyst thinks the themes fit together.

Once more, this level of analysis is not prescriptive and the analyst is encouraged to explore and innovate in terms of organizing the analysis. Not all emergent themes must be incorporated into this stage of analysis; some may be discarded. This in part depends upon the overall research question and its scope. It is as well to keep an open mind at this stage – in the light of work done on subsequent transcripts, you may come back to an earlier transcript to re-evaluate the importance of some themes. Effectively, however, you are looking for a means of drawing together the emergent themes and producing a structure which allows you to point to all of the most interesting and important aspects of your participant's account.

Here are two basic ways to look for connections:

- Type all the themes in chronological order into a list. Eyeball the list and move themes around to form clusters of related themes. Some themes will act as magnets, pulling other themes towards them.
- Print out the typed list of themes. Cut up the list so each theme is on a separate piece of paper. Then use a large space (e.g. the floor, a large piece of card or a notice board) to move the themes around. This enables one to explore spatial representations of how emergent themes relate to each other. Those themes which represent parallel or similar understandings should be placed together. Those themes which are in opposition to each other would be positioned at opposite poles of a spectrum, or opposite ends of a piece of paper. Like everything else to do with qualitative analysis, this approach will work well for some people and some projects; it will work less well for others.

We will now go through some more specific ways of looking for patterns and connections between emergent themes. Again, just to reiterate, we do not intend to be prescriptive. If these ideas inspire researchers to think of related ways that help the IPA analytic process, we will be happy.

Abstraction

Abstraction is a basic form of identifying patterns between emergent themes and developing a sense of what can be called a 'super-ordinate' theme. It involves putting like with like and developing a new name for the cluster. If we think about Jack's extract, there are a series of emergent themes around the impact of diagnosis: 'excessive thinking', 'mourning and grief', 'depression', 'shock', and 'loss of self esteem'. These can be grouped together under the super-ordinate theme title: 'The psychological consequences of HIV diagnosis'. The super-ordinate theme emerges at a higher level as a result of putting the themes together – see Box 5.3.

Box 5.3   Abstraction leading to the development of a super-ordinate theme

Psychological consequences of HIV diagnosis
Excessive thinking
Mourning and grief
Depression
Shock
Loss of self esteem

Subsumption

This analytic process is similar to abstraction but it operates where an emergent theme itself acquires a super-ordinate status as it helps bring together a series of related themes. Box 5.4 shows how 'Diagnosis as transforming the self' becomes a superordinate theme and brings together a series of clearly related other themes.

Box 5.4   Subsumption leading to the development of a super-ordinate theme

Diagnosis as transforming the self
Loss of self
Mourning and grief (of self?)
The questioning self
The self as performance
Work of managing the self
Denial as protecting old self
Disclosure as making diagnosis and new self real?
Loss of future/expected self

Polarization

It may be worth examining transcripts for the oppositional relationships between emergent themes by focusing upon difference instead of similarity. So, for example, set against the largely negative aspects of 'Diagnosis transforming the self', was another set of related themes elsewhere, which all detailed the positive aspects of self-transformation associated with HIV diagnois. For example, 're-affirmation of self', 'the constant self', 'rebuilding the self', 'being a better person', 'learning to live fully'. This oppositional relationship may itself then offer a higher level organizing device for the analysis.

Contextualization

A useful way of looking at the connections between emergent themes is to identify the contextual or narrative elements within an analysis. Attending to temporal, cultural and narrative themes in a proactive manner is useful as they frame many of the more local understandings presented within an interview. Because a transcript is shaped by the participant's narrative, it may be useful to highlight constellations of emergent themes which relate to particular narrative moments, or key life events. These may be dispersed across the transcript. For example, within the interview with Jack there is a series of critical 'events': the moment of diagnosis, his retrospective accounts of the moment of infection, his first disclosure of his status to a friend, his first visit to a support group, his first sexual interaction as an HIV-positive man, his disclosure to his family. Therefore it would be possible to organize the emergent themes in terms of the temporal moment where they are located.

Numeration

Sometimes we might be interested in taking account of the frequency with which a theme is supported. This is definitely not the only indicator of its importance, and should not be over-emphasized – after all, a very important theme, which clearly unlocks a further set of meanings for a participant, may sometimes be evidenced only once (e.g. perhaps *shell shock* could be one of these for Jack). However, numeration can be one way of indicating the relative importance of some emergent themes. Put simply, it reflects the frequency with which emergent themes appear throughout the transcript. Although at first this may appear unusually quantitative, it can also be thought of as a patterning within the emergent themes. If the interview style was particularly open-ended and unstructured, it makes sense to think of the frequency with which emergent themes appear as one (though not the only) indication of their relative importance and relevance to the participant.

Function

Emergent themes can be examined for their specific function within the transcript. For example, the interplay of meanings illustrated by organizing themes by their positive and negative presentation may be interpreted beyond what the participant presents in terms of their meaning, and rather as a distinct way of presenting the self within the interview. Thus, negative aspects of self-transformation following diagnosis can be seen as serving to position Jack as a 'victim' of circumstance (eliciting sympathy and care from the listener), while positive themes relating to 're-assertion of self' can be seen as a means of positioning himself as a 'survivor', or 'hero', within the narrative (eliciting praise and positive affect from the listener).

Although, at face value, this kind of analysis seems again to pull away from the focus upon the participant and their thinking, it also enables a deeper interpretation of the data. The function of the language use is inevitably deeply intertwined with the meaning and thoughts of the participant. Clearly this type of analysis is drawing on ideas from discourse and narrative analysis but here they are coupled with a commitment to the experiential. For us, these narrative positionings represent a part of the nexus of the self for Jack and in one sense he can be said to own them as opposed to them owning him. In reality of course the relationship is more complex – both/and rather than either/or.

Bringing it together

The above strategies are clearly not mutually exclusive. Use ones that work for you and the material you have. Organizing themes in more than one way can itself be creative and push the analysis to a higher level. Once the process of exploring patterns and connections has ceased and the analyst feels comfortable with the outcome, it is important to make notes about how this key stage of analysis was conducted. Indeed you may find it helpful to keep a research diary along the way, regularly recording descriptions of the analysis process and commentaries on your analytic work.

Next, the analyst should attempt a graphic representation of the structure of the emergent themes. This may be done through the creation of a table or figure, or the researcher may find other devices helpful. This can be useful in looking to the gestalt that has emerged from the analytic process. Box 5.5 illustrates an abridged table of emergent themes for one participant from a project looking at the psychological impact of back pain (for more details, see Smith and Osborn, 2008). It shows the development of three super-ordinate themes that emerged from the analysis, with the themes under each one. It is useful to annotate each theme with the page/line on which it is located and a few key words from the participant, to remind you later of the source of the theme.

Some other processes to help analysis

Compiling transcript extracts to make files of emergent themes.   To help with local analysis, sometimes it can be useful to construct files of transcript extracts. For each emergent theme open a new Word file, name it with the theme title, and paste all the relevant transcript extracts into this file identified in some way – e.g. with the transcript line number. Obviously, depending on the frequency of each emergent theme, the length and volume of such files will vary. This process can help one look at the internal consistency, relative broadness, or specificity, of each emergent theme. It can also help develop the local analysis of particular themes.

Commenting and thematizing on the computer.   So far we have been advocating working primarily with hard copy material. Some people are now moving

Themes	Page/line	Key words
Living with an unwanted self		
Undesirable behaviour ascribed to pain	1.16	It's the pain
Struggle to accept self and identity	24.11	who am I?
Unwanted self rejected as true self	24.24	hateful bit
Conflict of selves	7.11	me, not me
A self that cannot be understood or controlled		
Lack of control over self	24.13	can't help
Rejection of change	1.7	still the same
Avoid implication	10.3	no different
Undesirable feelings		
Shame	5.15	disgusting
Anger and pain	24.9	snappy
Lack of compassion	6.29	don't care

to conducting the whole of this process on the computer. We would not necessarily recommend this to the novice researcher unless this is very close to one's normal working practices. However, if you do work this way, it is possible to set up a series of columns indicating the flow of the analysis, in one direction, from the original transcript to the final super-ordinate themes, either for sections of text or for the whole manuscript.

Step 5: Moving to the next case

It is possible to write up a single case as case study report. However, more usually a project involves more than one case. So the next step involves moving to the next participant's transcript or account, and repeating the process. Here it is important to treat the next case on its own terms, to do justice to its own individuality. This means, as far as is possible, bracketing the ideas emerging from the analysis of the first case while working on the second. This is, of course, in keeping with IPA's idiographic commitment. During this process, you will inevitably be influenced by what you have already found (and in hermeneutic parlance therefore your 'fore-structures' have changed). However there is an important skill in IPA in allowing new themes to emerge with each case. The rigour of systematically following the steps outlined should ensure that there is scope for this to happen. This then continues for each subsequent case.

Step 6: Looking for patterns across cases

The next stage involves looking for patterns across cases. This usually means laying each table or figure out on a large surface and looking across them. What connections are there across cases? How does a theme in one case help illuminate a different case? Which themes are the most potent? Sometimes this will lead to a reconfiguring and relabelling of themes. This can be a particularly creative task. Often it helps the analysis to move to a more theoretical level as one recognizes, for example, that themes or super-ordinate themes which are particular to a individual cases also represent instances of higher order concepts which the cases therefore share. Some of the best IPA has this dual quality – pointing to ways in which participants represent unique idiosyncratic instances but also shared higher order qualities. The final result of this process can again be presented in a number of ways – for example it could be in the form of a graphic, but in this case showing connections for the group as a whole. Most usually it has been in the form of a table of themes for the group, showing how themes are nested within super-ordinate themes and illustrating the theme for each participant. See Box 5.6 for an abridged example taken from Pnina Shinebourne's project on the experience of addiction (in prep).

Box 5.6   Master table of themes for the group

A. Focus on addiction

Addiction as an affliction

Katherine: Addiction is like you have this big boil here and it's like full of poison	line 682
Tracey: I am on the floor, pissed and throwing up and crying	178–179
Susie: The paranoia and the fear every time I woke up without knowing where I've been	284–285
Meera: Just normal everyday things like bathing, like cooking. Didn't bother to eat properly	218–219
Claire: This feeling of complete despair … The only way I can deal with this is if I could kill myself	291–292

Intensity of engagement in addictive behaviours

Claire: I can't stop until there's nothing left or until I pass out	131–132
Meera: Was all all consuming as well, the alcohol consume me	44
Susie: I walked around with a bottle of vodka everywhere I went. I couldn't survive	259
Tracey: All I wanted was cocaine. I didn't give a shit about friends or anything	263
Katherine: I still force it into my body. My body tried to tell me no but I still do it	33–34

Addiction as support
Susie: My first, my only love which was drugs and alcohol   241
Meera: I drink alcohol sometimes to enhance whatever I am feeling   568–569
Julia: I didn't feel safe to face it sober, I mean it is also crutches   199
Claire: The way I got over that was to have a drink, it   70–71
made me more confident

B. Focus on self

Perception of self
Claire: I'd always kind of hit myself down for it, like   590–591
this isn't good enough
Susie: Felt I'm not good enough 'cause I always   304–305
compared myself to other people
Katherine: I never really liked myself in my life I   495
was never good enough
Tracey: Thoughts like oh I'm worthless or no one cares about me   537
Julia: I just wanted to block emotions   42

C. Focus on relationships

Dynamics of relationship in the family
Katherine: My mother had me on anti depressants when   44
I was very young ... my mother was an addict
Claire: My dad was an alcoholic but I didn't really see   60–61
him as one ... and then he left
Julia: I am like my mother ... I think we both had cycles of depression   177–178
Susie: My brother is an alcoholic, would get in to fights, we   290
colluded with each other
Tracey: I am so drunk and unable to look after the little one,   204–205
my older one has to look after the younger

Patterns of Relatedness
Katherine: I thought I was using men when I slept with   38–40
them ... I think because I was sexually abused
Claire: I had disastrous relationship with men all my   71–72
life ... always been like my father
Julia: People pleasing .... trying to live up to what everybody   97
else thinks of you
Susie: Careaholic, looking after everybody   70–71
Tracey: I like to take care of other people 'cause it gives   610–611
me a sense of well being
Meera: I just didn't want to see anybody or do anything   174–175
or have anything to do with anybody

D. Focus on recovery

Recovery as a painful/arduous process
Katherine: Pull myself up brick by brick with my finger   576–577
nails bleeding and taking everything I've got

Susie: It's an ongoing, well it's for the rest of my life	79
Tracey: You can't be mended quickly	838–839
Claire: It takes so long to get back to life	827
Meera: I still think it's early days	527
Support in recovery	
Katherine: For the first time in my life I felt I was around people who understood [in AA meeting]	272–273
Susie: For the first time I felt like I was been emotionally held	376–377
Meera: To have somewhere which is supportive	287
Tracey: When we come to these meetings, you express your feelings	435–436
Claire: It's scary but we're all scared together, we're all doing the same thing [recovering]	382–383
Julia: I go to the gym almost every day because that helps with the depression	173–174
Self-awareness in recovery	
Katherine: I realize now that I never drank because I enjoyed drinking. I drank to escape	30–31
Susie: It's also about trying to, um find out who I am	83–84
Tracey: I want to give up drinking completely really because I know I will slip back into my old ways	84–85
Julia: Figuring out what's going on with me	134
The meaning of recovery	
Katherine I feel like someone took the blinds off me and I can see	633
Susie: It's like starting over again, completely new	45–46
Claire: A completely different way of living	13
Meera: Just to be normal	942
Julia: Staying on top of things … being able to get on with your life a little bit better	33–34
Tracey: In five years time hopefully married and hopefully another little one and no drink	399

Such a group table should have a satisfactory sense of completion capturing the most important things you want to say about the participants and a suitable ordering of those things.

Taking it deeper: Levels of interpretation

One of the current issues in IPA is levels of interpretation. IPA is always interpretative, but there are different levels to that interpretation. In our experience novice researchers tend to be too cautious, producing analyses that are too descriptive. To help researchers dig deeper, we here present an analysis of one short extract which illustrates the different levels which are possible in IPA. This account first appeared in Smith (2004). We can look at this process in terms of the hermeneutic circle discussed first in Chapter 2 and where we also briefly first introduced this piece of analysis.

Up to this point in this chapter we have primarily been moving from the part to the whole – a slow, step-by-step process from the particular to the more holistic. Here we move in the other direction – having analysed a whole transcript, we notice a particularly resonant passage and so move to a deeper, more detailed, reading of the part. One of the exhilarating features of this type of process comes from the realization that often the increasing depth of analysis of the part, the short extract, illuminates and can be seen as integrally related to the analysis of the whole, the complete interview.

The passage comes from a study of the personal experience of chronic benign lower back pain Jonathan conducted with Mike Osborn (Osborn & Smith, 1998). During an interview discussing this, one woman, Linda, says:

> I just think I'm the fittest because there are three girls and I'm the middle one and I thought well I'm the fittest and I used to work like a horse and I thought I was the strongest and then all of a sudden it's just *been* cut down and I can't do half of what I used to do. (Osborn & Smith, 1998: 70)

We would suggest there are (at least) three levels of interpretation consonant with IPA here. First, Linda compares herself with her sisters and this is part of a set of social comparisons Linda makes in her interview. At the next level, we can examine how she uses metaphor. Linda compares herself with a horse and we interpreted Linda as using this metaphor to exaggerate the strength she had in the past in order to emphasize how weak she feels now. Relatedly, it is possible to read 'it's just been cut down' as also having metaphorical weight, as when we read it we saw an image of grass being scythed – a symbol of how flimsy Linda now feels.

The third level of interpretation moves to an even more detailed micro-analysis of the text, and here we offer an extended quote from Jonathan's paper (Smith, 2004):

> Look at the temporal referents in the passage. Linda begins in the present tense:
>
>> I just think I'm the fittest because there are three girls and I'm the middle one.
>
> So initially one might assume Linda is referring to herself now – well yes there probably are still three of them and her birth order won't have changed, but 'I'm the fittest?' Surely she means 'I used to be the fittest'? And indeed she then slips into the past tense:
>
>> And I thought well I'm the fittest and I used to work like a horse and I thought I was the strongest.
>
> This seems to confirm that Linda is referring to a time in the past when she had such great strength and which she has now lost. So how does one explain the apparent contradiction – 'I am the fittest', 'I was the fittest'? Well this seems to go to the heart of the psychological battle for Linda, as her sense of identity is ravaged by her back pain. Thus, on the one hand, Linda acknowledges that she has lost an identity – a strong, proud and autonomous self which has been replaced by an enfeebled and vulnerable self. On the other hand, Linda still 'identifies' with the strong self – so that in part her sense of who she is is still represented by the super-fit being in the image.

Thus Linda is struggling between being taken over by a new self, defined by her chronic pain, and hanging on to an old self, in spite of the pain she is suffering. This struggle is literally illustrated in the temporal changes in the passage itself. (p. 45)

Connecting the part back to the whole, this micro-analysis of a few words thickens our reading of the whole passage and the whole interview in turn. The readings presented above are consistent with and cast further light on the analysis which was emerging from the whole transcript, thus strengthening the confidence with which they are treated.

Finally we will contrast each of the levels of analysis presented so far with a fourth type of interpretation which could be offered and which we think marks a boundary for IPA. Here we continue with a quote from the same paper from Jonathan:

Finally, to clarify the bounds of IPA analysis, I would like to mention a fourth form of interpretation which was offered to me when I presented this analysis at a recent workshop. One participant suggested that a psychodynamic analyst could argue that the horse clearly symbolized Linda's sexual appetite, frustrated by her current condition. This to me illustrates the difference between a grounded IPA reading and an imported psychoanalytic one. I accept that it is possible to interpret the passage in the way suggested, but in order to do so, one is invoking a particular formal extant theory which is then 'read into' the passage. By contrast, I would argue that my account in terms of a struggle for identity is based on a close reading of what is already in the passage, helped by analysis of what the participant said elsewhere in the interview and informed by a general psychological interest but without being influenced by a specific pre-existing formal theoretical position. Thus the IPA and psychodynamic interpretations are coming from two different epistemological perspectives and each has its own explicit or implicit criteria for the validity of a reading. The direction looked to for authority for the reading is different – outside in the case of the psychoanalytic position, inside in the case of IPA.

That distinction has been presented in quite a strong form, for clarity. However, as ever, reality is fuzzier! First, I am not claiming all psychodynamic researchers would work in the way illustrated; I am saying some do. Many psychodynamically inclined researchers do include an analysis based on a close textual reading, foregrounding the presenting account itself.

Secondly, even though most IPA reading is operating close to the text, there is still a reader doing the reading and influenced by all of her/his biographical presence when doing that reading. There is a discipline, however, in staying grounded and attentive, checking one's reading again against the local text itself, and verifying it in the light of the larger text/what is said elsewhere in the interview and one's unfolding analysis.

Thirdly, occasionally one may wish to draw on a more specific theoretical account to assist. With an IPA analysis, this would be clearly marked by a difference in tone and as more speculative because of the distance between text and interpretation.

Fourthly, IPA does systematically make more formal theoretical connections, but this is more usually done after the close textual analysis and guided by that emerging analysis. So, for example, it is possible to connect this reading of pain engendering a struggle for identity with Charmaz' work on chronic illness as a threat to self (Charmaz, 1991). (Smith, 2004: 45–46)

This connects back to Chapter 2 where we stated that IPA involves a middle position between a hermeneutics of empathy and a hermeneutics of suspicion. One starts with a hermeneutics of empathy but it is fine for one's interpretation to become more questioning as long as it is prompted by close attention to the text itself, that is, that it still comes from within rather than from without. The psychoanalytic reading above is clearly coming from without and is an example of Ricoeur's hermeneutics of suspicion. One final complication! It is possible to couple an IPA analysis with one more formally adopting a hermeneutics of suspicion, for example from psychoanalysis, discourse analysis or critical theory. However, it makes sense to present the two readings separately so that the reader can see the different analytic leverage which is going on. For further discussion of how IPA connects with other theoretical approaches, see Chapter 12.

So what makes a 'good enough' analysis? Considering the levels of interpretation offered for the back pain extract, we would expect a student new to IPA to be working at something like the first level, that is, where we were considering the woman's social comparisons. We realize that the third level of interpretation involving the micro-textual analysis of the temporal status of her verb usage is quite sophisticated and we wouldn't expect a novice IPA analyst to be working at this level, though of course it is great if they are. Yet we would hope that as researchers become more confident and experienced that they can push the interpretative side of their work further.

Working with larger samples

Having zoomed in to look at a small piece of text in detail, we now move in the other direction, panning out to consider large sample sizes. We have suggested that for most first student projects, a sample size of up to six will be sufficient for a good IPA study and indeed we would often advocate three as an optimum number for such work. With these sort of numbers, the set of steps outlined above works well. It produces a detailed analysis of each case, resulting in a table or figure capturing the pattern for that particular person. It is then quite manageable to examine the table or figure from each participant to elicit the themes across the group.

If one has a larger corpus, then almost inevitably the analysis of each case cannot be so detailed. In this case, the emphasis may shift more to assessing what were the key emergent themes for the whole group. Here it may even be the case that one identifies emergent themes at case level but holds off the search for patterns and connections until one is examining all the cases together. As you can see, great variety is possible in terms of the detail of the particular analysis and the relative weighting to group and individual. However, even where the analysis is primarily at the group level, what makes the analysis IPA is the fact that the group level themes are still illustrated with particular examples taken from individuals.

For these larger studies, measuring recurrence across cases is important. The key decision here is how, for a particular study, the status of 'recurrent' is defined. So, for example, a decision may be made that for an emergent, or super-ordinate theme to be classified as recurrent it must be present in at least a third, or a half, or, most stringently, in all of the participant interviews. Counting like this can also be considered as one way to enhance the validity of the findings of a large corpus (see Chapter 11). Box 5.7 gives an illustration of establishing recurrence. This indicates whether the super-ordinate theme is present for each participant and then calculates whether it is therefore prevalent in over half the cases.

Box 5.7   Identifying recurrent themes

Super-ordinate themes	Fred	Bill	Sam	Iain	Dave	Present in over half sample?
Diagnosis and transformation of self	YES	YES	YES	YES	YES	YES
Re-assertion of self	YES	NO	YES	NO	NO	NO
Psychological consequences of diagnosis	YES	YES	YES	YES	YES	YES
HIV as catalytic in life change	NO	YES	NO	YES	YES	YES

There is no rule for what counts as recurrence and the decision will be influenced by pragmatic concerns such as the overall end product of a research project (e.g. a PhD thesis may have different requirements from a report for a funding body intended to affect policy). Also the degree of recurrence will be influenced by the level of commenting and theming. A super-ordinate theme expressed at a broad level is likely to have more instances in the corpus than one expressed at a more specific level. It is not that one level is more right than the other; it all depends on how the analysis evolves and what one is trying to do with it.

It is also important to remember that indicating a prevalence for a super-ordinate theme in the group still allows for considerable variation. Different participants may mainfest the same super-ordinate theme in different themes. And the same theme or super-ordinate theme may look very different in how it is evidenced across different participants. Doing IPA with numbers of participants constantly involves negotiating this relationship between convergence and divergence, commonality and individuality.

Having identified a set of criteria which can be used to identify recurrent themes, you may, as a final step, be able to find a way of showing the interconnections between the recurrent group themes graphically. Some of the processes described earlier, such as abstraction and subsumption, can again be helpful here. Studies with larger samples require considerable skill in retaining an idiographic focus on the individual voice at the same time as making claims for the larger group.

<table>
<tr><td>

SIX

</td></tr>
<tr><td>

Writing

</td></tr>
</table>

Introduction

Just as with every other stage of IPA there is not a single right way to write up an IPA analysis. Writing is a creative process, and authors, just like participants, have voices which will come out in the constructing of the account. Here we offer some guidelines to help this process.

There is not even a rule about the sequence for writing each section of the report. Our advice is to move straight from analysis to writing the analysis or results section because this keeps the momentum going. It is also the case that analysis continues into the writing phase so that as one begins to write up a particular theme, one's interpretation of it can develop. However, as intimated, this is not a rule. Sometimes people will wish to start from the beginning of the report and will therefore choose to write drafts of the introduction and method before moving to the results section. And it is also the case that drafts of the introduction and method may have already been constructed at an earlier phase – during or even before analysis. And wherever one starts, good writing almost always involves drafting and redrafting – one's analysis and argument will deepen and become clearer as one works.

Here we will follow the most common sequence by talking about analysis first and then considering the other sections of the write-up in which the analysis is embedded.

Analysis or results section

This is by far the most important section in an IPA write-up. It is where you show your reader what you have found. You have gone through a long and complex process of attempting to make sense of what your participants have said. You may have captured that process with various devices along the way.

However, your reader was not alongside you during that process and therefore you must present your results in a full narrative account which is comprehensible, systematic and persuasive to that reader who is coming to your study for the first time.

As we indicated in Chapter 3, the reader performs a critical role within the hermeneutic dialogue. Your analysis of your participant's sense-making is of no value unless your reader can make some sense of it too! And the only entrée the reader has to the lived experience of the participant is through what you tell them so the write-up is a critical part of the process of doing IPA.

It follows therefore that the results section of an IPA write-up is much more substantial, and much more discursive, than the results section of a typical quantitative report. A large proportion is constituted by transcript extracts whilst the remainder is your detailed analytic interpretations of the text. Your purpose here is twofold: you need to give an account of your data, to communicate a sense of what the data are like, and you need to offer an interpretation of your data, to make a case for what they all mean.

It helps to begin the results with an overview, a concise summary of what was found. This could be a list or an abbreviated table of the group themes or it could be a schematic representation. On the whole these summary devices should be simplified, helping the reader to get a broad sense of the whole, before getting into the detail of the first theme. You can present a more comprehensive table later or as an appendix and often a full model or figure is best left to the end of the results section, as a way of bringing the whole thing together.

Let us assume for now that you have completed an analysis of three participants and you have a table of group themes which has three super-ordinate themes. Not surprisingly the norm then is to take the super-ordinate themes one by one in a logical sequence and write them up in that order.

Taking the first super-ordinate theme, give a short statement outlining what it is. The aim is then to illustrate in detail how it applies to each of the participants in the study. There is considerable variation in how this might be presented and this again depends on both the writer and the material collected. The most orderly sequence is to take each theme in turn and present evidence from each participant to support each theme (case within theme). Sometimes, however, it could be that one favours an idiographic presentation where the participant is prioritized and themes for each person are presented together (theme within case).

The structure of the theme table will itself vary from project to project. Sometimes there will be a clear hierarchy where each super-ordinate theme has a set of nested themes, each applying to each participant. In other projects, the super-ordinate themes may be more powerful as an organizing device and it may be that, by the time of writing up, the important thing is to show how the super-ordinate theme is present for each participant, and that lower level themes have become redundant.

Either way, your task is to present a clear and full narrative account of what you have learnt about the participant. While writing, your thinking will draw on all the material you have accumulated – extracts, initial notes, themes, notes in research journal, and you need to support your account with plenty of quotes from the data. So each time you introduce a new theme or aspect of the data, you need to give evidence for it, from the participant's transcript. Remember both the I and the P of IPA; IPA is a joint product of researcher and researched. You are attempting to capture something of the lived experience of your participant but that inevitably invokes interpretations on your part. One way of looking at the write-up is to think of the extracts from participants as representing the P while the analytic comments on the material form the I. Thus an IPA narrative represents a dialogue between participant and researcher and that is reflected in the interweaving of analytic commentary and raw extracts.

Another reason for presenting extracts from participants is to make your evidentiary base transparent. That way the reader is in a position both to check the evidence for the claims you are making, and to either agree or disagree with those claims. And so, whether the narrative account is organized primarily by super-ordinate theme, theme or participant, in the case where there are only three participants, you would be expected to show evidence for each super-ordinate theme or each theme from each of the cases. Label each extract with the participant's pseudonym or unique identifier as this allows the reader to follow the story of each individual through the analysis. Having written up the first super-ordinate theme, one moves to the second and goes through the same process and then the same for the third one.

As stated earlier, there is not a clear-cut distinction between analysis and writing up. As one begins to write, some themes loom large, others fade, and so this changes the report. Even more commonly, some extracts will seem richer or more illuminating and so one finds oneself needing to say more about them. This is a bit like the magnet metaphor again (Chapter 5) – some extracts portray the theme better than others so they can begin to take centre stage and are then followed by other extracts in support.

It is often a good idea to try to draft a complete write-up quite quickly. Having achieved the whole, one can then go back with more leisure and decide what needs filling out and what can be discarded (you can hear the hermeneutic circle whirring again!). There is also a tendency among novice qualitative researchers for the first draft to be pretty descriptive and to have a lot of quotes from participants but not much analysis from the researcher. With a second draft this balance should shift as one finds oneself wanting to say more and, alongside that, either editing extracts or cutting some out. So the second draft becomes more interpretative, there is more of the researcher's thinking present. However, it is still important that each of the claims made is supported with material from the participants.

Of course another factor which will influence the shape of the analytic write-up is the number of participants. With one participant, there is an expectation of comprehensive detail for that individual. The larger the number of participants, the more selective one will have to be in choosing extracts. We discuss the issue of larger samples at the end of this chapter.

In Section B of this book you will find a number of examples of our own IPA studies written up, so once you have finished this chapter you will then be able to see the process put into practice.

Writing the other sections

Here we give shorter guidelines on the other sections of the write-up.

Title

The title needs to seize your readers' attention whilst informing them of your research project. As such, titles should succinctly capture the essence of your research project. Sometimes it is appropriate to use a short quote from one participant as the main part of the title. However, be careful, you should only do this if it really does encapsulate, as a gestalt, the most important thing you want to say. This is easier if you are writing up a single case study. Often the second part of the title will refer to the methodology you have used. So the title of an IPA study of loneliness might be: 'What it is to be lonely: An interpretative phenomenological analysis'.

Abstract

Your purpose here is to summarize the content of your paper as concisely as you can, for the benefit of someone who knows nothing about what you've done. You should:

1. Define the research question/problem and state why it is important.
2. Introduce the general subject matter.
3. Describe your sample.
4. Outline the data collection and analysis methods, and explain *why* you used them.
5. Summarize what you found.
6. Explain what you think this means, and how it relates to other research or practice.

Introduction

The introduction informs your reader what the project is about and explains the rationale for it. It also provides them with the background information to be able to make sense of what you have done. An introduction is not a literature review, but if you have previously prepared a literature review this can be drawn on. Link your paragraphs together with comments which show how your argument for the rationale is developing. You should:

1. State what your project is about.
2. Say why this is important, academically and perhaps personally, to you.
3. Use the literature concisely and critically to develop some picture of the current state of research in your particular area. Often this will give the flavour of work in the area, and if most of it is quantitative an indication of what a qualitative study can contribute.
4. Identify a particular issue (one which is problematic in, or absent from, recent research) which your study will aim to address.
5. Explain that you are using IPA and give a theoretical rationale for it, outlining how it is appropriate to your aims and to the phenomena under investigation. For a thesis, you will need to state why you have chosen this approach rather than alternative qualitative methods.
6. Finish with a statement outlining your research question. In a sense this is a natural culmination of what has come before. In the light of what you have already said, explain to the reader more specifically what you will be looking at in this study.

Method

This is a fairly straightforward section where you provide a step-by-step guide to what you actually did:

1. Outline how you chose and contacted your sample and what information they were given.
2. Describe your participants.
3. Explain how you developed your interview schedule or other data collection instruments and present the schedule (or it can go in an appendix).
4. Describe the interview process, your interview technique, and how data were recorded and transcribed.
5. Explain the sequence of analysis. The amount of detail depends on the outlet. If you are writing for a journal article, this will need to be short; if for a thesis, this should be more substantial and can include illustrations of the devices you constructed – for example, sections of annotated transcript, tables of themes.

Discussion

Usually in IPA studies the analysis or results section is discrete in the sense that the interpretative account provided is a close reading of what the participants have said. This is done without reference to the extant literature. Then in the discussion the register changes and you place your work in a wider context. Here then you engage in a dialogue between your findings and the existing literature. How does what you have found illuminate or problematize what other studies say? On the other hand, how does some existing work shed light on what you found? Some of the literature you will dialogue with will be found in your introduction. However, it is in the nature of IPA that the interview and analysis will have taken you into new and unanticipated territory. Usually the most exhilarating part of the analysis is that which is completely unexpected – themes that emerged during the process and which were not anticipated by your interview schedule. Therefore you are likely to need to do some extra literature searching after you have completed your analysis in order to frame this new angle that has developed. And with a qualitative write-up, it is fine to introduce some literature for the first time in the discussion. As with the introduction, this engagement with the literature should be selective not exhaustive. There will be a large number of literatures, and then texts within each literature, that you could connect your work to. You need to select some of that which is particularly resonant.

You should also evaluate what you have done. What have you learnt from the process? How might you do it differently now? What are the good points and the less good points in the work? How well does what you have done relate to the research question you started with? How has the research developed? Does your research have implications for practice? What suggestions would you make for future research? Consider what you have done in terms of the emerging criteria for validity in qualitative research – see Chapter 11 where we discuss this in detail. We do not subscribe to a checklist mentality with regard to these criteria. However, we do believe it is important that IPA is conducted properly and that there are a number of ways in which it can fulfil validity criteria.

A few other thoughts

Merging sections

Above, we suggested IPA studies normally separate discussion from analysis, and we would definitely recommend this for new researchers. However, it is possible, once you are more experienced, to choose not to have a clear demarcation between these two sections and rather to relate themes to the extant literature as you are going along. In this case results and discussion are merged into one section.

Horses for courses

Think about why you are writing and who you are writing for. Most IPA novices will be preparing their write-up as a thesis for a degree and usually there will be a handbook which outlines the requirements. These can vary from course to course and institution to institution and it is important to read them carefully.

Alternatively you may be writing up for publication. Here you should think carefully about which journal you intend to send your paper to and seek advice from a supervisor or other experienced researchers. Journals vary in terms of the type of research they publish and their submission requirements. Have a look at some issues of a journal you are considering to see what papers look like and the type of style employed. Can you write in the first person? Does the journal demand a more traditional approach to writing empirical work? For any journal, space is at a premium and there will be word limits, so you will need to write concisely. If you have completed a long thesis, you may also, therefore, have to choose carefully what you will submit for publication. It is often possible to divide a full analysis up into discrete sections so that each can form the heart of a journal paper. For example, it may be that your thesis is 20,000 words long and presents three super-ordinate themes from five participants in a results section of 10,000 words. In that case you may be able to write three papers, each about 6,000 words long, each presenting a different super-ordinate theme in a results section of 3,000 words which is then framed with other material from the introduction, method and discussion. Of course this needs to be done carefully and thoughtfully; having taken the trouble to produce a holistic account of one's participants, one does not want to fragment the analysis so much that it distorts the presentation.

In a journal article, there is less space to give a detailed rationale for choices, a description of the research processes or illustrations of the devices used. There is also less space for personal reflection and an evaluation of the research process. However, in a thesis there is space to do these things and indeed both examiners and institutions often expect this.

Writing up studies with larger samples

So far we have been thinking of studies with small samples, up to six participants, which we recommend for IPA novice researchers. What about writing up projects with larger samples? Here we offer a suggested sequence for doing this. Again this is not intended to be prescriptive but offers a heuristic to help.

Assuming you have a corpus of data from a large number of participants, it is likely that for each recurrent theme, the process of analysis will have produced a file of compiled extracts from the original transcripts: like has been put with like. Because the themes are recurrent they embody most of the participants speaking about their experiences in a similar way. Writing up a narrative account of a recurrent theme (in this case a group-level analysis) is about summarizing, condensing and illustrating what you consider the main themes to be.

Take the file of compiled extracts which constitute the recurrent theme and spend some time reading and re-reading them, thinking about what they say in their totality. Then close the file, or put the papers down. Start writing a summary of what your analysis of the shared experience was about. The focus of this task is to identify the key ways you, the analyst, thinks about the participants' experiences. This should produce some good generic writing, addressing the core of what the participants were thinking and experiencing. By focusing upon the generic you are writing at the level of 'most of the participants reported' or 'many of the participants'. Given that much of the analytic process was pitched at the idiographic level then this writing can feel strange because you cannot fail to be aware of the respective individual experiences which make up the totality of experiences which constitute the recurrent theme, but it is a good way to get the writing going and gain a sense of the whole picture that is necessary when you are reporting on a large number of participants.

The extract in Box 6.1, taken from Flowers, Davis, Hart, Rosengarten, Frankis and Imrie (2006), illustrates how the subject of the writing clearly relates to group level analysis and is here presented as generic text. Within this short extract there is a constant shift between an overall description of the shared experiences and an attempt to relate the findings to the group as a whole, illustrating the part–whole relationship of the hermeneutic circle yet again.

Box 6.1   Short extract from study with large sample

Within the interviews, HIV diagnosis is significant in terms of its deep impact and effect on respondents. The date of receiving positive test results was important for almost all the participants, reflecting the significance of the event in shaping their subsequent experiences and emerging social identity. Most of the participants received their positive HIV result whilst they were still physically healthy, and had no symptoms, although several were diagnosed with HIV-related illnesses. In terms of the psychological impact of diagnosis, there was a shared experience of initial shock and disbelief amongst all the participants. The moment of diagnosis was often described as having an immediate dramatic and negative psychological impact. The participants often struggled to take in the meaning of positive test results and, indeed, their implications for family, partners, children, life expectancy and future health.

As a next step, one moves to fill out some of the idiographic detail within the whole. The first thing to do is to choose a limited number of transcript extracts from the compiled file of extracts for each theme. These should be selected to, in some way, represent the range of views in the group. It may be helpful to select one typical extract which reflects the core of the participants' experiences. Other extracts can also be chosen because they are rich with emotion or metaphor, or elicit empathy, or capture the reader's (and analyst's) imagination. Another way of selecting extracts may be that they are good linking extracts which either illustrate the links between the previous or following recurrent themes, or indeed, also reflect other aspects of the analysis. And once a general pattern has been established, you may wish to choose some atypical extracts to illustrate contradiction and complexity. Of course if you are doing this it needs to be clearly stated.

This process may arouse anxiety. By limiting the number of quotes which may be presented, it forces the analyst/author to be more confident in their account of the analysis and not to rely on (or hide behind) multiple quotes and allowing a plethora of these to do the analyst's work. There is no point in employing a number of short repetitive extracts that all say the same thing. The process of analysis, particularly identifying recurrent themes, does this work. Presenting too many quotes can appear to a reader to be too defensive, implying that the analyst themselves does not trust their own analysis.

At the same time, it is important that the claims you make are accurate and evidenced. Thus if you say that a theme applies in the majority of cases, it is necessary to let the reader see this in some way. One possibility is to give an extended quote from one participant, short extracts from some others, and a cross reference to the theme table which indicates the presence of the theme in the remaining cases. This then allows the reader to check the generality of the claims you are making. Relatedly, you should not overdraw from a small number of participants. Thus overall in the write-up, the corpus should be sampled proportionately, so that each participant is given voice in your account.

Once the extracts have been chosen they should be connected to the generic text outlined above. The researcher should think about how each extract relates to the generic text which has been written. Again, then we are working within the hermeneutic circle, constantly and dynamically moving between part and whole. Moreover, you should think about how the extract illustrates and adds depth to what has already been written. Having linked it to the existing text, then begin thinking at the idiographic level. Ask yourself the following questions. What were the particularities of this participant? What does a reader need to know about this participant to appreciate the extract? What biographical information was important? Is this extract typical or atypical? Introduce the extract and the participant and then begin to think about writing some idiographic analysis. At this stage it is important to return to the original transcript and the original exploratory codes. Attend to the micro-analysis of personal meanings, language use and metaphor described within the exploratory noting. See Box 6.2 which shows an extract from one of our studies (Flowers, Smith, Sheeran, & Beail, 1997) and annotated comments illustrating how the writing works.

Because the task of writing necessarily re-creates the themes as if they were discrete entities it should be clear that the narrative – both the overall narrative of the paper, and indeed the smaller narratives of each recurrent theme – must compensate

Box 6.2 How the writing is working

Comments on writing

It appears that penetrative sex, within a relationship context, sometimes functions as an expression of commitment to that relationship and thus penetrative sex was seen as a kind of milestone. It is in the context of relationship development that penetrative sex comes to function expressively. In this way, in the following extract Peter illustrates a possible function of receptive anal intercourse. Central to his account of the significance of penetrative sex in his relationship, was the assumption that through allowing himself to be penetrated he expressed his total commitment to his relationship and his total self-involvement. This relationship was different from others, because, this time, he did not 'hold a bit of himself back':

Generic writing showing theme at group level

Writing at an abstract conceptual level

Introduction of Peter as a means to access the idiographic

Guidance through the extract closely tied to Peter's life.

Introduce key words used to illuminate Peter's life

It took me a long time to love John and that, I suppose for us to have anal sex it kind of, put the icing on the cake ... a sense, the relationship was complete because sexually we were ... I suppose sexually embarrassed to approach anal sex and then when we did do it, it got that obstacle out of the way. And also I wouldn't ... I've always held a bit of myself back, relationship-wise, because I've been dumped so many times.

---

for this fragmentation. Try and write narratives in ways that re-link themes and relate to the overall analysis. There should be a sense of the narrative developing across both the whole of the paper and indeed the different sections of the paper.

Concluding note

In this chapter we have considered how to write up an IPA study and have discussed different requirements for different outputs and different sample sizes. We have not given many illustrations of what IPA looks like when it is written up because this book has a number of chapters providing examples of what we consider to be good IPA writing. And, indeed, as this chapter marks the last one in the practicalities section, we now move to these worked examples within the next section of the book.

SECTION B

IPA Research

In this section we present some examples of what IPA studies look like once they have been written up. The aim is to give the reader an idea of what the procedures laid out in Section A are leading towards. Each of these studies is from our own work and each represents a study in its own right. We also think these are good examples of IPA. The examples are taken from Jonathan's work on dialysis treatment for kidney failure and on the transition to motherhood (Chapters 7 and 10), Paul's work on gay men's attitudes towards sex and sexuality (Chapter 8) and Michael's work on psychosis (Chapter 9). Thus they also illustrate the breadth of research topics IPA can be used for. Each chapter is also particular in that there are certain features of the IPA approach it demonstrates. These are summarized in a box at the beginning and discussed at appropriate points in each chapter. All names mentioned in the studies have been changed to protect confidentiality. And each chapter also contains a brief guide to some other IPA work in the area. The box below indicates the transcript notation we have used in these chapters.

Transcript notation used in quoted extracts in Chapters 7–10

…	significant pause
[ ]	material omitted
[*her husband*]	explanatory material added by researchers

SEVEN

Health and illness

Introduction

There is now a considerable body of work using IPA to explore issues in the personal experience of health and illness. This chapter will present a detailed illustration from a study by Jonathan examining one patient's experience of the psychological impact of haemodialysis treatment for kidney failure. What emerges from the analysis is the powerful ways in which the disease and treatment can be seen as undermining the patient's sense of identity. This example will illustrate what an IPA study looks like in practice but will also exemplify the approach's idiographic commitment as the data are drawn from a single participant. The particular features of IPA highlighted by this study are summarized in Box 7.1. At the end of the chapter is a short description of some other studies using IPA to explore aspects of health and illness.

Box 7.1 Particular features of this study

- Presents a single case study of one woman's experience. This is consistent with IPA's idiographic commitment and enables a detailed understanding of her particular experience but also an entrée to Warnock's notion of shared humanity.
- Illustrates Heidegger's notion of 'appearing'. One element of the woman's account seems, at the surface, not to be about dialysis at all but its latent meaning appears during the analysis.
- Offers a good illustration of the hermeneutic circle, as part of the material is seen as illuminating the whole and vice versa.
- Works towards a single overarching theme – 'the undermining of identity'.

Dialysis and the undermining of identity: A case-study of the psychological impact of haemodialysis treatment for kidney failure

Background

Haemodialysis is a treatment regime for end-stage renal disease (ESRD). During dialysis, the patient is connected to a machine which extracts, cleanses and replaces the blood, taking over the function of the damaged kidneys. Treatment sessions are long and frequent, commonly lasting three or four hours, three times a week, and can take place either in hospital or, if the patient has their own machine, at home.

Dialysis is a treatment which is protecting the individual from a life-threatening disease. However, research suggests the treatment can have deleterious psychological effects paralleling those associated with the condition it is intended to treat, and high levels of depression are reported (Watnick, Kirwin, Mahnensmith, & Concato, 2003). In health psychology, issues of perception of control are often important theoretical constructs. Dialysis treatment is typically correlated with high degrees of perceived external locus of control, that is to say the patient has very little sense of personal control (Martin & Thompson, 2000), and where internal locus of control is found it is coincident with positive adjustment.

Most existing studies on ESRD are quantitative, isolating discrete independent and dependant variables and modelling relationships between them. While these studies help provide an overview of the topic, their predominance has been at the expense of work which would attempt a more detailed examination of the phenomenology of the individual's response to ESRD – an equally valid psychological enterprise. A small number of studies have helped to provide a richer picture of coping with serious kidney disease, to supplement the broader quantitative canvas.

Reichsman and Levy (1972) followed ESRD patients for four years from beginning dialysis and found that, typically, patients pass through three stages in their response to treatment. A *honeymoon* period lasts up to six months as the patient expresses pleasure at being relieved from the serious acute condition which led to the requirement for dialysis. A period of *disenchantment* follows and this may last for up to a year, as the unrelenting burden of treatment begins to take its toll. During this period the patient may suffer severe depression or attempt to deny aspects of the illness. Finally a period of *long-term adjustment* ensues and the patient begins to accept their illness and the effect it is having on their life.

A grounded theory study by Gregory, Way, Hutchinson, Barrett, & Parfrey (1998) examined the responses of Canadian dialysis patients to their treatment regime. The paper discusses the range of emotional and physical reactions of participants, their attitudes to staff and family, and their beliefs about illness and treatment. The paper makes a useful contribution to the literature, grounded as it is in accounts obtained from patients from which illustrative extracts are provided.

From their content analysis of Swedish hospital haemodialysis petients, Hagren, Pettersen, Severinsson, Lützén and Clyne (2005) elicited three main themes. Participants spoke about the various restrictions dialysis placed on them, for example in terms of work and recreational activities. They described their reactions to the treatment process, for example in terms of emotional distance from the staff. They also pointed to ways of trying to manage the restrictions imposed by dialysis.

The study reported here intends to explore in detail the personal meaning of dialysis. It employs IPA in order to examine the impact of undergoing haemodialysis and how the patient attempts to make sense of it. We argued in Chapter 2 for the idiographic mode of inquiry and the important and neglected role of the single case in psychological inquiry. Thus, in order to capture in detail the experience of dialysis treatment, this chapter reports on one woman's account of it. However, as we argued earlier, the case does not exist in splendid isolation. It can then be used to dialogue with constructs in the existing literature and further, as Warnock (1987) suggests, the particular and general are not necessarily antagonistic. By learning in great detail about the individual case, we are thus better positioned to consider how, at the deepest level, we share much with a person whose personal circumstances may initially seem entirely separate from our own.

Method

Carole is the patient taking part in this study. She is 44 years old and has been dialysing in hospital for six months. Thus, according to Reichsman and Levy's model, she is approaching the end of the honeymoon period. Carole has a partner and two children. All identifying information has been altered in order to protect confidentiality. Carole was approached by the renal-unit counselling nurse to take part in the study and the counsellor explained that the study was being conducted by a researcher who had no connection with the hospital she attended.

Carole was interviewed in hospital before beginning one of her dialysis sessions. The semi-structured interview followed the guidelines outlined in Chapter 4. Examples of questions on the schedule are: 'What do you do when you are dialysing?' 'How does dialysis affect your everyday life?' The interview was audio-recorded and transcribed verbatim and the transcript was analysed according to the procedures outlined in Chapter 5. In this case, a single superordinate theme or gestalt 'undermining of identity' emerged through the analytic procedure. This appeared to make sense of the participant's experience and the analysis is therefore organized in terms of this concept. A small part of the data and analysis first appeared in Smith (1996).

Analysis

'Becoming part of this machine'.   While Carole recounts that she was positive towards the treatment when it began and was first experiencing relief from

the symptoms associated with kidney failure, by six months her attitude has changed dramatically and she vividly captures the physical demands of dialysis:

> I have become a bit more negative about it. [ ] I was really positive about dialysis [*in the beginning*] [ ] but now the feelings I have of, yeah loss of identity, being sort of tethered to one place and to this machine and becoming part of this machine. [ ] You're just so sort of passive in the whole situation cos once the machine is in operation you have to keep still and you can't move much otherwise the damn thing alarms all the time.

The dialysis is physically very restricting, allowing very little movement during the three hour session. The description suggests the confinement of a prisoner or even of a captured animal. The impact on self is clearly an important construct for Carole. The interviewer made no prior reference to identity. Carole herself brings it to the forefront of the discussion. Note also the direction of the process described. The machine is intended as an enhancement or extension of the self. However for Clare it works the other way as she is 'becoming part of this machine'.

The regime is unrelenting:

> At first it was a bit of a novelty and it was treatment that was doing me good. And now it's like as I say just repetitive and time consuming and the worst bit is like going home afterwards and feeling an absolute wreck you know really tired out and fit for nothing and totally drained. And when I go to bed that's my sort of lowest ebb of thinking oh God you know I feel like this again I've got to face it all over again in two days' time.

Thus the regularity of the dialysis treatment means as soon as Carole is over one session she is already preparing herself for the next one.

However, as Carole herself makes clear it is the institutional contextualization of the temporal and spatial entrapment that has the greatest impact on her sense of self:

> When you go on the machine you're a part of it. You haven't got an identity on that floor you know I'm sort of – I make music, got a family, but when I'm on that machine I'm just part of it to be dealt with and you feel tethered to it. You lose your identity.

Thus being attached to the kidney machine seems for Carole to have come to symbolize her becoming part of the bigger machine – the hospital regime. And Carole is explicit in pointing to how the institutional routine serves to undermine her identity. When dialysing, rather than being the person with multiple roles – mother, partner, artist – she perceives herself as becoming a patient, 'just something to be taken off the machine'. The use of 'tethered' continues the suggestion of a convict or trapped animal.

Carole suggests interaction with hospital staff only increases the process:

> You're up there like three times a week and you see the same nurses and so on and see the same other patients and there's only so far you can go with that relationship. But you're seeing them so often and yet it's always on this sort of 'Hello how are you today?' and sort of 'Oh well not all that'. 'Right you're on that machine' and you know (laughs) and you think oh here we go again it's – yeah get's sort of tedious really 'cos I suppose the – because the relationship or the experience doesn't deepen in any way.

Carole is frustrated by the discrepancy between the frequency of interaction and its superficial quality. Although Carole must spend a great deal of time at the hospital the relationship there fails to address her as a person with multiple roles and a full life outside. This is particularly marked because of the unusual nature of the situation. In one sense the nurses (and other patients) have, through the treatment, a considerable degree of physical intimacy with Carole. One does usually associate such familiarity with mutual and progressive disclosure within a close relationship.

Carole is able to put herself in the shoes of the staff and articulates some of the factors which she believes lead to such superficial exchanges:

> It's that jokey way of treating patients sort of to keep you on – there's some sort of level. [ ] They see lots of nasty things [ ] I suppose there's got to be maybe a standing back as well and protecting themselves throughout the day.

However recognition of the protective motivation, both towards self and towards patients, which may be prompting the perceived detachment, does not lessen the alienation Carole feels.

Carole is therefore trapped spatially, temporally and institutionally and perceives herself as having no control over the situation:

> I just hate that being out of control [ ] It's like being tethered to the situation (laughs) and not having the power to change it or to be perhaps a part of it. You just play your part which is quite a passive one and erm get on with it really.

So Carole sees herself as being both part of, and not part of, the system. Although she feels as though she is part of the hospital machine, she also feels detached from both the workings and management of that machine, rather perhaps like an outsider who intrudes occasionally. The net result appears to be induced and self-reinforced passivity:

> It makes you a little bit more passive in that when you come in you think right that's my place and I'll get on with it. You wait till you're told which one to go to and it's a bit like 'you're over there' (laughs) so you go and get yourself settled.

'It's waiting to hurt me'. Carole appears to project her current trepidation about dialysis onto the machine itself:

> Interviewer: How do you think of the machine?
>
> Carole: I think I find it quite harsh [ ] It's stuck up there or down there I think it's sort of waiting for me (laughs) waiting to hurt maybe and keeping me prisoner to it.

A presentation of the machine as malevolent seems to symbolize the entrapment Carole feels. Her sense of passivity and helplessness is turned, in the account, to her being a victim of the machine. Furthermore, while recognizing the good the dialysis machine is doing her, Carole is acutely aware of its invasive nature:

> It's sort of intrusive cos it's got these sharp needles of the thing that attaches you to it [ ] with the needling [ ] It can be quite painful and it's yeah that intrusion of metal into a very soft part of yourself.

And the needling is aversive not just because it is painful but because of the very real effect it is having on Carole's body:

> The arm is changing all the time now the veins are getting bigger and it's getting a bit sorer and it bruises and so you know you've got this part of you that's being um deformed.

Thus, as well as operating at the level of Carole's perception of the social and psychological impact on her, the assault on self is also more literal, manifested physically as Carole witnesses the negative impact of dialysis on part of her body.

Paradoxically, although the machine can be personified as evil, it is also characterized as impersonal. Thus, mirroring the superficial exchanges with the nursing staff, the connection with the machine remains detached:

> Interviewer: I got the impression you don't necessarily know which one you'll be on? [ ]
>
> Carole: No and it's not always in the same place either. [ ] You wait till you're told which one to go to.[ ] I mean I don't mind in different places particularly but it's just coming on to the ward I suppose yeah maybe it would be nice if it was the same one yeah maybe that would be good psychologically.

'When I get it home and it's mine'. The intention is for Carole to transfer to home dialysis some time in the near future and during the interview she alludes to this future a number of times. Much of Carole's view of home dialysis produces a symmetry with her description of hospital treatment and is clearly therefore also a commentary on the current regime. Looking ahead to the difference home dialysis will make, Carole says:

> I'm not dominated by it and dialysing at home would be – I'm still being myself I've still got my identity but I'm just giving myself some treatment that evening.

Again Carole points, unprompted, to the degree to which hospital dialysis undermines her sense of identity. She thinks that once she begins dialysing at home it will become more incorporated into her everyday life, transformed from hospital ritual to 'just … some treatment'. Thus as the centrality of treatment fades, so Carole's sense of being a person separate from a dialysis patient can be foregrounded once more. Again Carole's views of dialysis are captured in how she talks of the machine:

> I think when I get it home and it's mine and I get it on my own premises and it's a part of my life and put in it's place it's little back room then I think yeah it's under my control and I use it.

Ownership, place and control are intimately linked. Rather than Carole having to enter the machine's territory – the hospital – the machine will be installed in Carole's home and will become hers. Consequently the machine (and dialysis) will be relegated to its subordinate status, as it is 'put in its place'. Carole clearly perceives the greater control this will bring her as being a crucial element in asserting her sense of identity. And the assertion of self, and the establishment of agency, is manifested in the resurgence of the active voice in these extracts contrasted with the predominant passive in much of her description of hospital treatment. Carole is clearly looking forward to a time when she perceives herself as being able to take control of her life again.

A further advantage she perceives with the move to home treatment is more flexibility:

> I'm not having to go through all this rigmarole of hospitals and all that it entails. [ ] I can come to it when I want you know when the time I think oh in the evening time right I think I'm ready to dialyse now. [ ] So yeah that's flexible, so you can actually fit things around or the dialysis fits around you.

Thus temporal flexibility also has implications for personal control and agency. Whereas in hospital the person is fitted into an externally controlled schedule, at home 'the dialysis fits around you'.

Finally, dialysing at home will let her get to know the machine on her own terms.

> Carole: I think it would become more user friendly, that it would be my machine and I'd clean it down and maybe get to know it a bit better.
> Interviewer: What would that mean?
> Carole: I think it would mean that I'm not dominated by it. [ ] Have a bit of poke around and see what this and that is.[ ] As long as you're in sort of total control then it'll be better.

This suggests part of the reason Carole feels intimidated by hospital dialysis is her lack of knowledge of the equipment and its workings. At present she is dependent on the staff who operate the machine and her lack of knowledge disempowers her. Once she is dialysing at home, her sense of personal control can also be enhanced by greater knowledge of, and responsibility for, the process.

'I dreamt about the devil'. It is clear from her responses in the interview that Carole is concerned about how dialysis treatment is affecting her and the cumulative account suggests that the impact on self is a particularly important construct for her. Final evidence for the pervasive nature of Carole's concern is suggested by her recounting the following dream during the interview:

> I'd dreamt about the devil that was my latest real bad nightmare where my husband had to wake me up 'cos I was um whimpering he said and I was in a room with my Mum [ ] clinging to one another in a room, small room and my name being called by this um nasty spirit outside the room. And then it would suddenly rush in through the walls and then through my body and out the other side and when it rushed through it was like a nervous um an electric shock. And it was very painful this sort of rushing through. And then it would call my name again sort of very quietly I thought I was safe and it would call – I knew it was going to happen again.

Now consider the parallels between Carole's dream and her experience of dialysis. Box 7.2 shows the text of the dream on the left side, alongside extracts from Carole's account of dialysis but sequenced to enable comparison with the dream.

Box 7.2 Dream and dialysis

The dream

I'd dreamt about the devil that was my my latest real bad nightmare where my husband had to wake me up 'cos I was um whimpering he said and I was in a room with my Mum [ ] clinging to one another in a room, small room and my my name being called by this um nasty spirit outside the room.

And then it would suddenly rush in through the walls and then through my body and out the other side and when it rushed through it was like a nervous um an electric shock. And it was very painful this sort of rushing through.

And then it would call my name again sort of very quietly. I thought I was safe and it would call – I knew it was going to happen again.

The dialysis

It's sort of waiting for me (laughs) waiting to hurt maybe and keeping me prisoner to it. When you come in you think right that's my place I'll get on with it you wait till you're told which one to go to.

It's sort of intrusive 'cos it's got these sharp needles of the thing that attaches you to it. With the needling it can be quite painful and it's yeah that intrusion of metal into a very soft part of your self.

Thinking oh God you know I feel like this again I've got to face it all over again in two days' time.

The parallels are so striking that a reasonable interpretation seems to be that the dream symbolizes Carole's perception of dialysis, pointing to just how extensively dialysis pervades her thinking. She isn't even able to escape it when asleep at night. And the symbolism of the dream serves to highlight how devastating the impact of dialysis treatment is for Carole.

Summary

What clearly emerges from the data is the way in which Carole feels her sense of identity is being undermined by the treatment. She discusses the spatial and temporal restrictions imposed by the dialysis regimen and how this is transformed, through her perception of the institutionalization, to an invasion of self. Thus she seems to consider that her sense of being a person with a set of roles and activities in her life becomes lost in the hospital situation. Carole also feels she has no control over this process. Carole's perception of the invasive nature of the regime is symbolized by her account of the machine itself which is described as both malevolent and impersonal. Carole looks forward to dialysing at home, which she feels will allow the re-establishment of her sense of identity, as the machine becomes incorporated into her everyday life, and she retakes control.

Discussion

Charmaz (1983, 1995) has written extensively about the relationship between chronic illness and the self. Her 1983 paper is based on a study of chronically ill people with a range of different conditions, and she suggests a number of sources of suffering can be discerned in the patients: (i) living the restricted life imposed by chronic illness is perceived to undermine autonomy; (ii) persons with chronic illness receive various discrediting definitions of self, for example, from being talked down to; and (iii) chronically ill people feel they are becoming a burden as they lose their ability to control their life in the way they are used to and had hoped to continue. Charmaz theorizes these sources of suffering in terms of a loss of self.

Charmaz's work provides an important context for the existing study. Her methodology is consonant with this project; she conducted semi-structured interviews with patients but employed grounded theory to analyse the material. The study presented here is able to complement the work of Charmaz by providing an even more detailed picture of how some perceived 'sources of suffering' can lead to a loss of self for this particular person. Thus we have seen how Carole describes the effects of temporal and spatial restrictions and their institutional contextualization on her sense of identity and how she perceives herself to have little control over her situation. Qualitative research can valuably make a two pronged contribution to the psychology of chronic illness by documenting detailed processes occurring in particular individuals and by discerning patterns at the broader level within different patient groups.

Dialysis treatment has, for Carole, come to mean restriction, entrapment, a lack of control, passivity, invasion, and fear. These are not descriptions of the treatment itself, but rather of how Carole construes the meaning of the treatment for her at this stage in time. And it is these particular constructions that play into the undermining of her sense of identity that Carole experiences. Other constructions may be, and are likely to be, different – perceptions of other patients or perceptions of Carole at other times. Indeed she suggests she had a more positive view of dialysis when it began and looks forward to a more positive conception in the future when she begins home dialysis.

This emphasis on the individual making sense of their health predicament points to the possibility of a fertile dialogue with quantitative models in health psychology. Sense-making is crucial to how we have framed Carole's experience of her treatment and it is also central to many of the models used by health psychologists to examine individuals' behaviours. Therefore mixed methods studies combining quantitative instruments like the illness perception questionnaire (Moss-Morris, Weinman, Petrie, Horne, Cameron, & Buick, 2002), and in-depth experiential qualitative methods like IPA, could lead to an enhanced understanding of individuals' reactions to changing health status. See Smith (1996) and Chapter 12 where this potential relationship is discussed more fully.

What implications does this study have for practice? First, a note of caution. This is the case study of only one woman, and, as stressed at the outset, it is not argued that she is necessarily representative. However, the strength of the control construct for Carole and its prominence in the literature, both generally and with regard to dialysis, suggests one can perhaps look to possible implications of the study.

Certainly for Carole the re-establishment of a sense of personal control is a priority and she perceives that this will be facilitated by her change to home dialysis. However, not all patients can dialyse at home and nor is that the point of making this observation. It is quite possible that different individuals will perceive control and how to gain it in different ways. Thus it is important to take heed of individual accounts in order to determine effective intervention. As Kirschenbaum (1991) points out there are various ways hospital dialysis treatment could be modified to make the patient feel more involved and more in control. One could speculate, for example, that were Carole to continue with hospital dialysis, providing her with a greater understanding of the machine's workings and including her more in the physical tasks involved would enhance her sense of control. Consistent with the thrust of this study, we would urge that when considering interventions or changes two things are emphasized, firstly that it is the patient's perception of control which is important rather than control per se and, secondly, that individual perceptions of what can enhance control will vary so that patients should be closely involved in the discussions about possible changes that could be made.

Thinking about where to go next with this study, there are a number of possibilities. Playing to the strength of its idiographic potential, it would be interesting to follow Carole through time and see how her experience changes, particularly once she starts home dialysis – comparing this with her expectations. An alternative would be to include an ethnographic arm, observing what happens on the ward and possibly talking to the health professionals about their perspective on caring for Carole.

We would hope readers can see the value of a detailed case study such as that presented here in helping to understand what it is like to have a major personal experience. We would also hope that even though they may not share the content of the experience of Carole they nevertheless feel a resonance with the way it impacts on her existentially. We would concur with Warnock (1987) in arguing it is the very detail of Carole's case which allows for this potential for an understanding of a shared humanity.

The case also provides a good example of some of the elements of hermeneutics outlined in Chapter 2. First it illustrates Heidegger's appearance. At one level, Carole's dream is not about dialysis at all. And yet equally one can say it is all about dialysis. Therefore, the phenomenological importance of the dream is suggested by the manifest content but its latent force appears or comes to the fore during the process of analysis. By establishing a trusting and intense research relationship with the participant, the interviewer has been able to facilitate her disclosing personal material which can then be interpreted to help deepen our understanding of the phenomenon.

We can also see the dream acting as a 'part' to the 'whole' of the case study. The dream sequence is powerful in its own right but its meaning is strengthened when one recognizes it as contributing to the whole – the understanding of the personally debilitating impact of dialysis for Carole. And of course the horror of the dream becomes even more vivid when one realizes that much of what it seems to be about is the dialysis treatment.

Other research on health and illness

Health psychology is the area of psychology where IPA first became established (see Brocki and Wearden (2006) for a review). Therefore there is now a considerable number of studies examining, for example, the patient's personal experience of particular conditions, treatments and decision making. There are also studies exploring the perspective of the carer and the health professional. This section will present short summaries of some of these studies to give a flavour of the work which has been done. Reference will also be made to other related studies.

The experience of chronic fatigue syndrome

Arroll and Senior (2008) conducted interviews with eight people who had had chronic fatigue syndrome for many years, in order to learn about their experience of the condition. The interviews were analysed with IPA. This paper usefully illustrates the shared themes of the respondents but also the particularity of individuals' experiences. The paper is constructed in terms of the illness trajectory – from the initial experience of symptoms to a diagnosis and treatment.

Participants describe the complex patterning of symptoms. As part of this, Gerald points to the lack of precision in the term used for the condition:

> The thing that really spoils your life is what I call lack of stamina. I don't like this concept of chronic fatigue, I'm not tired all the time, sometimes I'm not tired at all. If I do nothing I often feel pretty well, as soon as I start doing something it tired me too quickly. (Arroll & Senior, 2008: 448)

The paper also captures the difficult process of trying to make sense of the problem, for example assessing the symptoms and considering them in relation to possible causes:

> When I first became ill, I wasn't sure it was ME and I was overseas [ ] I think I had gut problems initially but of course in the less developed countries there are those things around, parasites and other bits of stuff so I think my weak area for a while had been the gut which of course doesn't give you much energy and its sore so I suppose for a while I thought that was the main issue and it may have been to begin with. (p. 450–451)

This is followed by a careful examination of participants' descriptions of the problems involved in obtaining a medical diagnosis for their condition.

For other examples of studies on the personal experience of serious health conditions, see these papers on: bone marrow transplantation (Holmes, Coyle, & Thomson, 1997); chronic back pain (Smith & Osborn, 2007); multiple sclerosis (Borkoles et al., 2008; Reynolds & Prior, 2003); osteo-arthritis (Turner et al., 2002); spinal cord injury (Dickson, Allan, & O'Carroll, 2008); and vitiligo (Thompson, Kent, & Smith, 2002).

Deciding whether to attend a cardiac rehabilitation programme

A significant part of the process of dealing with illness is decision making on the part of patients and professionals. Wyer, Earll, Joseph and Harrison (2001) investigated factors influencing whether people who had had a heart attack attended a cardiac rehabilitation programme aimed at helping participants with exercise, lifestyle and stress management. Semi-structured interviews were conducted with nine attenders and 12 non-attenders and the researchers compared participants' responses in relation to the components of Leventhal's self regulation model of health behaviour. Thus the paper is an interesting example of IPA working closely with quantitative models in health psychology. Attenders and non-attenders differed in a number of ways. For example, attenders typically had a more psychological model of health and illness while non-attenders tended to have a more medical model:

> I think you can make yourself well. You just have to get on with it. You've got to be positive. (attender, psychological model) (Wyer et al., 2001: 181)

> I rely on the doctors and nurses to look after you. It's their job to look after my health. (non-attender, medical model) (p. 182)

Similarly the paper illustrates differences between the groups in terms of their coping style, with attenders displaying approach coping and non-attenders avoidance coping:

> I want to get better and I want to do everything right. I'd rather someone who's got more knowledge told me what to do. (attender, approach coping) (p. 183)

> I didn't ask anything. It's better to let the body carry on with it. You're better off not knowing. (non-attender, avoidant coping) (p. 183)

Wyer et al. are able to use these differential responses to construct a model of the decision-making process in patients. Other IPA papers on decision making in health are Daniel, Kent, Binney and Pagdin (2005) on the decision making in families where elective surgery for short stature is available for their children, and Smith, Michie, Stephenson and Quarrell (2002) considering the decision-making process for the genetic test for Huntington's disease.

The psychology of being a carer

Most IPA research in health has examined the personal lived experience of the patient. This is not surprising as it represents the core concern for a phenomenology of health and illness. However, illness has a broader relational and social context and it is also important to explore the personal experience of carers. Hunt and Smith (2004) conducted detailed semi-structured interviews with four carers of recent stroke survivors. Interviews were conducted while the patient was still in hospital. Each of the carers was the family member who would take primary responsibility for the patient on release from hospital. Three super-ordinate themes emerged during the analysis: uncertainty, personal impact, strength of relationships. There was a pervasive sense of uncertainty in participants' accounts as they tried to make sense of what was happening to their parent or spouse. Carers were clearly deeply concerned for their loved one but then went on to discuss the way in which the situation was affecting them personally. Carers felt tired, stretched and under pressure to attend:

I don't like to neglect him 'cos if I do I feel, I don't want to, I do feel guilty. I don't, I shouldn't feel guilty. I think, ah, he's got no one visiting him. (Hunt & Smith, 2004: 1005)

Three of the four carers describe being within a nexus of close relationships within their family, both with the patient and with others:

I'll do anything for her and I don't mind either, if it's going to make her happy and it makes me happy. (p. 1007)

We have been a very close brother and sister, we always have been [ ] even before my mum had a stroke we always spoke on the phone every day. (p. 1007)

The strength of the relationships offers support to the carers but can itself sometimes become a source of tensions. The findings are related to other studies on carers in the literature. A related paper is by Glasscoe and Smith (2008) on the parental experience of caring for a child with cystic fibrosis.

EIGHT

Sex and sexuality

Introduction

One key area of IPA research is concerned with sex and sexuality. In this chapter we present a small piece of analysis from Paul's study of gay men living in Scotland who have been diagnosed with HIV. The chapter focuses upon their sexual decision making and addresses the super-ordinate theme, or organizing concept, of the meanings of sex and risk. Although this was a relatively large study and involved different analysts working on the data, it illustrates IPA's commitment to an inductive approach, asking the participant (as an expert) to talk about the way they think about an issue, rather than using a priori hypotheses to make assumptions about how people think, as much of traditional health psychology does. Along these lines, in this study, unstructured interviewing was adopted as a means of harnessing the capacity of IPA participants to set their own agenda; talking about their own priorities, in their own terms. The data and analysis presented here have not been published before.

It may be worth noting that Paul is a very experienced interviewer and also that he is very familiar with the population and the specific issues of HIV and gay men. The participants often took part explicitly to share their knowledge, to bear witness to their experiences, and pass on some sense of their expertise to other gay men. As gay culture is a particularly sexualized culture there are pre-existing norms to talk about sex and sexual activity in very frank and detailed ways.

Whilst showing what IPA does in practice in an applied piece of health psychology research with one key goal being to shape health promotion resources and potential interventions, this chapter also exemplifies the approach's commitment to dialogue with existing theory. However, as an engagement with the analysis will show, this is clearly quite different from using these theories, or theoretical constructs from them, to shape questions used within the interview, or indeed searching for traditional concepts during the process of analysis. Compared to Jonathan's chapter which also touched upon health psychological constructs, this chapter is far more engaged with health psychology theory. Yet, as the reader can see, this occurs within the introduction and the discussion sections. Box 8.1 summarizes the way the study in this chapter illustrates particular features of IPA.

Box 8.1   Particular features of this study

- Relatively large sample size for an IPA study – illustrates how to draw on different participants' accounts in constructing an analysis.
- Illustrates unstructured interviewing – successful here because Paul is a very experienced interviewer.
- Shows how IPA analysis can be used to problematize extant theory.

The meaning of relationships to HIV-positive gay men

Background

Globally HIV remains a growing public health issue. Although HIV treatments are available in the West they are unattainable to the vast majority of people living with HIV in other areas. Although on a global scale HIV is primarily a heterosexual epidemic, in the West it is associated with men having sex with other men (usually gay men) or intravenous drug users. More recently, in the UK at least, the epidemiology of HIV has changed with around half of new diagnoses being associated with people being born in sub-Saharan Africa who have moved to the UK (see Flowers et al., 2006). The remainder of these new diagnoses remain with men who have sex with men, who largely identify as gay. It was amongst gay communities that the largest ever change in health behaviour was recorded (Stall, Coates, & Hoff, 1988) as communities responded to the threat of HIV with the adoption of condom use for anal sex. However, in recent years, there have been major increases in reports of unprotected anal intercourse in most communities of gay men across the world and an increase in men testing HIV-positive.

In the era before there were effective treatments for HIV, psychological approaches to understanding HIV risk behaviours were widespread. Models developed and utilized to understand a broad range of health behaviours were adapted to understand sexual health decision making and particularly to understand the use and non-use of condoms (see Flowers et al. (1997) for a quantitative review). Such approaches drew upon models such as the Health Belief Model, Protection Motivation Theory, or the AIDS Risk Reduction Model.

These models share many variables, such as knowledge of HIV, perceived susceptibility, perceived severity, social norms, self-efficacy and attitudes towards condoms. The models are operationalized through individuals completing questionnaires or structured interviews, at usually one point in time, and essentially attempt to map out the relationships between health cognition and health behaviour (in this case the use of condoms). By employing aggregate statistical nomothetic analysis they compare those who engage in risk behaviours with those who do not and identify which cognitions are associated with reported risk behaviour. Thus, although these approaches aim to divide and compare large samples by self-report of sexual behaviour, the unit of analysis is the individual and their thoughts. However, these thoughts are only understood in terms of the questions that were asked which in turn only relate to the operationalization of the specific variables taken from theories.

As such, these approaches map out the possible ways that people make decisions regarding safer sex within the constraints of the limited scope of the cognitions taken from the models such as perceived risk or knowledge of HIV. The individual is understood as an agentic, rational decision maker, weighing up the costs and benefits of each cognition in order to maximize health and minimize the risk of HIV. In this way condom use is understood as the dependent variable; it is the end point of sexual decision making and the constellation of health beliefs are understood to predict it. This study takes a different tack: its research question is making sense of how gay men themselves talk about and conceptualize their sexual decision making.

Method

The participants in this study were 16 HIV-positive men recruited from a variety of sources: groups and agencies dedicated to HIV-positive people, adverts placed within the gay and the positive press, and postcard adverts placed in gay venues within Scotland. Participants were interviewed by Paul in a variety of places ranging from their own homes to rooms within HIV agencies to rooms within a university setting. The interviews for this project were unstructured, with the only set question being 'What do relationships mean to you?'

Analysis

The analysis detailed a number of recurrent themes. Here we present two strong recurrent themes which relate directly to HIV risk management and the meaning of sex and risk. The participants described a broad range of risk management strategies. Here we concentrate on participants' accounts of current risk management (as positive men). It is important to remember that all such decisions were located within historical contexts, with several participants remembering the introduction of condoms in the early 1980s as well as contemporary accounts of HIV risk-related decisions.

The relational language of sex acts: 'I was giving him myself'.   This theme addresses those times that the participants talked about sexual decision making and HIV risk-related decisions in ways which related to the meaning of sex acts and the meaning of risk within 'romantic' relationships. Several of the participants talked about being in sero-discordant relationships (where one partner is positive and one is negative). Whilst initially HIV risk management was important in terms of the overall relationship, over time, as the relationship progressed, HIV took on less significance. The importance of risk seemed to diminish as time went on. As Terry says:

Terry:	He knew the risk, and he chose not to do anything about it.
Interviewer:	How did you feel about that?
Terry:	Um, I really liked the guy, um first I was really annoyed, but then it just got to a stage where it just became normal for us.

There are several important issues to note within this brief extract. Terry's initial reaction to his partner's desire not to use condoms was annoyance, reflecting the work Terry was doing in minimizing risk. In addition Terry almost qualifies this annoyance with a caveat of 'I really liked the guy'. Lastly, it is important to engage with the passage of time in understanding the reported changes in risk management: HIV risks became normalized and risk management dissipated. This sense of relationship development being associated with diminishing risk management seemed a common occurrence. There was a tendency for sexual acts to sometimes be associated with expressions of love, trust and commitment. Across the history of a relationship there can be a sense of progression with sex acts, sometimes culminating in unprotected sex. Below, we see how, for Jack, the context of a romantic relationship led him to move from condoms for oral sex to having unprotected anal intercourse:

Jack:	It had been a long time since I'd been using flavoured condoms for oral sex, and I'm not really sure that anybody really does actually... I've found that now, since, whenever I've kind of put them forward as an option people are just like disgusted by it. And you think well I'm only doing it because I want to protect you, but more importantly myself. So it's really strange, but it had been maybe a couple of years since I'd been like that and, the change happened, I suppose because I was deeply in love with the person, and that's why, that's the reason. It didn't feel like sex, it didn't feel like we were having sex, it felt like we were making love and it didn't feel that I had anything to worry about so ... That's kind of what it was, it was never painful, he was the best, best, the best lover that I'd ever had, it was the most enjoyable, satisfying sexual relationship and I didn't think that I had anything to worry about so ... I suppose I wanted to I wanted to please him, I wanted to, I suppose it was something that I could give him that ... I felt nobody else could, I suppose that was my way of trying to show him how much I cared.

Interviewer: So what...
Jack: I shouldn't have done but ...
Interviewer: ... What were you giving him, to show him how much you cared?
Jack: I was giving him myself, um I was giving him what he wanted, I didn't realize that at the time but um ... I was giving him my unprotected sex, which had never been an option in my mind before, before I met him, um ... but then I'd never met anybody that wanted to have unprotected sex, with me before.

The extract above illustrates the simultaneous engagement with HIV risk reduction on the one hand and relational, romantic dynamics on the other. Clearly for Jack the romantic dynamics shaped the sexual activity. He describes his willingness to engage in unprotected anal intercourse as making a 'gift' of himself. For him, this exceptional behaviour represented his exceptional feelings. This idea is critical to understanding the ways in which gay men can communicate within relationships. At times it is almost as if actions are speaking louder than words, or expressing things that words cannot. There almost seems to be a deep symbolic language which people can draw upon. Jack, who was infected by his long-term partner, goes on to emphasize the difference between having sex and 'making love'. He clearly outlines this sexual activity as non-corporeal as it is concerned with spiritual or religious matters:

Making love was more of a kind of spiritual or even religious experience rather than being in your body having physical pleasure, I had complete pleasure throughout my whole body, I was making love. I was in love with him, I felt that he was in love with me. I know that he was, he was in love with me, I wouldn't have felt like that if if it wasn't both ways of ... when we were making love I didn't I wasn't aware of myself as a person, I was more aware of the two of us together, and it was a different, different level of consciousness I would I would think as well.

These extracts describe the ways in which sexual conduct can be understood within a relationship. Ideas around making a gift of the self and indeed not being aware of the self as a person illustrate the magnitude of the feelings involved. Given the reported intensity of these emotions it is not surprising that condoms can be thought of as problematic. As Lee explains:

A condom's great for protection but it's it takes away the ... intimacy, the closeness the oh just everything. you can't get any closer than your body fluids interacting with each other I mean it's just ... the thought of that is just, fantastic.

In summary this theme has highlighted how within romantic relationships the meaning of sex acts can change across relationship development. Unprotected sex can be understood as relating directly to notions of closeness, intimacy and direct expressions of love. Participants' willingness to engage in behaviour which they have always previously avoided (namely unprotected anal intercourse) expresses their commitment and trust to a particular partner.

The relational language of risk: 'It would bring us closer together'. Given the currency that unprotected sex can have, and indeed the notion of giving the self as a 'gift', it is not too surprising that amongst the participants there were incidents in which potential, or actual infection, or indeed even the knowledge of risk, were also used in a similar way to express the depth and magnitude of emotion. Sam describes the reaction of the first man he discloses his HIV-positive status to:

> Was like: 'oh I don't care if you're positive' and wanted to have unsafe sex! And I was like, I'm the one again who's taking responsibility and saying no, you know, and it's like for fuck's sake you know, like my head's spinning already anyway and then this person wants to come back and say to me: 'Oh well, you know I don't mind you know, I'll take the risk because I'm, I'm really into you.' And blah blah blah, and you think for fu ... I mean it's just as well in a way that I was kind of like not really into him, in in the way that would all, would allow me to have kind of like say: ok I'll go for it, you know. Um because I think I could have easily have been seduced into the idea that if I if I was so kind of um smitten and he was willing to like kind of abandon all the ... You know I might have felt pretty difficult and awkward and guilty about it, but I don't know I might have might have succumbed as well you know.

This extract again draws our attention to the time frame of relationship development. It is 'after a while' that this issue becomes a central feature of this discordant relationship. We see that a negative partner expresses the degree of how much he is into Sam by harnessing the power of the risk of HIV infection. Although Sam was tempted by this behaviour, the partner's feelings were not reciprocated by him. Sam went on to explain how such an incident (i.e. the partner being infected through sex with Sam) would perhaps also have cemented the relationship, but with problematic ideas (on Sam's part) of obligation and 'commitment':

> There's an assumption inbuilt there that somehow, I don't know maybe maybe it is something that they feel will then tie them for life, if they become you know, or maybe it's it's the the sense of um I'm I'm prepared to kind of do this for you as it were.

Similarly below, Andy describes a situation in which a positive partner, pretending to be HIV negative, used the idea of potential infection as a means to express commitment to the relationship. This highlights the particular valence of risk:

> Rick, when I met him, was HIV but wanted to have unprotected sex with me and then wanted to become HIV and not telling me he was already HIV that we could be closer. That kind of did my nut in.

Later the same partner said that:

> Life would be much easier if he was positive and that it would bring us closer together.

It is the very fact that Rick, although already positive, pretends he is willing to become positive that illustrates the importance of using a language of risk within an apparently discordant relationship. The extract below details how, for Andy, risk behaviour changed across another relationship's development, from the one incident of unprotected anal intercourse before HIV status disclosure, to a period of condom use and then to increasing levels of unprotected sex:

> Because then he started to insist that he never wanted to use a condom. That he hated condoms. And that he felt, by not using a condom, it would bring us closer together. And that ... and I kind of swayed back and forwards between it and ... for a quiet life, sometimes, let it go, let it slip and let him do it. Em ... but ... with that ... any time we had an argument, he would use that against me ... Eh, obviously it was me to blame as well because I let it happen, it takes two to tango.

Eventually the future of their relationship depended upon his partner receiving negative results. When he did test negative, this partner begged to stay in the relationship and on returning home, as Andy says:

> The first words he said was 'I want to show you how much I love you, I want to fuck you without a condom' and I was just like ... 'Here we go' and then all I thought was ... 'as soon as I get out, they pull me back in'.

Frank adds to this way of thinking in describing how he felt within the relationship with his positive partner, prior to becoming infected himself. Similar to other respondents, Frank describes how he understood engaging in unprotected anal intercourse with his partner as an indication of his investment in the relationship, but in addition, he harnessed the dynamics of differential risk as a means to also expressing perceived power within the relationship:

> I feel it almost could created a, well upper hand's not the real, the right thing because it wasn't kind of like I was seeking the upper hand, but I fe, I felt I obtained one somehow, you know had some kind of, I had some extra thing that I was putting into this relationship that he wasn't, which was a [unclear] of this extra um and dangerous, I suppose, thing. [ ] Yeah but not, but not calculatingly looking at it I mean I did, I felt I felt it existed, I felt it became that, you know it it was, you know, almost like well he had, he's got more to lose, if he split up he's got more to lose than I've got, you know, that kind of thing ... it's not how I really saw, it's not how I saw myself viewing a relationship, and all of a sudden there was the, there was extra little mechanisms starting to kind of build up, in the way that I viewed it.

Whereas Frank expressed a subtle change in feelings of power within the relationship, other partners used the positive status of their partner and the potential risk of infection to destructive and manipulative ends. As Andy says:

> One thing he loved to do was go into the kitchen and ... if he was upset with me, was drop things on the floor and if I used to go to step towards him, he'd drop something

else. One time, he was smashing things in the kitchen and he cut himself, and he had beaten me up and I had bled into him ... so, I've bled into many times or our blood has been mixed many, many, many, many, many, many times.

In summary, this theme illustrated the valence of risk within sero-discordant relationships. There are clear parallels with the previous theme although here much 'darker' relational dynamics are at play. Risk was sometimes used instrumentally, as a means to a set of very diverse ends. Within this study, risk was used to express a spectrum of meanings involving relational commitment, relational power and manipulation.

Discussion

The analysis has demonstrated, first and foremost, that condom use, or unprotected anal intercourse, is anything but a simple health behaviour. From this analysis, sexual conduct emerges as meaning-laden, joint behaviour; it is 'relational', both conceptually and in a literal sense (the concept of relationality is explored in far greater detail in Chapter 10). Although the points raised by the analysis may seem obvious, they have profound implications for how health psychology could, or should, theorize and research sexual conduct. The implications are profound because the understandings of sex and the accounts of sexual decision making differ so widely from those described by traditional health psychological models.

On its most basic level the analysis shows how 'relational' decisions around sex and risk are on a number of levels; they relate to the sexual dyad and they also often relate to communication within that dyad. Traditional approaches to sexual health understand decisions about condoms as being made by individuals and that these decisions relate to understanding sex as a 'health' issue. Although some of these models do have some '*social*' variables, for example, the 'subjective norm', from the theory of reasoned action (Ajzen & Fishbein, 1980) or perceived behavioural control (which attempts to define the scope of agency or capacity to enact an intention), they are still anchored firmly to the individual. Thus the analysis is showing a fundamental dissonance between how health psychology constructs sex and how gay men report thinking about it. See Flowers et al. (1997) for more on this.

Moreover, when talking about sex and sexual decisions, the participants highlighted a range of very powerful and complex meanings. These meanings clustered around giving the self as a gift to demonstrate commitment, love and intimacy, and using the potential threat to the self to do likewise. For the most part, these powerful meanings did not relate to health, although a good understanding of the health implications of HIV transmission was core to some of the meanings which were being made. For example, to demonstrate that a willingness to engage in unprotected anal sex can be a measure of love only makes sense if the perceived severity and susceptibility of HIV transmission is acknowledged.

Thus, although the risks of HIV infection are ubiquitous, they are often not the major factor shaping sexual decision making, or indeed the end point of any costs and benefits analysis. Yet, the participants do report engaging in costs and benefits analysis, but these relate to the costs of risk versus the benefits of emotional fulfilment, or the future of a relationship. They relate to a rationality of overall life priorities not to a specific health rationality. As the analysis described it is precisely *because* HIV risk behaviour is dangerous and should be avoided that some men actively use it to accomplish relationship-oriented ends.

These findings point to the limitations of the static and linear health rationality employed within traditional approaches to explaining gay men's condom use. They highlight complexity, ambiguity and variability within decision making, something that is difficult to capture within cross-sectional quantitative research design. Condom use or unprotected anal intercourse emerges as having context specific meaning and decisions are based within an understanding of those meanings.

Other research on sex and sexuality

IPA has been widely adopted in terms of studying sex and sexuality, perhaps as a direct result of the sensitive nature of the subjects involved. IPA is particularly suited to researching sex and sexuality in that it can challenge understandings which are based around 'othering' people, or medicalizing and pathologizing behaviours. In the remainder of this chapter we give a flavour of the variety of sex and sexuality studies in which IPA has been adopted. Three papers are summarized and key points drawn out. Each addresses both the inter-psychic aspects of the social nature of sex and sexuality and the intra-psychic processes of internal conflict and identity.

Women's experiences of living with HIV

Jarman, Walsh and De Lacey (2005) present an analysis of HIV-positive women's experiences of partner relationships. The study is interesting as it explores an under-represented group of positive people (women) and examines their experiences within the context of their relationships. The study highlights the importance of 'protection' as an integral aspect of living with HIV; protection of both the self (from stigma) and of others (from concomitant worry and concern following status disclosure) and eventually the risk of infection. The authors describe how this protection is often experienced in direct conflict to the need to share and discuss the psychological burden of the impact of HIV and indeed attain access to broader sexual and emotional intimacy. Moreover, the study examines these issues in both relationships in general and then in partner relationships in particular. In partner relationships, there was the opportunity for the women to experience openness, acceptance and 'normality' if partners were also positive, or if a status disclosure had occurred. Yet for one woman who had not disclosed her status:

> I know that part of me has just felt ugly, dirty, erm unattractive, diseased you know, erm and obviously I've never been able to discuss those kind of things with my present partner because I've not disclosed my status. (Carol) (Jarman et al., 2005: 543)

This extract hints at the broader issues which the paper addresses, the difficulties of starting and finishing relationships and the moral quandaries the women express:

> I couldn't sleep with someone and then tell them after, it's not right is it? Because you haven't given them that choice? (Kate) (p. 543)

Being in a relationship and having a sense of being accepted led to the salience of HIV and the associated distress diminishing. Throughout the paper the aspects of partner relationships which contexutalize the meanings and impacts of HIV diagnosis are clear. However, for the participants these become tangible only when starting and ending relationships. As one participant said regarding the end of a relationship:

> I was absolutely devastated. Er, I've never been as angry in my life, I hated him, devastated, because it threw up, the HIV hit me. It hit me because all of a sudden I were facing a future on me own, and I'd never thought about that before. It were only, it were always, it had been me and Rob, and all of a sudden this were a real thing that me and Rob might have split up and I'm [states age] and HIV. (Laura) (p. 545)

The experience of inorgasmia

Lavie and Willig (2005) present a study of women's experience of inorgasmia. Again this study is important as it charts an under-researched area and presents a particularly gendered perspective. Like many IPA studies regarding sexual issues, it problematizes understandings of the phenomenon in question as being about physical sensation or a medical condition. It shows how the participants' own meanings and experiences may challenge readers' understanding of an issue in ways which stress the role of personal and relational meaning, and indeed show the inappropriateness of unitary or singular understandings. The paper details how inorgasmia can have deep repercussions on women's sense of self. Inorgasmia was understood to affect self-image and self-identity. It was also clearly understood within a social context, at the level of both peer-comparisons and within the wider culture, where inorgasmia carried stigma and a pejorative identity. As one participant put it:

> I felt also like I am a person with a problem and also I sort of really don't see the real truth, er, it's somehow to do with myself ... like, I see myself opposite them. They're people who come and I am not. (Beth) (Lavie & Willig, 2005: 120)

The participants also stressed the importance of inorgasmia within their sexual relationships. Its relational meanings included both orgasm as an indicator of women's satisfaction but also as a symbol of men's own performance and achievement. In addition to outlining what a lack of orgasm meant to the participants, the paper also addresses what orgasms could mean. As Ana said:

> It seems like a divine thing, mystical, some kind of hovering (...) I imagine, it seems to me an internal thing, a pinch in my heart (...) the sense of connecting with the one who is next to you. Orgasm is having sex while the person facing me looks at me and sees me in my peak. It seems to me like the most amazing thing. Kind of giving a present to the one who is next to you, not only to yourself. (p. 123)

The authors stress how orgasm almost illustrates the relationship between the partners, that it is firmly about connection and the idea of giving.

Negotiating cultural, religious and sexual identities

Coyle and Rafalin (2000) present a study of the interpersonal and conflict-ridden experiences of holding the somewhat irreconcilable identities of being both Jewish and gay. Both the gay cultural context and indeed the religious and cultural context of Judaism shaped the internal identity struggles of the participants. As a result the participants reported identity conflict, as Nathan said:

> I just thought 'God [ ] Jewish people aren't like this' [ ] If you're Jewish [ ] you know, you could not be gay. (Coyle & Rafalin, 2000: 29)

This oppositional dynamic was understood to pull the participants in different directions. As Joshua said:

> I was an unhappy ... almost suicidal young man ... I suppose that was partly due to being ... to having these two forces. (p. 31)

The authors go on to say that these identity conflicts had ramifications for a range of social relationships. Among these, community and parental relationships were important. For the latter, concerns about the continuation of the family or the faith were important. Sam described his father's distressed response to him coming out:

> I think the fact that my father lost so much family in the Holocaust was ... I was going to continue that family and having a son was very important and having the name was very important. (p. 34)

Participants reported managing their identity conflict and identity threats with a variety of strategies, often including maintaining a distance from other people, or feeling obliged to lie. This often involved compartmentalizing aspects of their lives:

I've lived with all these in various separate compartments for so long, I don't think I can remember much of another way of life. (p. 37)

However, others reported drawing upon their experience of difference and disconnection with the wider society on account of their Jewishness. In this way there was a sense of parallel or a model for coping with devalued difference. As Jeff reported:

If you can say 'I'm different' once in the face of that, then you can say 'I'm different' again in a different light [ ] And it really really helped. (p. 39)

Other IPA work

Here are details of other IPA studies on sex and sexuality. Research has looked at: gay men and their sexual decision making (Flowers et al., 1997; Flowers, Marriott, & Hart, 2000); gay men and their understandings of the HIV antibody test (Flowers, Duncan, & Knussen, 2003); heterosexual women's understandings of the impact of chlamydia diagnosis (Duncan, Hart, Scoular, & Bigrigg, 2001); the experience of living with HIV amongst black Africans living in the UK (Flowers et al., 2006); the impact of sexual assault (Connop & Petrak, 2004); lesbian planned parenting (Touroni & Coyle, 2002); and men talking about Viagra (Rubin, 2004).

NINE

Psychological distress

Introduction

Increasingly IPA is being used to examine the experience and context of psychological distress. This chapter presents an example from Michael's work. This is a case study exploring the experiences of a young man with psychosis and is published here for the first time. This example will allow us to explore and illustrate some of the contributions which IPA can make to clinical psychological research. Following that, we will briefly examine examples from three different threads of IPA research in the clinical psychology domain.

Box 9.1   Particular features of this study

- Shows how IPA analysis can be used to understand experiences which, at first glance, may seem to present a challenge to empathic, phenomenological understanding.
- Presents in-depth analysis of a single case.
- Illustrates the balance between phenomenological and interpretative aspects of IPA analysis.
- Demonstrates how a creative and interpretative focus on metaphor (and the use of other cultural resources) can offer powerful insights into the lived world of a research participant.

Metaphor and psychosis: A case study

Background

This section will draw upon some extracts from a single interview, partly in order to illustrate some of the insights that IPA can offer, and partly as a platform from which to identify and discuss some of the challenges which face phenomenological researchers in clinical settings.

The participant in this case study is a young man, known here as Syed, who has recently experienced episodes of psychosis. The account offered here draws on a single interview, which is taken from the first phase of a wider study. The study looked at the experiences of some of the young British-Asian people receiving support from an Early Intervention (EI) service in the West Midlands (Latif, Newton, & Larkin, 2004). The later phases of the study examined the experiences of the young people's families (Penny, Newton, & Larkin, in press) and of the staff on the EI team itself (Bhogal & Larkin, in preparation).

Psychosis. Psychosis is usually understood to refer to an episodic change in one's state of mind or way of being. This change is typified by a loss of contact with reality as most other people would usually or easily recognize it. These episodes sometimes occur only once, but more usually they will recur. Episodes are often characterized by unusual beliefs and preoccupations, and sometimes hallucinations (e.g. hearing voices), but they may also include a loss of insight, and impaired reasoning, communication and motivation. The impact upon people with psychosis, and their families, can be very distressing. Developmental delays and accumulated cognitive and social deficits may prove to be debilitating in the long term, particularly in the wider cultural context of shame and stigma. Thus, psychosis is a complex event, affecting a person's thoughts, feelings and behaviours, their everyday functioning, and their relationships with others.

Until relatively recently, experiences like Syed's have been situated firmly within the disease-model of 'schizophrenia' (e.g. see Boyle, 2002a, 2002b) rather than the broader term 'psychosis', and medication and hospitalization were its preferred interventions. These have their place, but a well-developed, multidisciplinary critique has identified major limitations to their widespread use (e.g. Johnstone, 2000). Stigma, institutionalization, dependency and serious physical ill-health, have all been negative consequences for many people with psychosis. Schizophrenia, however, is not only a highly stigmatizing term, with some threatening medico-social consequences, its diagnostic validity is also the object of a considerable conceptual critique:

> In the last 25 years, the scant evidence for the validity of schizophrenia as a coherent disease entity has been comprehensively undermined (see Bentall, 2004; Boyle, 1990; Read, Mosher, & Bentall, 2004; Sarbin, 1990). Of course, this does not mean that people do not experience problems and distress (all of these critiques acknowledge that they do). (Newton, Larkin, Melhuish, & Wykes, 2007: 128)

Critical psychiatrists and psychologists have observed that, firstly, the experiences and behaviours which have conventionally been labelled as 'schizophrenia' are so varied, and so context-sensitive, that they are unlikely to be the 'symptoms' of a single disease. Secondly, they have argued that, once conceptual assumptions and methodological flaws are taken into account, there is no persuasive evidence to suggest a single underlying neurological etiology for these experiences and behaviours. More recent research has taken a number of interesting turns – towards cognition, social and family contexts, life history and trauma – in order to address the complexity and variability of experiences which are now more commonly referred to by the broad umbrella term, psychosis.

On the whole, these new models, and the research which underpins them, have tended towards recommending interventions which move away from diagnosis, and towards problem solving. Here, the role of psychologists and psychiatrists is to help clients to identify and understand their problems, and to intervene, where possible, in ways that support change and/or coping – in psychological, medical, social and vocational domains. It is a key tenet of these critical approaches that psychosis is an *understandable* experience. Delusional beliefs, for example, are not held to be simply meaningless, and talking about them is not held to be pointless – or dangerous. They are also not confined to people who come to be labelled with mental health problems – many people have 'strange beliefs' which cannot be easily verified or tested. These new approaches to psychosis therefore resonate strongly with phenomenological research.

Psychosis and phenomenology.   There is a long association between the 'topic' of psychosis and the phenomenological approach. Psychosis was once thought, most notably by the influential psychiatrist Karl Jaspers, to serve as a sort of 'threshold of empathy' for phenomenological inquiry (Bentall, 2004). Jaspers felt that the empathically-minded person might well enter into the world of a like-minded person, but not that of a person with psychosis. His contemporary, the existential psychiatrist Ludwig Binswanger, strongly disagreed with this. Partly in response to Jaspers's claims, Binswanger (1975/1963) went on to develop a hermeneutic and existential approach to therapy and research, which continues to have resonance for current approaches to psychosis.

Both points of view merit some brief reflection here. The focus of the IPA researcher can be thrown into some considerable uncertainty in clinical settings: the claims made by participants may be very moving but they may also be confusing to comprehend and this can easily lead us away from 'sense-making' (which is where our focus should be) and towards 'causality' and 'veracity' (wondering how this came to pass, or what *really* happened). It may even prompt us to become excessively absorbed in trying to understand our own experiences and reactions. A certain amount of reflection is a helpful and necessary part of phenomenological and hermeneutic inquiry, as is made clear in Chapter 2, but as we also indicated earlier, too much reflection takes us away from our object of inquiry – 'the thing itself'.

Binswanger offers us a helpful framework for thinking about these matters, by placing empathy ('being-with') at the core of his practice, whilst simultaneously attempting to understand the *position-and-context from which a person's claims make sense*:

> [Binswanger] emphasises the need to live in the world of the *'Mitsein'* ('being-with'), where one becomes an equal, so to speak, of the person one is analysing. Standing shoulder to shoulder in the *mitsein*, the person's world becomes intelligible as a series of 'modes-of-being-together' (*miteinandersein*). (Ghaemi, 2001: 57)

Indeed, his adoption of the concept of 'being-with' foreshadows the 'insider's perspective' which is one core element of IPA, *and* the phenomenological turn in recent work on psychosis. See, for example, Bentall's emphasis on the personally, relationally and biographically meaningful nature of 'symptoms': 'We should abandon psychiatric diagnoses altogether and instead try to explain and understand the actual experiences and behaviours of psychotic people' (2004: 141). Thus Binswanger makes a deliberate attempt to transcend the point where empathy (particularly in psychosis) becomes most challenging, and to enter into the internal logic and the life-historical context of the client's world. This is the stance from which interpretative phenomenological work begins. It is the stance which we aim to take up over the following sections, as we introduce, contextualize and explore the case study example for this chapter.

Early intervention.   In clinical practice, a move away from diagnosis has been encouraged and embraced by Early Intervention (EI) services in the UK. These services work with young people during the three-year period following a first episode of psychosis. Psychiatrists and multidisciplinary teams are encouraged to work in a climate of 'diagnostic uncertainty' and to treat what they see, using a combination of pharmacological, social and psychological interventions, in accordance with the presenting difficulty described by the young person (see e.g. Birchwood, Fowler, & Jackson, 2000).

This service model has been adopted nationally as a key approach to psychosis (NICE, 2002; IRIS, 2006). It works on the principle that there is a 'critical period' lasting two to five years, beginning with the first experience of problems (and possibly before the first full 'episode'), and during which the effects of interventions are likely to be most beneficial in reducing secondary difficulties (e.g. poor self esteem, suicide risk, socio-economic decline), and in promoting recovery. It has also been suggested that primary positive symptoms may be more responsive to treatment during this critical period. Thus, EI involves:

> offering effective treatment at the earliest possible point [ ] ensuring that intervention constitutes best practice for this phase of illness, and is not just the translation of standard treatments developed for later stages, and more persistently ill subgroups, of the disorder. (McGorry, Edwards, Mihalopoulos, Harrigan, & Jackson, 1996: 305)

It is therefore crucial that EI services respond effectively to the psychosocial needs of their clients. This requires an understanding of the cultural and relational frameworks within which people make sense of their experiences of psychosis and recovery. As a result, the research questions of our three-phase study were primarily focused upon the participants' experiences of the service, and of their understandings and evaluations of its model of working (e.g. see Penny et al., in press). For the purposes of this chapter, I want to consider the relationship between Syed's experiences, their context, and the cultural resources which he uses to make sense of them. The reader will note that, while the Asian aspect of Syed's identity is clearly important, this certainly does not mean that 'Asian cultures' are the only resources from which he can draw.

Method

Syed is a young Muslim man, whose parents emigrated to the UK from South Asia. He was born and educated in the UK. His mother speaks no English, and his father only a little. He began to experience psychological and social problems in his late teens and at the time of interview had been under the care of the EI services for slightly more than the three-year period usually adopted.

The interview was carried out by Sabah Latif, a student working with the EI service, under the supervision of Elizabeth Newton (an EI psychologist). The interview was semi-structured, following a simple series of open questions, which asked, principally, about how the person came into contact with the EI service, what was happening in their life at that time, what the early intervention team did, and what things they should do differently. It was conducted in Syed's home and was subsequently transcribed verbatim.

Analysis

The phenomenology of emasculation and threat.   Later on this chapter will work towards an analysis of the central, organizing metaphor which is employed by Syed and which very effectively communicates and binds together the principal aspects of his experiences of psychosis and recovery. Before we introduce this metaphor, and begin the more interpretative work, it is important to establish the phenomenological core of Syed's account – that is, to identify his primary claims and concerns.

Syed offers a complex and multi-layered account, which, in addressing Sabah's questions about how he came into contact with the EI service, and what he gained from them, also reveals his attempts to account for the origin of his problems. His concerns coalesce around one major super-ordinate theme, disempowerment, which, his account suggests, could be understood as profoundly emasculating, in the context of a threatening and violent socio-cultural environment (Box 9.2).

Box 9.2   Emasculation and disempowerment in Syed's account

Sexual injury	E.g. 'I used to get bullied, punched on the testicles'. – Accident on the ice. – Assaulted by bully.
Girlfriends	E.g. 'Every girlfriend I had, someone took me away from her'.
Threat to property and security	E.g. 'People nicking my furniture'.
Worries and stresses	E.g. 'People are stronger than me'.
Racism	E.g. 'Oh you fucking Pakis, you need to get out of this country'.
Identification disappointed	E.g. 'I used to watch a lot of cowboys and Indians movies. Now I hardly watch them.'

This theme of disempowerment in general – and emasculation in particular – helps us to understand Syed's experience of psychological distress. One of his prevailing concerns is that he might have received some form of sexual injury. At various points in his interview, he suggests that such an injury may have been sustained in either an assault by a school bully, or an accident on the ice, two events which he recalls from his earlier childhood. Here, for example, he describes the assault:

> When I was hit right in the centre of my testicles, my life was going like a film and it stopped. And my thoughts – my thoughts were beyond imagination, you know what I mean? It's like the pain barrier [ ] I don't feel pain [*now*]. Not the same pain that I have when I was hit at school. I remember then, that I went into the boys' toilet and I'm not sure, but I think that I pissed a bit of blood in the urine, in the urinals, and I was crying at the same time. I was crying and crying and then I stopped crying and um I started – I just went into my shell, you know what I mean?

The physical and experiential impact of this event was clearly very powerful. Syed associates his persistent fear, that he may now be impotent or infertile as a result of this injury, with his experience of psychosis. Syed also offers the event as a potential turning point in his narrative, a point beyond which he was psychologically-changed. The shell motif is repeated on several occasions, and on several levels ('in school someone cracked my shell') to describe the isolating and damaging aspects of his psychosis experience, which, for Syed, may stem from this moment. And he has not yet been entirely reassured by medical advice on the matter of the physical injury:

I've had all these scans done on me, and all this monitoring, and I've – I'm really happy that I can get it off my chest, you know what I mean? 'There is probably something wrong, or there probably isn't something wrong.' But that kind of swelling around my body kind of thing [*points towards groin*] is – I um – I don't know what it is. I can't explain it, because I'm not a doctor. And um I think that doctor said that what happened down there is a kind of cyst or something, but I'm not sure.

Alongside the two childhood incidents which underpin his worries about the possible persistence of this sexual injury, Syed speaks about his childhood experiences of racist abuse and, movingly, about the disappointment of his failed attempts to find a positive, powerful and attractive 'Asian' model of masculinity with which to identify. He describes having often watched and enjoyed old Westerns on the television as a child, and how he admired the 'Indians' in these films:

I felt like a warrior; a peaceful strong, warrior, like a Native American. I used to love them people, riding on the horses; you know, with nice brown eyes and light brown skin. That was my idol. I was brought up on them.

Later, he realizes that the 'Indians' in these films were not intended to be the objects of his identification, but were more usually the 'villains' of the genre. Syed reflects rather wistfully upon his disenchantment ('now I hardly watch them').

There is a broader cultural context, too, in which 'madness' is associated with the propensity for violence:

I used to know psychosis as mad. This is before I knew what it really meant, you know. You know, like the craz – Charles Bronson and Mad Frankie Fraser, that is the kind of madness I knew, that people would talk about when I was younger and that I would see on the TV. You know, like people getting locked up in prison, and getting punched and kicked, because people didn't understand what was wrong with them; that they were ill, not mad. People who are aggressive: streetfighters, and knucklefighters, boxers, that's what madness I knew.

In this context, Syed finds that his relationships with women seem always to be vulnerable to violent competition from others. He speaks of lost, and violated, girlfriends. Syed repeats these claims several times, in passing, as incidental to his main story, and without a great deal of further information. He communicates a sense of the frailty of his relationships with women, and the frequency with which those relationships have been disrupted by others.

This is a good point at which to remind ourselves that veracity (with regard to *events*) is not our concern here. We simply don't have enough information to know whether these events occurred, or how often. What is important, however, is that they are meaningful to Syed. From Syed's point of view, they can be understood to contribute to the wider experience of threatened masculinity which underpins his understanding of his vulnerability to, and experience of, psychosis.

In line with this, Syed expressed a further concern, about the people living in his neighbourhood, and the threat that they appear to pose to his belongings, security and health. He does this in an account which also captures his escalating confusion and stress during the onset of his first episode of psychosis:

Syed: A housing manager, for the area that I was living in, told me that I had to see a psychiatrist. Well, basically there was a lot of shit happening in my life, you know what I mean? And I just couldn't cope.
Sabah: Can you explain what you mean by 'shit happening in my life'?
Syed: You know, like – like people trying to beat me up in my flat, people nicking my furniture and um you know, nicking my carpet and um you know, leaving fumes going up in my flat and no money to live on. Just buying enough to live on, you know, like bread, milk, cheese. A bit of money for fags and basically trying to chase the meter for the electricity, because every time I put the bloody thing in, the money, it's gone back to zero again and um I'm chasing again. And um basically, I was in all directions, getting stressed. I wasn't sleeping, I wasn't eating properly, and um I wasn't even having a bath, and I was trying to keep all the dust off the flat, and there was a lot – a lot of um – a lot of um inconvenience in my life. I couldn't understand what was going on.

Thus, in his account of his episodes of psychosis, Syed emphasizes the negative effects upon his day-to-day living. Later, he describes the cost, or threat to, his relationships with friends ('My friends said that, "Oh yeah, you're stupid"') and family ('With a lot of Asian families, they kind of always think that it is black magic or things like that ... their families do neglect them sometimes'). These are very common features of the negative motivational, social, relational and self-care aspects of psychosis.

Syed does not describe any of the major 'positive symptoms' of psychosis (such as delusional beliefs, or auditory hallucinations). It may be that he avoids this out of awareness of the stigma often attached to such experiences (he is, after all, speaking to a young woman of his own age, who shares his religious and ethnic identities), or it may be that, for Syed and his family, these were not the most salient or pervasive consequences of his psychosis.

So Syed offers a range of possible explanations for his episodes of distress. These explanations tap into familiar cultural and psychological narratives which account for anomalous experiences and behaviours. As it happens, they are also considered by many professionals to be viable alternatives to a reductive, 'brain disease', medical model of schizophrenia (e.g. see Read et al., 2004). Thus, Syed considers that he may have been traumatized by a violent attack, or by a painful accident, in his childhood; he wonders whether a consistent and permeating atmosphere of threat (from racism, and from 'bent dictators firing bombs'), which make him 'feel scared, as a Muslim', might be the source of his difficulties; and he describes a range of psychosocial stressors (being underpaid, having to work unsocial hours, having noisy and disruptive neighbours, and so on) which cause him a barely-tolerable level of 'inconvenience' and 'stress'.

To summarize then, the prevailing psychological experience of psychosis, as Syed describes it, combines a retrospective awareness of his earlier lack of insight ('I got carried away kind of thing and I didn't realize what I was doing'), with a feeling of agitation and vulnerability ('I was thinking this and that, and making up that – it was really bad'), and confusion ('There was a lot of shit happening in my life that I didn't understand').

Syed's account of his recovery is consistent with this. Recovery is indicated both by the return of his ability to look after himself ('I have managed to sort out all my debts, and managed to eat well, catch a bus, and um get a bus-pass, and sometimes um catch a taxi and claim it back or whatever'), and by increased confidence in his relationships ('I broke down and I'm glad that my family accepted me back'). He is beginning to make plans for his life, to feel considerably less agitated and confused ('My stress level has kind of got better'), and feels confident about his ability to cope with any future episodes ('If madness comes again, you can cope, 'cause you have already had it, that stress').

Note that, so far, we have explored some of the explicit claims and concerns expressed by Syed. We have stayed relatively close to the language which he used, and attempted to give a 'faithful' account of his stated experiences and understandings of psychosis and recovery at the time of interview. In this sense, we have attempted to stay close to the ethos of empathic *mitsein* advocated by Binswinger. However, as we noted in Chapter 2, we may also want to work less 'descriptively' and to enter more into the hermeneutic circle at a more interpretative point. The development of this next level of analysis need not necessarily lead to a 'suspicious' account, however. If it did, we would have difficulty resolving two very polarized narratives – and we want to be able to connect our interpretations very clearly to the 'phenomenological core' of the participant's world. The 'faithful' account established so far can be extended via a hermeneutic stance which takes an inquisitive and speculative approach to understanding someone's meaning-making. Through this, we attempt to illuminate – or better, *amplify* – something of the psychological and cultural meaning of Syed's stated experiences and understandings. See the related discussion in Chapter 5 where we explore levels of interpretation in analysis.

Metaphor and hermeneutics: The 'Lonely Man'. In order to extend this account's engagement with Syed's meaning-making, we will now look more closely at one of the central, organizing metaphors within his account. Early in the interview, Syed has been talking about the difficulties he has experienced through psychosis. Sabah asks him if there have been any other problems, and he responds, not by expanding upon his difficulties, but by trying to make sense of them:

> I used to get bullied at school [ ] and that was um at what is it called the primary school, yeah primary school that is. And once I fell on the ice and um I kind of like experienced something really weird. It was like um like when I was ten, I fell on some ice and I stopped breathing for about a good 30 to 40 seconds. I haven't told my keyworker that but I just thought I would mention it now, for the record, you know. Obviously, I got punched in my testicles and I've been in shock for most of the time. I was I think 15, yeah 15 when I got punch[ed] in my testicles and um I kind of lived the Incredible Hulk life, you know, walking down the road, dreaming along. And [af] every inconvenience, I get angry, you know, and then I get back to normal.

As we might expect, after five years, Syed has a number of theories of his own, and he begins to share some of them here. This might have come about, he says, because of a traumatic event: perhaps because he was bullied at school, and subjected to a painful assault; or perhaps because of an accident that he had, when he was ten. These are separate events, but they do come out rather jumbled together here.

Particularly interesting, from the point of view of our hermeneutic task, is the closing metaphor. The Incredible Hulk is a *Marvel Comics* character. Readers may be aware that, in the comic (and the later television and cinema adaptations of the story), the core element of the story is that a government scientist, David Banner, is exposed to 'gamma radiation' in a laboratory accident. Subsequently, the irradiated Banner finds that he is subject to a dreadful metamorphosis, whenever he experiences pain or anger. On these occasions Banner is transformed into the Incredible Hulk, an enormous, raging, green giant. In his initial attempts to reverse the procedure Banner's laboratory is destroyed, partly through the unwitting interventions of a journalist, and in this second accident a fellow scientist is killed. The journalist witnesses the Hulk's escape. Banner takes the opportunity to allow people to believe that he has been killed too, and departs *incognito*, on a quest to find a cure for his condition. He is pursued by a number of people (reporters, agents and military officials) who are all seeking the Hulk, as the likely perpetrator of the scientists' deaths.

There are clearly two complementary and very powerful components to the 'Hulk life' as Syed experiences it. The first aspect very poignantly captures the loneliness and isolation of early psychosis. In the television series of *The Incredible Hulk* (Rathwell, 2007), which was first screened between the late 1970s and the early 1980s (when Syed was growing up), each episode closed with a familiar, downbeat montage of image and sound. This recurring motif combined shots of a resigned David Banner walking, solitarily, down a dusty road, alongside the programme's famously atypical superhero music (the 'Lonely Man' theme). (See Box 9.3 for some further recurring themes of the series, each resonant with Syed's experiences).

Box 9.3   The Incredible Hulk – common narrative features

No privacy or stability; wrongful pursuit; constant threat
Every week, David Banner would make his way to a new town, searching for a cure for his condition and taking odd jobs along the way to survive, while always being pursued by investigative reporter Jack McGee, and not far behind him, General Ross and Major Talbot, the men charged with capturing the Hulk.

Conspiracy; and sexual competition
Talbot was not only convinced that Banner was secretly working for the Soviets, but also had designs on Banner's sweetheart, Betty.

Concealed power; rage and transformation
Without fail, Banner would find himself caught up in the tribulations of the local towns-folk, who when threatened by thugs or bullies or natural disaster would find themselves receiving some much-needed assistance from Banner's green-skinned alter ego.

A recurring cycle; the romantic outsider
Once the Hulk had been spotted, Banner knew McGee would not be far behind, and he'd have to hit the road again, accompanied by the tinkling notes of the haunting 'Banner leaves town' piano theme.
(Adapted from Tipton, 2003.)

Banner's 'Hulk life' appears to offer a romanticized view of the outsider ('Walking down the road, dreaming along'). We can see how this might be particularly appealing to adolescents and young adults. Banner is pursued, and an outcast, because he is *misunderstood*, after all, and adolescence/young adulthood is a time of individuation and identity formation. Indeed, disruptions to these processes are a common feature of psychosis (Harrop & Trower, 2003). The transformative capacities of comic book heroes can be said to act as metaphors for the trials of adolescence. Hence, the 'Hulk life' is not entirely a desirable life, but it is a fantasy of exclusion-as-heroism, which renders Syed's experiences more palatable, and which adds a layer of meaning and illumination to them.

One of the reasons that Banner's exclusion is attractive, of course, is because he is also very powerful. This second aspect of the metaphor is bound to the first: it is the cause of Banner's exclusion and the source of people's misunder-standings of his actions and motives, just as psychosis is for Syed. Thus, when Syed says, '[At] every inconvenience, I get angry, you know, and then I get back to normal', he evokes the threat of the Incredible Hulk. When Banner is provoked to anger (by injustice, violence, pursuit or captivity) he is transformed into the Incredible Hulk, the muscular green giant who is the personification of righteous rage, but whose actions are often misunderstood.

There is ambivalence here, however. Syed's experience of psychosis has included some explosions of temper, as he demonstrates in this section, which begins when he mentions having made a 'bad mistake':

> Syed: So really, me parents had to call the police 'cos they didn't understand my behaviour.
>
> Sabah: Can you tell me about this mistake?
>
> Syed: Yeah, my mistake was that I was in the garage and I was arguing over a cassette with my sister. My sister is only small, I think she is about 18 or something or 16 or whatever. And I – stupidly enough, I just slapped her, 'cos I got so agitated. It's like that music. That cassette that she wanted helped me relax, and at the time, cos of my problems, I needed that music. And I made a stupid mistake, which Inshallah [*God willing*] I'm never going to make again.

Thus, the transformative capacity of the Hulk metaphor captures something of Syed's own problematic experiences of aggression, and more generally, of the shame which is experienced by many people after episodes of psychosis (Birchwood, Trower, Brunet, Gilbert, Iqbal, & Jackson, 2007). In Syed's case, the metaphor fits on more than one level, because his 'shaming' experience is a loss of control (over his temper) and respect (for his sister), it is a consequence of masculinity gone awry.

Alongside this, however, there are also some potentially empowering aspects to the Hulk imagery. Sexuality and masculinity are important topics for young adult men, and they are already amplified in Syed's experience (the injury to his testicles; the bullying; the lost and violated girlfriends). Here, then, is a potent symbol of masculinity regained, which captures not only the frightening transformations of adolescence, but also those of psychosis. As with the first aspect of the metaphor, this second aspect permits a certain amount of the identity which has been 'spoiled' by psychosis to be repaired and reclaimed. The connection between Banner's weekly warning to his tormentors ('You won't like me when I'm angry'), Syed's experiences of racism and bullying, and his initial understanding of psychosis ('people who are aggressive') seems clear. Underneath the vulnerable exterior, Syed can nurture a version of himself which is physically powerful, invulnerable and aggressive. The metaphor thus functions as a direct *sense-making* response, to a threat which is experientially *real*.

The Hulk metaphor communicates a great deal about Syed's experiences of psychosis and of the personal meaning of that experience for him. In terms of what it claims (about being misunderstood, excluded, at the mercy of events and circumstances; and also about perseverance, resignation, resilience and strength), it tells us a great deal about the difficulties faced by young people with psychosis, and the qualities which they may draw upon to cope with those difficulties.

Despite its considerable sustaining and illuminative power, this metaphor is a holding strategy for Syed, not a guide to the future. When Syed's psychosocial needs are finally addressed, the Hulk is abandoned:

> Sabah: What did the Early Intervention team do?
>
> Syed: They um actually, um they give me a CPN which is a psychiatric nurse and they gave me Sanj as the social recovery groups. Sanj is also a nurse but helps in activities. And he took us swimming and um. You know in the first few years it was

really good, you know, I was like well-chuffed – taking us swimming and um I kind of got happy in my life. It doesn't matter about the medication, I can take any medication but the happiness started coming out of me. I was coming out of my shell. I was in the system and I was getting helped. [ ] And I started befriending, opening up and um they used to pick me up and take me to the day centres and take me [to the] pictures. I'm glad that they took me out of that life I was living as lonely, living like an Incredible Hulk type of life, walking down the road and not realizing how far I got to, walked to, where I'm walking to, what I have to do.

Discussion

So what have we gained, through taking this interpretative phenomenological approach to a single case? We have seen that the careful identification of claims and concerns, and the focused description of a 'phenomenological core' in the analysis, can be very valuable and revealing. Being able to understand Syed's gendered and contextual experiences of vulnerability (i.e. of masculinity under threat) is an important precursor to being able to understand how his metaphorical description of his psychosis experiences (via the Hulk motif) works as a *meaningful response to* those experiences. That is, we have seen that psychosis is not inevitably an insurmountable barrier to empathy, or meaning-making – and this is consistent with current psychological thinking on the topic (e.g. see BPS, 2000). We have also seen that metaphors can be important aspects of phenomenological analysis. In fact, Binswanger himself described metaphor as 'foundational' (Lanzoni, 2005).

Other research on psychological distress

There is a growing body of work using IPA to examine aspects of psychological distress: the phenomenon itself; experience of recovery; professionals' understanding; and the institutional and cultural context. In the remainder of this chapter, we provide three brief examples of further studies in this field, to give a flavour of the kind of work which has been conducted.

Client perspectives: Women's experiences of brain injury

Howes, Benton and Edwards (2005) describe the experiences of six women with traumatic brain injury (TBI), recruited purposively via a district general hospital. They were interviewed twice, at one-year intervals, to track the evolution of their experiences over time. The study reports four main themes at its clearly articulated 'phenomenological core': awareness of change; emotional reaction; the struggle to make sense; and acceptance and adaptation. The first of these themes charts the women's sense of cognitive and physical changes post-injury. These are largely experienced as losses. The 'emotional reaction' theme picks up on their responses to these changes:

Anger was one of the intense emotional reactions experienced by the women and seemed at times directed inward, and at times directed at those nearest to them, or those involved in their care [ ] Sometimes the women seemed to get stuck at the angry stage, unable to move on to later reactions, which might be further emotional distress such as anxiety and/or depression. [ ]:

> Things that didn't ever use to bother me that I used to cope with and never think twice about, now I get really anxious about. It's silly trivial little things that are really just of no significance, I can build them up into real big issues and worry about them. (Howes et al., 2005: 134)

In the discussion, the authors go on to relate this to the work of Parkes (1998) and Charmaz (1989) on the emotions that arise as people struggle to make sense of other kinds of losses, such as bereavement and chronic illness. They recommend the development of interventions designed to help women in such situations to regain some of this control, and to take up a position as an 'active problem solver'.

Professional perspectives: Clinical decision making

Kam and Midgeley's (2006) study offers us a good example of what can be learned from research which examines professionals' perspectives. They explore when and how mental health professionals decide whether or not to refer a child for individual psychotherapy. Making a strong case for their idiographic and contextual focus, Kam and Midgeley interviewed five 'referrers' within a single Child and Adolescent Mental Health Service: counsellor, psychiatrist, psychologist, family therapist, social worker. As a result, this study provides an interesting example of how it can be possible to balance some degree of multiperspectival design against an acceptable level of homogeneity.

Kam and Midgeley outline three main themes in their participants' responses: child psychotherapy as 'precious'; 'what I would recognize as a child psychotherapy case'; and 'an idea about readiness.' Each of these has interesting implications for the provision and development of child psychotherapy services, but the first theme is perhaps the one most immediately striking. There are both positive and negative constructions of child psychotherapy as precious. Thus it can be construed as 'valuable and special', or as 'rigid about its way of working and too sure of its own [psychodynamic] perspective'.

In their discussion the authors draw together a series of similar ambiguities across all three themes, and make some interesting observations about the relationship between referral decisions and the evidence base for those decisions. This is a good example of the way that relatively localized phenomenological explorations can give rise to more general critical observations:

> It was clear [ ] that the children referred for individual psychotherapy did not reflect the recommendations of the evidence base in any straightforward way and that clinicians were not basing their judgements on these guidelines to any significant degree. This was partly related to the paucity of relevant (or methodologically acceptable) research

in the field of child psychotherapy outcome, but there was also a distrust of research in general that seemed to reflect a perceived disparity between the complexities of the clinical situation compared to the relative crudity of evidence-based guidelines. (Kam & Midgeley, 2006: p. 40)

In this way, the study also suggested some of the limits of the evidence-based approach per se. For example, most evidence-based guidelines are organized around the evidence for particular treatment modalities for specific psychiatric diagnoses. But this study suggests that psychiatric diagnosis is not always central to clinicians' thinking about the appropriateness of a particular form of treatment for a particular child. Rather, there is a much more complex interplay between the referrer's broader perception of a certain treatment modality, the specific difficulties that the child exhibits, and the stage of work that a therapist has reached with a child and his or her family.

User-led research: Recovery from psychosis

One notable and relatively recent development has been the adoption of IPA as a method for user-led investigations:

The term 'user-led research' refers to research where service users control all stages of the research process, including design, data collection and analysis, writing-up and dissemination (Rose, 2003). Service users, rather than being the objects of research, become active agents in decisions about the research process. This benefits the research by ensuring that the work done is relevant to the concerns of service users. In addition, the rapport developed by user interviewers can lead to the collection of data not otherwise accessible. (Pitt, Kilbride, Nothard, Welford, & Morrison, 2007: 55)

This exciting approach has the potential to be applied across various dimensions in the field of psychological distress. Pitt et al. offer an excellent example. Their study explored the subjective experience of recovery in people who had experienced psychosis. The research question, design, data collection and data analysis were led and primarily conducted by two user-researchers (with research supervision from three clinical psychologists, and input from a service-user steering group). They carried out seven interviews, and analysed the transcripts using IPA.

Their analysis describes recovery from psychosis as 'complex and idiosyncratic' and their themes focus particularly on the experience and process of rebuilding and empowering the self, rebuilding a life and social support and relationships, and of the commonly expressed hope for a better future.

Within the theme 'rebuilding social support', the authors point to the value of professional, voluntary sector, and social network support. Regarding the last of these, one participant says:

I got ill and they [*her parents*] realised I was ill and then started reading literature about what I was going through so they understood what was happening. They ... just don't see it as anything wrong with me really, just think its me and support me completely. (Pitt et al., 2007: 58)

The research also pointed to the importance of wider social change to help combat stigma and misunderstanding:

> I think they [*her friends*] were very scared of it, hearing voices. They just don't understand it at all. Just think it's really bizarre to their experience and I think they think I might go and kill them or something. Just don't understand it at all. I think it's bad but I think there should be more education about it. (p. 58)

The study links these thematic outcomes to a number of recommendations for improvements in clinical interventions.

The paper is a good illustration of the fact that, while prior experience of a phenomenon should not be seen as either a requirement or a barrier to exploration and understanding, it is also obvious that user-led research has the potential to offer some powerful insights. Insider status is not clear-cut, and does not transmit automatic authority or insight, but it does provide the user-researcher with a further point of comparison in the hermeneutic circle.

Other IPA work

Other studies employing IPA to examine topics in psychological distress are concerned with clients' experiences of processes of change and recovery (Macdonald, Sinason, & Hollins, 2003; Newton et al., 2007); professionals' understandings of their practices and decisions (Carradice, Shankland, & Beail, 2002; Golsworthy & Coyle, 2001); the institutional context of certain kinds of experiences (Larkin, Clifton, & de Visser, in press; Schoenberg & Shiloh, 2002); and cultural understandings of mental health issues (Roose & John, 2003; Swift & Wilson, 2001).

TEN

Life transitions and identity

Introduction

One of the interesting things to emerge from the growing corpus of IPA studies is how often identity becomes a central concern. For example the three preceding chapters, although ostensibly about other topics, all have identity issues running through them. An even more specific commonality is that much IPA work is around identity changes associated with major life transitions. In one sense this is not surprising. If one embarks on an in-depth inductive qualitative study of a topic which has considerable existential moment, as is often the case in IPA research, then it is quite likely the participant will link the substantive topic of concern to their sense of self/identity. What is noticeable, however, is that this striking feature of IPA work is not at all prevalent in many other approaches to psychology.

The centrepiece of this chapter is an example from Jonathan's early research on identity change during the transition to motherhood (the original papers from the study can be found in Smith 1994a, 1999a, 1999b). While Jonathan had interests in identity when embarking on the project, the construct took on a life of its own during the course of the study. We include the study here as, in addition to illustrating a different domain where IPA has been employed, the study has a number of distinctive characteristics. The study illustrates how IPA has been used longitudinally and with an intensive idiographic focus based on a wide range of data collected from each participant. During the course of the study, about 20 pieces of data were obtained from each woman. The chapter also illustrates a project which pushes the I in IPA quite far and where the material is used in dialogue with a strong theoretical framework and where the analysis illustrates a slightly different way of working than shown so far. Box 10.1 shows the main features of IPA this study illustrates. After the main study, the final part of the chapter considers some other IPA studies which have focused on identity.

Box 10.1   Particular features of this study

- Collects multiple sources of data for each participant: interviews; diaries; personal accounts; repertory grids; and follows participant over time.
- Engages strongly with a theoretical framework.
- Formulates the cross case analysis in a novel way drawing on a form of analytic induction.

Identity change during the transition to motherhood

Background

Becoming a mother represents an important transition for a woman, when a number of significant personal, social and biological changes coincide. The study reported here follows a small number of women through pregnancy and the transition to motherhood and explores the women's personal accounts of the experience.

When this study was conducted, the existing research was predominantly quantitative. And much of that quantitative research operated from a medical or psychiatric model and focused on problematic pregnancies (see Smith 1999a for more discussion of this). The aim of this research was to explore pregnancy and the transition to motherhood as a normative process, one that most women go through without long-term physical or emotional problems.

It was considered that a qualitative methodology was best suited for the project because of its concern with the detailed examination of personal change. The project was also constructed from the outset to be heavily idiographic – collecting much data longitudinally from a small number of women rather than surveying a larger sample. Some opportunity for triangulation was offered as the study used multiple methods – interviewing, diaries, personal accounts and repertory grids.

The project was inductive. While the researcher was familiar with theories of life span development, for example Erikson's (1980) psychosocial model of identity development, and therefore anticipated that the transition to motherhood may be marked by personal change, there was no expectation of how this change might be manifest and there was a readiness to accept that major changes might not be reported.

The study was also influenced by the arguments of a number of feminist writers who had reservations about much of the existing work on the transition to motherhood, in part because of its operating within the medical or a positivistic model of inquiry. Nicolson (1986) pointed to the value of 'woman-centred' studies which focus on the first-hand accounts of women themselves and assume 'that whatever individuals report about their experience should be taken *as their interpretation of reality*' (p. 146). Nicolson (1989) used such an approach in her work around post-natal depression. And when looking at the existing work on the transition to motherhood, some of the most compelling and insightful analyses appeared in the published personal accounts of women themselves (e.g. Rich, 1977).

Method

The aim was to find a small group of women who were comparable in terms of obvious factors, following the principles of purposive homogeneous sampling explained in Chapter 3. Careful selection led to a group of women sharing the characteristics outlined in Box 10.2.

Box 10.2 Purposive sampling criteria

- Aged 25–30.
- In full-time employment.
- In long-term heterosexual relationship.
- First pregnancy.
- No previous miscarriage or termination.
- Not an unwanted pregnancy.
- Within the first trimester.

Each woman was visited four times: at three, six, and nine months pregnant, and five months after the birth of the child. Each woman was interviewed on every visit and kept a diary for the whole period. The interview was intended as an exploration of the woman's personal experience of pregnancy and how it was affecting the way in which she thought of herself. Instructions for the diary were left very open, the woman being asked to record things she thought and felt during the pregnancy, related to the topics discussed in the first interview. Women were asked to make entries once a week and most did so. Repertory grids were also constructed with each woman at each visit. These produce idiographic quantitative data which can be built into the case study. The grid data will not be referred to further here (see Smith 1994a, 1999a for more on how they were used in this study). The names of the women and members of their families have been changed to protect confidentiality.

Each case was then written up as a longitudinal case study in its own right in order to to do justice to the large amount of rich data obtained from each woman.

Cross case analysis. After each case had been written up separately, a second-order, cross case analysis was conducted and the process here is rather different from that described in Chapter 5. Again, then, it illustrates the flexibility of IPA. The procedures are different but still operate within the principles of IPA.

The sequence of analysis is important as it points to how the subsequent second-order analysing was prompted by, rather than pre-empting, the researcher's response to the material in the individual cases. The cross case analysis involved a form of micro theory development drawing on ideas from analytic induction (Robson, 1993; Smith et al., 1995) whereby provisional hypotheses are modified in the light of checking each case. This means the theory development is itself idiographic as each case is used to refine it. The aim is to produce theoretical statements which are true for all cases in the data set, or every case with clearly articulated exceptions, rather than the actuarial claims of orthodox psychological methodology. In practice, this involves a constant move between the individual cases and between levels of analysis, drawing on the complete studies, detailed sub-sections and abstracted comparison matrices.

While the terminology is different, the logic is not that different from the generation of super-ordinate themes as described in Chapter 5. A super-ordinate theme is a construct which usually applies to each participant within a corpus but which can be manifest in different ways within the cases. Similarly, the theoretical statements generated in this study applied to all participants (or to all with clearly marked exceptions where this applied) but the way the statement worked varied considerably between participants. Just as with group super-ordinate themes, this chapter illustrates how a well wrought IPA study will show both convergence and divergence, patterning but also individual nuance, as the write-up points to what the participants share at the same time as illustrating their individuality.

During the analysis of the individual cases, Jonathan was struck by how the women often referred to their relationships with significant others. This had not been a research question going into the study and the interview schedule did not have questions on personal relations in it. However, consonant with a hermeneutic phenomenological perspective, the woman were the experiential experts and the flexible inductive methodology allowed them to bring relationships in as a core element of the project and one which featured strongly in the individual case studies.

Prompted by this central concern with relationships, during the cross case analysis, Jonathan consulted literature in this area. George Herbert Mead (1934) proved an extremely useful source. Thus, a dynamic relationship exists between the comparing of individual case studies and the writing of Mead. His thinking provides an overall theoretical framework for the second-order analysis but the analysing and the specific content are driven by the material in the cases. Again we see IPA working creatively here. The first-order case studies were entirely inductive in the classic IPA style. However, as the analysis moved to the second stage, external theory came in at an earlier point than is typical of IPA. However, the crucial thing is that this dialogue with theory is still consistent with the principles of IPA as it was prompted by attending closely to the women's accounts and the emergent case study analysis. Therefore the theorizing is still 'from within' rather being imported 'from without', a distinction described in Chapter 5.

Mead's conception of the self was symbiotic, with it coming into being through social interaction with others:

> The individual experiences himself [sic] as such, not directly, but only indirectly, from the particular standpoint of other individual members of the same social group, or from the generalized standpoint of the social group as a whole to which he belongs. For he enters his own experience as a self or individual, not directly or immediately, not by becoming a subject to himself, but only in so far as he first becomes an object to himself just as other individuals are objects to him or in his experience; and he becomes an object to himself only by taking the attitudes of other individuals toward himself within a social environment or context of experience and behaviour in which both he and they are involved. (1934: 138)

Mead's view of the self is both relational and symbiotic:

> Selves can only exist in definite relations to other selves. No hard-and-fast line can be drawn between our own selves and the selves of others, since our own selves exist and enter into our experience only in so far as the selves of others exist and enter as such into our experience also. (p. 164)

For the analysis across cases, the author began by writing a generic summary statement encapsulating the overall meta-theoretical framework guiding the analysis and closely influenced by Mead's position but also by the emerging theme in the individual cases:

> *First statement:* Conception of self and of other are dynamically interdependent.

One case was then reviewed in the light of this general statement and a more specific provisional theoretical statement was constructed. The other cases were examined again in the light of this statement which, in turn, was modified as a result of this search. Thus, theoretical statements were produced, reviewed, modified and honed in the light of empirical data.

Four theoretical statements regarding the relational self were produced through this process. Here we present and illustrate two of them. The full account of the relational self can be found in Smith (1999a). The main study had a number of these inductive theoretical paths. See Smith (1994a) for the other main theoretical paths written up in full. It concerns self reconstruction during the transition to motherhood.

Analysis

The symbiotic psychological relationship of self and other is facilitated and accentuated during the pregnancy by social occasions. It may be that when individuals face major life transitions, the symbiotic relationship of self and other is accentuated and may facilitate the individuals' development through the transition. The women in this study show evidence of considerable reflection on the relationship between self and other selves. This is particularly noticeable after attending significant social gatherings. This is shown in the following passage from the original paper (Smith, 1999a):

> Clare has been to her step-daughter's wedding and, at the end of a diary entry, writes:

>> It struck me again as I watched Paul [her partner] give his speech at the reception about the nature of all our relationships with the advent of this second family. It is important to me that Laura and Mark [Paul's children from his previous relationship] are happy and accepting and it seems that they are.

> So this family wedding leads to awareness of inter- and intra- family connections. The network is complex. 'All our relationships' entwine. 'This second family' could refer to a number of relationships.
> Attending a friend's wedding has a rather different effect on Diane:

>> Thought a lot about being paranoid today. Last night Keith and I went to a friend's wedding, and I got very jealous over him talking to a friend of mine. At the time I was convinced something was going on behind my back. Today, after talking to Keith, I could see how paranoid I am. Keith forgets to tell me that I'm still attractive to him, and that I still look nice. Of course he's been fussing over me today and I feel that I've been ridiculous.

> In this case then there is a perception of a separation of Diane from others at the wedding, rather than the connection felt by Clare. What the two cases share is the process involved, whereby the women use the public event to reflect on their own sense of self and relations with partner.
> Equally these public events can serve as a forum for acknowledgement of the woman's growing identity as a mother. Seven months pregnant, Clare writes in the diary:

>> I managed to get Paul to go to one of the parentcraft sessions run at the health centre. [ ] Somehow I wanted the reassurance of public acknowledgement that we're going through this together, it's as if sometimes I feel like I'm running to catch up with him on the experience stakes – pretty inevitable really when you consider the circumstances!

> Clare requires recognition, 'the reassurance of public acknowledgement' of commitment to the relationship, and the mutual production of this child, partly necessary because Paul, unlike Clare, has been through this process before.
> Finally Angela writes in her diary:

>> We went to a friend's wedding yesterday. Usually Michael always cracks a joke about it being the worst thing that ever happened to him. He was very conscious of my presence and said how great we get on and that he feels very proud of my pregnancy. I was quite surprised. He is usually very private and does not show many feelings publicly.

> As with Clare, some weight is given to a public statement of commitment by the partner (Smith, 1999a: 415).

Thus in each case there is a pattern. Spontaneously the women write in their diaries about significant 'family' events which, through the process of enhancing social contact with important others, lead to a reflection on their own identity and their own family roles.

The increasing psychological engagement with significant others during pregnancy can facilitate the psychological preparation for mothering. Women are able to use their engagement with significant others during pregnancy as part of their developmental psychological preparation for becoming a mother. The loosening of the self/other distinction and the heightened awareness of interpersonal connections mean that women have the opportunity to take shifting perspectives on what it is to be a mother.

Here we explore how this works for Diane. It is suggested that significant others (her partner and young brother) take, along with Diane, changing roles in a family drama, enabling her to play out important family roles while she is still pregnant. We trace this development through the interviews and diaries, in another passage from the original paper, (Smith, 1999a):

> Diane is very close to her brother, David, who is twenty years younger than she is [he is 8 years old]. At interview one (three months pregnant), she suggests that this relationship is somewhat maternal and states:
>
> > How I've been with David is how I want to be with my own children.
>
> Perhaps looking after and growing fonder of David has been symbolic preparation for mothering her own child. This theme becomes further developed and localised in the pregnancy.
>
> Diary one includes a long entry (at four months) which introduces the family motif so central to Diane's accounts:
>
> > David had asked [ ] if Keith and I were getting married before or after the baby is born. Keith asked him whether he thought it made any difference and David shrugged his shoulders. [ ] But it made me think whether the baby would worry about it when he or she grew up.
> >
> > Another thing that happened today was that I banged my head as I went up the stairs. Keith and David were drilling the concrete out in the hallway. I sat on the steps and started crying like a baby. Keith came up and started rubbing my head and looking for any cut. I really behaved like a small child begging for sympathy. Keith kissed me and I stopped crying. Any other time I would have just sworn, rubbed my head, and gone on. I don't know whether I was just tired or after a bit of attention.
> >
> > Recently I've been making a clown mobile for the baby's room. Keith had taken David to the pub garden to play Aunt Sally, I was cooking the dinner and cutting out my clown. They arrived home and I went to check the dinner. When I entered the front room, Keith had cut the hat so that it fits the clown's head. I went mad, and screamed at him for touching my belongings. I said 'what's the point of teaching children, not to touch other people's belongings if even he can't do it'. Keith was astounded at my reaction and laughed at me. But I felt quite angry about it.

Notice how individuals' family roles change within the extract. It begins with Keith playing an adult role and Diane being like a child. In the third paragraph, Keith plays 'father' to David's 'child' but then, in a sense, seems to regress to himself being a child scolded by Diane or 'the mother', after which he is transformed to the worldly parent again.

So the roles are quickly interchangeable. Diane is baby and mother, Keith is carer, child and cynical adult, all within the space of one episode. Perhaps Diane is here psychologically exploring these different family roles, and particularly what it means to be a child, from a number of different perspectives and it is the symbiotic connection of self conception with conception of others which allows this to happen. David has a particular role in this psychological preparation for motherhood. In the first paragraph, his talk leads to Diane thinking about her child's attitude. In the playing, his presence helps facilitate the taking of different roles. This connection is made more explicit in a later entry (six months):

Keith's taken David to the club with him. [ ]It's so lovely to see Keith taking so much interest in David, it shows to me what he will be like with our own child.

Diary two (seven–nine months) shows a development of the symbolic motif as the nuclear family itself begins to take symbolic centre stage. This begins in the first entry (seven months):

Mum got me a pushchair/pram from Mark's and Spencer's yesterday. I put it all together and wheeled it about the kitchen. Keith laughed at me and said I thought the baby was already in there. I suppose I did.

Keith seems to be more excited by the soon to be arrival. He kisses my tummy as well as me in the mornings now. I love it. It makes us feel like a family already.

So the missing child is now included in the greeting patterns as if they are 'a family already'. Later, at eight months, there is another self-contained, lyrical entry:

David stayed last night. Keith and David were driving me mad this morning, play fighting on the bed and hence on top of me. I ordered them out of the room, to play elsewhere. After a while I went downstairs. Keith had prepared the vegetables, and David was sat at the table drawing. Keith had given him some tracing paper and a pencil. I began to make the batter pud mixture. Keith was showing David how to make moving pictures. I suddenly felt how right everything was. [1] That it seemed like a real family together.[ ] [2] I suppose having David here makes me feel like a real mum, or what it will be like when the baby is born and grows up.

In a sense, this entry itself captures the developmental, psychological preparation being suggested. Initially we see Keith and David like the children of the Diary one entry. During the entry, however, Keith becomes a more responsible 'new man', preparing vegetables and being a 'father' to David. Chaos is replaced by order and a 'real family' has been constructed. [ ] Diane's words provide support for the notion of symbolic preparation, making explicit at [2] the process of family construction. The use of 'real' here and at [1] underscores the bridge between symbol and reality. [ ]

So the drama is replayed a number of times but the narration has a cumulative development so that the evolution of a new 'ordered' family occurs as part of Diane's psychological preparation. The nuclear family arises again in the final entry of Diary two (nine months), though by here the entry is less lyrical and more explicit:

> David wants to spend more and more time around here with us. Keith spends a lot of time with him. [ ] It shows me what a good Dad Keith is going to be. He's got his faults but he cares a lot about bringing up the baby and David for that matter, cos he seems to be more and more involved with our little family than his own.

By now, Keith is presented as fully socialised. He has learnt how to become a good father. By nine months pregnant, talk is short and to the point:

> We love David so much and, you know, I think it would just fit in nicely if it was a boy (Smith, 1999a: 419–421).

Thus it is suggested that Diane's accounts point to a rehearsal for mothering as she is involved in family role play exercises with her partner and young brother. The entries show both internal narrative progression but also contribute to a cumulative development so that, by the time the birth is impending, Diane has more confidence about how the new family will work.

The diaries of Angela paint a similar picture and contribute to the cumulative power of this theoretical account. In the analysis of Angela's diaries, much attention is paid to ambiguity in how she makes reference to 'the baby' leading to uncertainty about whether she is referring to her own unborn child or to others she encounters. It is argued that this referent ambiguity is consonant with the identity fuzziness purported to be prevalent during pregnancy and illustrates another example of the opportunity offered to women to practise being mothers before they are faced with the reality of it. See Smith (1999a) for the full analysis.

Discussion

This study has suggested that pregnancy provides the opportunity for important psychological preparation for mothering. How does this relate to existing writings? Antonucci and Mikus (1988) draw on Markus's notion of 'possible selves' to suggest that pregnancy offers an opportunity for a woman to invoke her future mother self. One can see the potential for a useful dialogue here between quantitative work producing constructs, and qualitative work providing some of the detail to fill them out and also offering a more dynamic picture of the process.

The work also offers a dialogical exchange with Mead. Empirical results led to Mead as a fertile source to help explain and frame the analysis. In turn, the detailed analysis from the cases can be seen as illustrating how Mead's ideas can become manifest in practice. The study also connects with the work of Gilligan (1982), Gergen (1987), and others who champion a model of human development which emphasizes the relational and connected over the individualistic and autonomous.

Of course this is an abridged version of the complete analysis. Hopefully there is sufficient here to enable the reader to see how the analytic process was conducted, how the interpretative part of IPA works, and how the material illustrates the concept of the relational self. The strength of the conceptualization is cumulative and the reader may be interested to read the complete analysis (Smith, 1999a) in order to see the whole theoretical pathway. Another extended piece of analysis from the original study which has not been included here has also been used to illustrate the value of hermeneutics to contemporary qualitative research. This can be found in Smith (2007).

At this stage, the theoretical model is only making strong claims for the immediate population from which it is derived. We would argue that there is a need for theories of human functioning and social interaction which are founded on, and grounded in, the detailed analysis of individuals' accounts of their psychosocial world. The resultant micro-level theorizing should be richly informative of those particular individuals and may well be fairly modest in its claims to generalization. Indeed, such idiographic theorizing is primarily concerned with documenting the existence of actual patterns of life, not with measuring actuarial incidence.

However such models also offer a wealth of potential for subsequent theoretical development as outlined in the section on idiography in Chapter 2. So, for example, this micro-idiographic, theory-modelling work could be used in a subsequent study to help the generation of grounded theory (Charmaz, 2008; Chapter 12; Henwood & Pidgeon, 2006).

Other research on life transitions and identity

Migration and threat to identity

This study by Timotijevic and Breakwell (2000) explores how migration impacts on identity. Immigrants to the UK from the former Yugoslavia were interviewed about their perceptions of the homeland they had left and the country they had joined and the decision to move. The responses revealed a rich patterning of identifications.

Different people used different category membership strategies in relation to their former home. While some people identified as Yugoslavian and emphasized their own ethnic group as being an important element in that Yugoslavian identity, others stressed their own ethnic identity at the expense so the greater national identity:

> I identify as a former Yugoslavian [ ] I am proud to be a former Yugoslav. I am not ashamed. I think that the Serbs and Montenegrins appropriate this sense of Yugoslavianism undeservedly, they have no right to do it. That's not fair. I am angry about it a little bit. (Timotijevic & Breakwell, 2000: 364)

I hated the former Yugoslavia. I hated the whole system, this idea of Yugoslavia could not work and I had to go to war to defend my country [*Croatia*] against it [ ] I am a Croat and this means everything to me. It is the place you were born, the food you eat, the music you listen, it is your roots. (p. 364)

Thus the category Yugoslavian is not fixed and as a result can be invoked in different ways as part of the process of asserting one's identity, either as part of the category or as outside the category.

The relationship to the new host country can be similarly complex:

I am a refugee and that sounds terrible [ ] When you say to the people here that you are a refugee everyone turns their head away from you. But I understand those people. I could never imagine myself as a refugee; that just happened to me. I was at the wrong place, wrong time [ ] Sometimes when you watch TV and see people leaving their homes in their villages, you hear they say they are refugees and then you realize that you are a refugee as well and I don't want to be seen like that. (p. 366)

One can hear the participant thinking through the changing identifications. In the past, he, like his new neighbours, would have seen the refugee as other. And he therefore shares some of the negative views attached to the concept. As part of the assimilation process, he has tried to distance himself from that identity category. However, watching television, he is reminded that indeed he is now a member of the group he at one time saw himself as distinct from. The paper neatly captures this complex and dynamic process of identification and relates it to various theories of identity, including social identity theory and identity process theory.

Impact of homelessness on identity

Homelessness is another form of spatial dislocation which can have a serious impact on a person's sense of identity. Riggs and Coyle (2002) report a study based on in-depth interviews with four young people who faced the experience of homelessness in adolescence or early adulthood. The report presents their accounts as a series of case studies and then makes connections across cases. The case of Paul, in particular, shows how devastating homelessness can be to one's sense of identity. Paul says:

You *lose* who you are and people impress upon you who you *are* just by walking past you in the street ... their opinion of you ... and you adopt that identity. (Riggs & Coyle, 2002: 8)

Thus one's own sense of identity fades away as other people impose their own set of attributes associated with the state of homelessness. Indeed, so strong is this process that it can reach the point where one's identity appears to completely disappear:

You become like a non-person, you know. People don't bother with you ... talk to you, look at you ... which crumbles down any self-worth. (p. 8)

Part of the problem arises from losing a connection with a sense of place. John states:

> When you've lived somewhere for that long it's got your *character* in the house as well. (p. 11)

Eventually finding accommodation, John says:

> I'm filling my flat with my character as quickly as I can. (p. 11)

Thus the paper nicely points to the various negative impacts that homelessness can have on identity and also describes the coping strategies employed by participants.

Masculinity, health-behaviour and identity

The aim of this study by de Visser and Smith (2006, 2007) was to identify how young men's patterns of health related behaviour are related to their beliefs about masculinity, and the importance of drinking to their masculine identities. The study included both individual and focus group interviews with young men aged 18–21 in London. Participants were from a range of SES and ethnic backgrounds. The analysis showed that men indicated a range of ways in which masculinity and health behaviours were related. De Visser and Smith (2006) report a case study of one man, Rahul, an Asian student. The analysis illustrates how he can be seen to be constructing his own masculine identity by negotiating the various elements of masculinity which are available to him.

Rahul takes pains to emphasize his difference:

> I went to school in a pretty much 99 per cent majority white population [ ] I grew up in a different way to a lot of people especially at [*university name*] who are at this university um a lot of the Asians and stuff who grew up in other, around other Asians and stuff, I have a much different perspective to them due to the fact of having not grown up around that. So – not that that's a bad thing. I enjoyed it. (de Visser & Smith, 2006: 689)

So Rahul is doubly different – he is different from the white majority but also different from the Asian minority. Rather than feeling alienated by this difference, Rahul celebrates it, enjoying the lack of fixity that ensues:

> I'm unclassified, my whole thing. And I personally I love it ... because you can mix everything from, or you can take all the best things from all the different cultures. (p. 689)

Rahul demonstrated a similar strategy of careful negotiated identification when talking about health-related behaviour. Thus describing his drinking, Rahul says:

> I enjoy drinking … ah … just socially. I wouldn't enjoy … I don't really go out and say 'Oh I'm going to go out and get really plastered tonight' [ ] Obviously I've tried it and didn't enjoy it too much [ ] I just do it to relax with my friends and chill out. Not go crazy. Though you know we do go crazy but it's on rare occasions not every night kind of thing. (pp. 689–690)

So Rahul smoothly navigates around the various positions associated with alcohol in relation to masculine identity. He presents himself as having a mature perspective in contrast to the implied behaviour of those who are less mature and 'go out and get plastered'. However, to counter the notion that he is therefore not a normal male, he also points out that he can engage in the more extreme masculine behaviour, used to do so in the past, and still does occasionally now. Thus Rahul skilfully succeeds in presenting himself as combining two potentially contradictory elements of masculinity. He is both mature versus naïve and fun-loving versus boring. In the remainder of the interview, he demonstrates similar dexterity in relation to other components of maleness. The paper relates these findings to discursive and psychoanalytic accounts of masculinity.

SECTION C

Current Issues for IPA

In this section we present chapters dealing with some current issues for IPA. Qualitative researchers have fairly recently become particularly interested in the question of validity in qualitative research. In Chapter 11 we discuss how IPA addresses and can be seen in relation to validity. In Chapter 12, we look at the relationship between IPA and a number of what might be described as core concerns for a broad psychology. These include cognition, language and embodiment. We also consider IPA in relation to other phenomenological and hermeneutic approaches. Finally we offer some concluding comments and thoughts for the future in Chapter 13.

ELEVEN

Assessing validity

In this chapter we first set the scene for assessing validity and quality in IPA. We will then consider how IPA studies can meet the criteria offered by one recent guide to validity and qualitative psychology by Lucy Yardley. We will then describe the independent audit as a powerful way of thinking about quality in IPA research.

Assessing validity and quality in qualitative research

There is now considerable discussion among qualitative researchers about the assessment of quality of qualitative research. This has been prompted by growing dissatisfaction with qualitative research being evaluated according to the criteria for validity and reliability which are applied to quantitative research. Many qualitative researchers would assert that validity and quality are indeed important considerations but that qualitative research should be evaluated in relation to criteria recognized as appropriate to it.

A number of guidelines for assessing quality or validity in qualitative research have been produced. The way some of this work has progressed has been towards easy-to-use checklists against which a qualitative paper can be assessed by examiners, by reviewers or by editors. The danger here is that the assessment procedures become simplistic and prescriptive and that the more subtle features of qualitative work get missed out. We particularly like two approaches which present general guidelines for assessing the quality of qualitative psychological research and have a more sophisticated and pluralistic stance (Elliott et al., 1999; Yardley, 2000, 2008). First, their suggested criteria are broad ranging and offer a variety of ways of establishing quality. Second, they attempt to offer criteria which can be applied irrespective of the particular theoretical orientation of a qualitative study. Both are also presented in an accessible style. In this chapter, we focus on Yardley's criteria.

Yardley's criteria and how IPA can meet them

Lucy Yardley (2000) presents four broad principles for assessing the quality of qualitative research. We will go through each in turn and illustrate how IPA can address them. The first principle is *sensitivity to context*. Yardley argues that a good qualitative research study will demonstrate sensitivity to context. She offers a number of different ways in which such sensitivity can be established. The researcher may show sensitivity to, for example, the socio-cultural milieu in which the study is situated, the existing literature on the topic, the material obtained from the participants.

IPA researchers start demonstrating sensitivity to context in the very early stages of the research process. Sometimes the very choice of IPA as a methodology, the rationale for its adoption, will be centred upon the perceived need for sensitivity to context through close engagement with the idiographic and the particular. Because IPA tends to recruit purposive samples of participants who share a particular lived experience, they can be more difficult to access than other kinds of samples and sustained engagement, in terms of establishing access or a rapport with key gate keepers, may well be central to the very viability of an IPA project from the outset.

Sensitivity to context is also demonstrated through an appreciation of the interactional nature of data collection within the interview situation. Conducting a good IPA interview requires skill, awareness and dedication. An IPA analysis is only as good as the data it is derived from and obtaining good data require close awareness of the interview process – showing empathy, putting the participant at ease, recognizing interactional difficulties, and negotiating the intricate power-play where research expert may meet experiential expert. A researcher who navigates successfully through the terrain laid out in Chapter 4 and produces a good interview will definitely have shown sensitivity to context.

And, as shown in Chapter 5, this sensitivity to context continues through the analysis process. Making sense of how the participant is making sense of their experience requires immersive and disciplined attention to the unfolding account of the participant and what can be gleaned from it.

From the reader's or reviewer's perspective, much of the sensitivity so far will be judged indirectly – in the sense that a compelling and convincing IPA study is likely to have required the researcher to have shown the degree of sensitivity to context described in order to produce it. However, this can also be manifest explicitly in the written report or paper itself. It can be argued that the strongest context which a good piece of IPA research will be sensitive to is the data. Because such care is taken with the collecting of data from participants and with grounding analytic claims in the data obtained, a strong IPA study will thereby be demonstrating a sensitivity to the raw material being worked with. So a good IPA study will always have a considerable number of verbatim extracts from the participants' material to support the argument being made, thus giving participants a voice in the project and allowing the reader to check the interpretations being made. And good IPA is written carefully, making claims appropriate to the sample which has been analysed. Interpretations are presented as possible readings and more general claims are offered cautiously.

Researchers can also show sensitivity to context through an awareness of the existing literature and this in turn can be either substantive or theoretical, the former related to the topic of investigation, the latter to the underpinnings of the research method itself. In IPA the relevant substantive literature is used to help orient the study and the findings should always be related to relevant literature in the discussion. As we have seen, often this discussion will include a dialogue with literature which was not referenced in the introduction to the study.

Yardley's second broad principle is *commitment and rigour.* Commitment can again be demonstrated in a number of ways. With IPA there is an expectation that commitment will be shown in the degree of attentiveness to the participant during data collection and the care with which the analysis of each case is carried out. Thus to conduct an in-depth IPA interview well requires a considerable personal commitment and investment by the researcher in ensuring the participant is comfortable and in attending closely to what the participant is saying. We expect IPA researchers to take the business of doing experiential qualitative research seriously, to realize it requires certain skills and to make efforts to realize those skills. The complex nature of those skills means that one can begin to see an overlap in how IPA addresses Yardley's criteria. For some elements of the research process, a demonstration of commitment can be synonymous with a demonstration of sensitivity to context.

Rigour refers to the thoroughness of the study, for example in terms of the appropriateness of the sample to the question in hand, the quality of the interview and the completeness of the analysis undertaken. Thus, one would expect the sample to have been selected quite carefully to match the research question and also to be reasonably homogeneous, according to the principles described in Chapter 3. As we have seen, data for IPA are usually obtained through in-depth interviewing. Conducting a good interview will be a demonstration of rigour as well as the commitment addressed above. One needs to be careful to keep the balance between closeness and separateness, to be consistent in one's probing, picking up on important cues from the participant and digging deeper. Novice researchers find doing this demanding, and training and supervision is important in helping to ensure qualitative psychology is done rigorously.

As Chapter 5 demonstrated, the analysis must be conducted thoroughly and systematically and with IPA there must be sufficient idiographic engagement. The analysis must also be sufficiently interpretative, moving beyond a simple description of what is there to an interpretation of what it means. Good IPA studies tell the reader something important about the particular individual participants as well as something important about the themes they share. Also, as readers of an IPA study, we would in the results section expect the corpus to be drawn on proportionately, as touched on in Chapter 6. Thus, imagine a study with a small sample size of four participants where the analysis has led to the deployment of three major themes which the researchers argue are present for each participant. Because the numbers are manageable we would expect to see extracts from each participant to illustrate each theme. However, if the study has a larger number of participants and/or themes, there will probably not be space to provide an extract from each participant for each theme. In this case the researcher should judiciously select good and appropriate illustrations for each theme, as discussed in Chapter 6. We would expect each theme to be supported with quotes from a number of participants and that, in the overall narrative, participants' accounts will be drawn on pretty even-handedly.

Yardley's third broad principle is *transparency and coherence*. Transparency refers to how clearly the stages of the research process are described in the write-up of the study. A researcher using IPA may attempt to enhance transparency by carefully describing how participants were selected, how the interview schedule was constructed and the interview conducted, and what steps were used in analysis. Tables can be included to detail each of these features – the participants, the schedule, elements of the analytic process.

The coherence of a piece of qualitative research can itself be thought of in a number of ways and much of this is judged by the reader of the finished write-up. So it is important to read one's draft thesis or article carefully and to put oneself in the shoes of the reader.

Does it present a coherent argument? Do the themes hang together logically? Are ambiguities or contradictions dealt with clearly? It is not that contradictions shouldn't be in the data, they are often the richest part of the text, but the analysis of the contradictions should not in itself be contradictory! Good IPA like any good qualitative work requires careful writing and usually considerable drafting and re-drafting. As we said in Chapter 6 analysis and writing up overlap, and as one redrafts the analysis will become clearer.

Yardley suggests coherence can also refer to the degree of fit between the research which has been done and the underlying theoretical assumptions of the approach being implemented. So, when reading the report of what is claimed to be an IPA study, one would expect it to be consistent with the underlying principles of IPA rather than it seem to be adhering more closely to the expectations of a different qualitative approach.

And if the study is claiming to be IPA or to have IPA as one of its touchstones, the phenomenological and hermeneutic sensibility should be apparent in the write-up. Thus, the paper or write-up should have as its focal topic a significant experiential domain for the participants, and the writer should be able to demonstrate a commitment to attending closely to this 'thing itself'. At the same time, the writing should be nuanced and cautious and should also manifest an awareness of IPA as an inherently interpretative activity. The reader should be aware that they are positioned as attempting to make sense of the researcher trying to make sense of the participant's experience. In this way the reader can be convinced that the research has been conducted according to the principles of IPA. If evidence of these principles 'appears' within the write-up, it therefore acts as a testament to the complete research project.

Of course it is also possible for a study to be mixing methods and to present a hybrid. In this case the author should be clear about stating the approaches being drawn on and how they have been mixed in this particular study.

Yardley's final broad principle is *impact and importance*. She makes the important point that however well a piece of research is conducted, a test of its real validity lies in whether it tells the reader something interesting, important or useful. We think this is true of IPA as well and that the IPA researcher should be aspiring to do this.

The independent audit

We think the independent audit is a really powerful way of thinking about validity in qualitative research. Yin (1989) suggests that one way of checking the validity of one's research report is to file all the data in such a way that somebody could follow the chain of evidence that leads from initial documentation through to the final report. Thus, if one thinks of an IPA interview project, the trail might consist of: initial notes on the research question, the research proposal, an interview schedule, audio tapes, annotated transcripts, tables of themes and other devices, draft reports, and the final report.

Doing this is in itself good discipline for the researcher. By putting oneself in the place of someone having to make sense of the final report and check that a coherent chain of arguments runs from the initial raw data to the final write-up, one is forced to check the rigour of one's claims. At this level, the audit is hypothetical or virtual. The researcher files the data in such as a way that someone else *could* check through the 'paper trail'.

Of course one can go further and actually conduct an independent audit where the file of material, sequenced as above, is given to a researcher who has played no part in the project. Their task is to check that the final report is a plausible or credible one in terms of the data which have been collected and that there is a logical step-by-step path through the chain of evidence.

An independent audit is not at all the same thing as inter-rater reliability, commonly used when quantifying the analysis of open-ended material. The independent auditor is attempting to ensure that the account produced is a credible one, not that it is the only credible one. This speaks to the particular nature of qualitative inquiry. The aim of an independent audit is not to produce a single report which claims to represent 'the truth', nor necessarily to reach a consensus. Instead the independent audit allows for the possibility of a number of legitimate accounts and the concern therefore is with how systematically and transparently this particular account has been produced.

The independent audit can be conducted at a number of levels. It is possible in the most complete form to indeed pass all the box files at the end of a study to a researcher who was not involved in the project and ask them to conduct an 'independent audit'. At the other end of the spectrum, supervisors can conduct mini audits of their students' work by, for example, looking at the first interview transcript annotated with the student's initial codes, categories or themes. The supervisor can then check that the annotations have some validity in relation to the text being examined and the approach being employed. During this early apprenticeship phase, it is also appropriate for the supervisor to offer occasional additional notes on what he/she thinks is interesting or important in the transcript. This is with a view to helping the novice see good practice in action and so will help them develop their own skills. Thus we see the independent audit in the same way as Yardley's criteria. It is a flexible creature offering a range of opportunities to help the IPA researcher demonstrate the validity of their work. Thus, even just conducting a virtual audit shows considerable commitment to quality and validity.

Concluding thoughts

We think it is important that IPA researchers take quality and validity seriously and we have suggested some of the ways in which this can be addressed in an IPA study. Of course one of the primary reasons for writing this book is to help people conduct high quality IPA, and so indicators of quality can be found throughout.

At the same time it is important to remember two things. First, IPA is a creative process. It is not a matter of following a rule book. Therefore criteria for validity will need to be flexibly applied; something that works for one study will be less suitable for another.

Second, we need to get the balance right. There is now a large corpus of IPA research out there. Up to this point, we have felt it important to encourage people to have a go so that qualitative psychology becomes much more visible. Now there is a body of work, it is easier to begin to think of quality markers. What makes study A better than study B? We can envisage this corpus being a very useful source for such evaluation and that this will help feed into markers of good practice and illustrations of how IPA studies meet criteria for validity.

When we talk about getting the balance right, we mean the balance between pushing for the work to be of very high quality and recognizing when something is 'good enough'. Indeed we discussed this topic in Chapter 5 when considering levels of interpretation and what to expect of a researcher new to IPA. For the novice qualitative researcher, knowing what does make a piece of work good enough can indeed be one of the most difficult things and is where the role of the supervisor can be crucial. Looking ahead then, we look forward to more of both types of IPA: (a) work from new IPA researchers which can be seen to meet the types of criteria outlined in this chapter, which shows commitment and rigour and is therefore good enough to be written up; and (b) work which is pushing the boundaries further and producing research which is becoming better than good enough and thereby contributing to a body of IPA research studies which is outstanding.

TWELVE

The relationship between IPA and other approaches

In this chapter, we pick up on some of the issues first introduced in Chapters 2 and 3 which relate to IPA's position in psychology and its relationship with other approaches within qualitative psychology. We have also then seen these issues arising or flagged at various points in the rest of the book.

From the outset (Smith, 1996), IPA has been positioned as an integrative approach. IPA aims to allow the researcher to develop an analytic interpretation of participants' accounts which should be prompted by, and clearly grounded in, but which may also go beyond, the participants' own sense-making and conceptualizations (see also Larkin et al., 2006; Smith, 2004). Thus at the heart of an IPA study must be a commitment to the three key principles outlined in Chapter 2. The study must be concerned with examining 'the thing itself', the phenomenological experience of the participant. This requires an intense interpretative engagement with personal verbal material obtained from the participant. Each case is examined in detail as part of the process of analysis. If these three basic principles are adhered to, then IPA researchers may draw upon a considerable interpretative range and make connections with an array of other theoretical positions as part of the process.

One of IPA's main attractions, particularly for applied psychologists amongst whom it has been most popular (see Brocki & Weardon, 2005; Reid et al., 2005), has been its capacity for making links between the understandings of research participants and the theoretical frameworks of mainstream psychology. Fertile theoretical connections with other qualitative approaches are also now being developed by IPA researchers. We have already seen instances of both of these type of connections in the chapters in Section B. This chapter will be organized in terms of IPA's relation with a number of core constructs within the broad field of psychology: cognition; language, culture and narrative; embodiment and emotion. The context of our discussion here is rather different from that in Chapters 2 and 3. Those chapters are primarily offered with theoretical contextualization and research decision making in mind and, in turn, aim to help the reader see what is distinctive about IPA. Here we are beginning to think about connections as well as distinctions and to point towards possibilities for more integrative psychologies. This is a broad remit, and the following discussion is by no means exhaustive!

At the end of the chapter we consider the relation between IPA and some other approaches to phenomenological psychology. A final section will consider the relation between IPA and grounded theory because there is a degree of overlap between the approaches.

IPA and key domains in psychology

Cognition

From its inception, IPA has included a concern with cognition (Smith, 1996). What do we mean by this and how does it relate to phenomenology and hermeneutics? As will be seen throughout this book, IPA is concerned with examining how a participant makes sense of, or sees meaning in, their experience. We have suggested that sense-making is indeed a core human activity and one that participants share with researchers; hence the double hermeneutic whereby the researcher is trying to make sense of the participant making sense of x. However, some writing on phenomenology seems to emphasize a focus on immediate pre-reflective experience. How does this sit with IPA's concern with cognition, which would appear therefore to be reflective?

Clearly the primal experience of the flow of consciousness is a significant focus for phenomenological thinking. An example of this form of immediate experience would be walking in contentment down a country lane, putting one foot in front of the other, receiving a constant but changing flow of visual and aural stimuli as we move. Thus we catch glimpses of each tree as we pass, occasionally hear the rustling of leaves and chatter of birds, but these stimuli barely register for us and we do not attend to them. This is more or less an example of Dilthey's generic flow 'experience', as first discussed in Chapter 1.

Much phenomenological writing has been concerned with the most basic pre-reflective features of experience. An example we met in Chapter 2 would be the process of a hand reaching out to touch something as described by Merleau-Ponty. And it is also the case that much of our life is taken up with the mundane and ordinary sort of experience – the kind which is 'not thought about'. A phenomenological analysis has much to offer the elucidation of this taken-for-granted realm of experience.

However, it is important not to assume that it is only such basic, immediate, unmediated domains which are of concern to phenomenology. As we have seen in Chapter 2, Heidegger and Sartre also turn our attention towards the things which matter to us – the people, objects, places and relationships which constitute our lived existence, and Husserl was very interested in the array of mental processes involved in human life. Much of what is important to us involves bigger concerns with life goals, relationships, personal and professional projects, and with the factors that facilitate or inhibit them. And when it comes to these arenas, we naturally engage in considerable mental activity. Phenomenology is also interested in those experiences which register as significant for the participant, those which become 'an experience' of importance rather than remain as just 'experience'.

It is these bigger and more significant experiences which IPA is almost always concerned with; experiences where the individual is prompted to contemplate, take stock, worry, and try to make sense of what is happening. Indeed, each of the experiences recounted in the chapters in Section B of the book is of this order: major things happening to the person, which have existential significance and which engender a considerable amount of mental activity.

So what about the issue of pre-reflection? Is it the case therefore that phenomenology is interested in both the pre-reflective and also in the reflective? Well yes indeed. We consider the natural attitude of everyday experience, which is the site for phenomenological inquiry, to have a wide spectrum or bandwidth and that it contains within it both pre-reflective and reflective activity. We want to make a distinction therefore between what can be described as informal or intuitive reflection, which is occurring spontaneously within the person's natural attitude, and formal or phenomenological reflection which is being produced by the researcher conducting a phenomenological inquiry. The thoughts of two phenomenological philosophers are helpful here. Reviewing a book on Husserl, Mohanty (1975) writes:

> Natanson suggests that the natural attitude already includes reflection. There is a spontaneous 'becoming aware that one is aware.' We may call this the reflexivity of our conscious life. But one needs to distinguish between pre-reflective reflexivity and the reflective 'glancing at' a pre-reflective experience. Again one may have to distinguish between that reflective glance which ordinarily and spontaneously 'irrupts' into natural life, and that deliberate, methodologically controlled reflection which philosophy needs ... The first two sorts of reflection are located within the domain of everyday life. (p. 543)

This is complex, but then the phenomenon we are talking about is complex. Mohanty is suggesting that ordinary life can contain reflection and he introduces two layers of reflection within the natural attitude, which therefore contains both 'pre-reflective reflexivity' and 'the reflective "glancing at" a pre-reflective experience'. We have tried to spell this out more fully in Box 12.1, and in the process, have added an additional layer to the pre-phenomenological reflection.

Box 12.1   Layers of reflection

1. *'Pre-reflective reflexivity'*. Sartre argues that even in the most immediate flow experience, there is a minimal level of awareness, as we are 'conscious of being conscious' (1956/1943: 11). Walking down the country lane, I have this minimal level of awareness which does not interfere with the flow of experience and would not even be registered by me as awareness.

2. *'The reflective "glancing at" a pre-reflective experience'*. This involves intuitive, undirected reflection on the pre-reflective, as when we engage in daydreams, imagination and memory. Walking in the lane, I become aware of the warmth of the sun on my left shoulder and am reminded of swimming in the Mediterranean the year before.

3. *Attentive reflection on the pre-reflective.* My leg starts to ache and I begin to wonder what is wrong. Is this a recurrence of the injury I had three months ago, which meant I had to stop running, and led to many painful sessions with the physiotherapist? If so, what does it mean is happening to my body and does it have implications for other aspects of my life? 'Experience' becomes 'an experience' of importance as it is registered as significant and requiring attention.

4. *'Deliberate controlled reflection'*. This is phenomenological reflection. Later on in my office, I decide to reflect on the morning's events. I deliberately mentally replay the sequence of events and conduct a formal analysis of the content of my pre-reflective reflections on those events. My analysis represents a phenomenological reflection on my spontaneous reflection on what has happened to me.

Box 12.1 aims to illustrate what we mean by the bandwidth of reflection. Rather than there being a binary distinction between a non-reflective natural attitude and a reflective phenomenological attitude, we would assert that there is a wide range of related activity going on here, comprising a sequence of layers, with each representing an increased degree of reflection. There is a boundary between the 'natural' reflection of everyday life in layers 1–3 and the phenomenological reflection of layer 4. But the fact that the domain is layered rather than binary also points to the fact that this phenomenological reflection has some relationship to the everyday reflection.

In other words 'being phenomenological' involves taking a quality which occurs in everyday life, honing it, stretching it, and employing it with a particular degree of determination and rigour. And of course there are individual differences to be factored into the matrix. Different people will evidence these different layers to different degrees. Most of the time, most of us do not engage in the more formal and systematic reflection of layer 4.

You will have realized that Box 12.1 presents the bandwidth for the individual doing their reflections alone. In this case it is similar to the way Husserl might describe the process for his own phenomenological investigations. However, as we have discussed in Chapter 2, doing psychological (or any other human or social science) research involves another individual, the researcher, entering the reflective loop. Within the research encounter then, the researcher will facilitate the participant in providing an account of their reflections.

This then introduces another intricate set of complexities to the equation. What we are saying is that the participant, prompted by an event of significance happening to them, will spontaneously, and on their own, engage in the type of reflections we have described as layers 2 and 3. Then, when being interviewed by the phenomenological researcher, they will recount some of this reflection that they have already done. In addition, however, the interviewer may well spark additional new reflections by the participant. Some of these will again be relatively unselfconscious (layers 2 and 3) but some will be a form of phenomenological reflection in their own right (layer 4).

Thus the interviewer is facilitating some self-conscious phenomenological reflection by the participant. For example, if I was to participate in a phenomenological study, the researcher might ask me to do some thinking about the experiences described in Box 12.1:

> Think back to that moment when the sun on your arm reminded you of swimming in the Mediterranean. Tell me about the point at which the association happened. What was the sensory relation between the two events? What emotional quality is attached to the association? (*layer 4 reflection on layer 2 reflection*)

> Take me through the process of the experience of your leg aching. At what point did you become conscious of it as a problem and what specifically was it that led you to start worrying about it? How did the sensations perceived at the time compare with those when you had the leg injury? What form did your worries take – what was their content, quality, prevalence? (*layer 4 reflection on layer 3 reflection*)

Here the previous unselfconscious reflection by the participant becomes material for conscious reflection, again by the participant, and prompted by the researcher.

Then later, the researcher will conduct the full, layer 4, formal, reflective, phenomenological analysis on the transcript which is a record of the participant's layered set of reflections. This connects with our description of the IPA researcher as engaging in a double hermeneutic, where the researcher is trying to make sense (layer 4) of the participant trying to make sense (layers 3 and 4) of what is happening to her/him.

Layer 3 in Box 12.1 is, of course, the site where the material for an IPA analysis is primarily located, and, as we have said, the reflection here occurs spontaneously (that is without deliberate self-conscious prompting) as participants reflect on and try to make sense of what is happening to them. And, going full circle and connecting IPA's project with that of Husserl, here is a quote illustrating how he too was indeed centrally concerned with these spontaneous reflections (layers 2 and 3):

> While observing, I perceive something; in a like manner I am often 'busied' with something in memory; while quasi-observing, I follow in inventive phantasy what goes on in the phantasied world. Or I reflect, I draw conclusions; I take back a judgement,

perchance 'abstaining' from making any judgements at all. I am pleased or displeased, I am glad or sad, I wish, or I will and I do something; or, again, I 'abstain' from being glad, from wishing, willing and doing. In all such acts I am present, I am *actionally* there. Upon reflecting, I apprehend myself as the human being who is there. (1982: 190)

This implies that within the natural attitude one can remember, fantasize, reflect, make judgements, come to conclusions, have volition – all of which are examples of mental or cognitive processes. This, then, is what we mean when we say that IPA is concerned with cognition. This cognition occurs within the informal, intuitive domain of reflective activity in the natural attitude. It is dynamic, multi-dimensional, affective, embodied, and intricately connected with our engagement with the world, and we would therefore argue that this cognition is at the heart of the phenomenological project.

There is an additional, more specific context for this debate about cognition and IPA. When Jonathan wrote his paper 'Beyond the divide between cognition and discourse' (Smith, 1996), he was writing within a particular intellectual climate. Discourse analysis (DA) was emerging as a successful and radically alternative approach to the experimental paradigm which dominated psychology. This DA could be described as one instantiation of a critical psychology seemingly determined to expunge cognition as a marker of its separation from mainstream psychology.

Within British social psychology, in particular, there then appeared to be two main and incommensurate paradigms, the social cognition models of mainstream experimental social psychology and DA. At that time, Jonathan was pointing to a third, less separatist way, an experiential psychology which retained a concern with mentation and which could therefore connect with the constructs of mainstream psychology but which offered a more dynamic processual model of human being, and which therefore connected to the micro qualitative analysis of DA.

We are arguing that cognition is and can be a significant site for phenomenological inquiry but that does not mean that we share the vision of how cognition has been operationalized by mainstream psychology. As we have described above, we are interested in cognition in the sense of cognition as a complex, nuanced process of sense- and meaning-making – the very activities that Bruner (1990) considered central to his model of cognitive psychology. This conceptualization of cognition is dilemmatic, affective and embodied. It is complex, changeable, and can be hard to pin down, but it is cognition none the less. From the perspective of IPA, like phenomenology more broadly, cognitions are not isolated separate functions, but are one aspect of being-in-the-world, and are accessed indirectly through people's accounts and stories, through language, and ultimately, meaning-making.

Thus, faced with a dominant model of the construct of cognition in psychology we are faced with two choices. We can choose to excise the construct from our conceptual framework or we can choose to use it, but to use it in a different way from that manifested in the dominant paradigm. Because we feel the term has significant intellectual leverage, and because we want to re-appropriate it or thicken its signification in psychology, we have chosen the latter course of action.

Of course, cognition is operationalized rather differently in mainstream psychology and IPA. Certainly, the aim of much experimental psychology has been more concerned with attempting to make direct claims about cognition-as-process, than it has with understanding the meaning or contents of thoughts. Cognitive psychology tends to come with certain assumptions (i.e. inferring cognitive processes from measurable behavioural responses), metaphors (the mind-as-computer, and consequently, an information processing account of cognition), methods (primarily experimental or questionnaire) and boundaries (e.g. the separation of cognition from emotion). The field is obviously broader and more complex than this (e.g. see Bruner, 1990, or Gallagher & Zahavi, 2007), but for the purposes of this chapter, it may be helpful to work with this simpler characterization.

Nevertheless, people's interpretative activities are still integral to certain aspects of cognitive psychology. This is particularly the case in social cognition models, memory research and applied cognitive psychology. For example, think of concepts like salience and priming in the study of prejudice, or the reconstructive aspects of remembering, or the complex relationship postulated between 'beliefs', 'attitudes', and 'behaviours' – all of these are about meaning-making, and all can be re-viewed anew, in the light of insights from more open-ended experiential psychological investigations. Thus we might say that, conceptually, certain forms of IPA research and certain strands of cognitive psychology ought to have something constructive to say to one another. And we would like to see more of this dialogue in the future.

In practical terms, this has most often been played out in terms of mixed method studies and programmes (e.g. see Flowers et al., 2003; Flowers et al., 1997; Michie, Hendy, Smith, & Adshead, 2004; Newton, Landau, Smith, Monks, Shergill, & Wykes, 2005; Newton et al., 2007). The power of mixed designs lies in the combination of insights and leverage which can be offered by IPA when it is used alongside quantitative approaches. So, phenomenological work can be used to explain and make sense of quantitative findings. For example, in Newton et al. (2005), the quantitative part of the study is largely concerned with demonstrating that a psychological intervention has, for the most part, been effective. In the companion paper (Newton et al., 2007), the phenomenological analysis helps the reader and researchers to understand *how* this psychological intervention has worked, from the perspective of the clients who received it. But here, IPA also illuminates something of the experiences of those 'less typical' participants, who can so easily disappear in the aggregates of statistical analysis. The intervention studied in the two papers has been more successful for some participants than for others, and the IPA work actually leads to a persuasive experiential, relational and contextual explanation for this.

Alongside the potential for complementary (and also contradictory) perspectives on a topic, there is one obvious further attraction here, which is purely pragmatic. Mixed methods approaches may have considerably more capacity to bring about change (in practices and policies) than singular designs. This may seem obvious for qualitative studies – their place in the 'hierarchy of evidence' is still not widely understood, and so quantitative studies are often assumed to offer 'better' evidence, even when basic standards of design, measurement and statistical analysis have not been met. Quantitative studies really do benefit from the presence of qualitative perspectives, too, however. IPA can offer insights into experiences of events and processes, and the personal meaning of various 'outcomes', which can help researchers to interpret their quantitative findings and to illustrate them for a diverse audience. This has been exemplified very effectively in some of Paul's work on sexual decision making (see Chapter 8).

The key to success here is that the IPA component must, at the very least, be seen as an equal partner in the design and resourcing of the research. Indeed, in Paul's work it has generally been positioned as the primary element. In studies where qualitative components of the design are given only 'exploratory' or 'auxiliary' status, their potential to transform and illuminate is greatly diminished.

We hope this extended discussion of IPA's position on cognition will help address the concerns of Willig (2001) and Langdridge (2007) who see IPA's engagement with cognition as problematic. We have shown how we have a model of cognition much broader than that which is usually explicated in mainstream cognitive psychology. The cognition we are talking about includes the range of layers of reflective activity which make up part of everyday experience and which can therefore form the focus of a phenomenological inquiry. It also includes the additional formal reflection and other activities conducted by researchers as they carry out interpretative phenomenological analysis. Box 12.2 shows a list of terms describing both the 'content' and the 'process' of IPA which are also contained within the category of cognition.

Box 12.2 Cognition and IPA

Everyday cognition as 'subject' for IPA
pre-reflective reflexivity
intuitive reflection
awareness
consciousness
hot cognition
rumination
sense-making
meaning-making

Self-conscious cognition as 'process' of doing IPA
analysis
interpretation
sense-making
formal connecting with theory

And, as we pointed out earlier, we don't see this cognition as a compartmentalized activity – it is dynamic, emotional and embodied. The concerns of hermeneutic phenomenological psychology and standard cognitive psychology are clearly distinctive (they are interested in acquiring different sorts of knowledge, in making different levels of claims, and they employ different definitions of the terrain) but they do overlap at certain key points. We also hope that we have established through the book that the most obvious point of contact is sense-making and meaning-making. People make meaning. For IPA researchers, the sense-making activities of people (in conversations, diaries, group discussions or other forms) are the basis for learning about their relationship to the world. From this position, IPA research can clearly 'speak to' cognitive psychology. As we develop accounts of what an identifiable experience (an event, process, or relationship, etc.) has come to mean for particular people within certain contexts, our analyses can be related back to existing theoretical accounts from psychology.

Language, culture and narrative

Meaning-making clearly takes place using certain kinds of resources (narrative, discourse, metaphor, etc.), and within certain sorts of contexts (interactions, such as interviews, and settings, such as universities or hospitals, for example). Cultures are, effectively, frameworks for meaning-making (Much, 1995). Thus, while IPA's primary purpose may lie elsewhere, with understanding experience, it is inevitably 'always already' enmeshed with language and culture. As we have seen in Chapter 2, these concepts are familiar to phenomenological and hermeneutic philosophers. Moreover, when Heidegger writes of language as 'the house of Being', he points out that our interpretations of experience are always shaped, limited *and* enabled by, language. We have seen this illustrated in the case study in Chapter 9, where Binswanger's view of metaphor-as-foundational is applied to an analogy ('the Hulk life') used by a research participant, in order to better understand the experience and life-world of that participant.

Similarly, when Heidegger writes of Dasein as being *thrown* into the world, he gives us a metaphor for understanding our relationship with cultural objects and resources. The physical, social and cultural world has an existence which precedes us, and which constrains what we can do, be, and claim. Remember also, that Heidegger's world is a 'with-world' (Mitsein, *being-with*, is a further characteristic of Dasein). Our understandings of our experiences are woven from the fabric of our many and varied relationships with others. Crucially, accounts of enculturation and intersubjectivity which are broadly consistent with these positions can be drawn from symbolic interactionism (Mead, 1934), developmental psychology (Trevarthen & Aitken, 2001) and cultural psychology (Cole, 1996). These are important, because they give us an account of how the *situated* and *related* qualities of human understanding come about.

Thus, we can say that IPA research is, in part, an inquiry into the cultural position of the person, and that to understand the experiential claims being made by a research participant, we also need a certain level of cultural competence. This doesn't necessarily mean that we have to be cultural 'insiders', but it does mean that we may need to do some work of our own in order to properly understand our participants' terms of reference.

This is not the same as saying that IPA has the same deconstructive aims as discourse analysis, however. Discursive approaches now occupy a range of epistemological and methodological positions (e.g. see Wetherell, Taylor, & Yates, 2001), but can be very loosely categorized (e.g. see Burkitt, 1999) according to their primary interest in either power (after Foucault) or interaction (after Garfinkel and Sacks). In the case of Foucauldian discourse analysis (FDA), 'discourse' is understood to be a body of knowledge (a way of understanding), and these bodies of knowledge are held to be constitutive. The other major strand of discourse analysis has developed broadly within the ethnomethodological tradition, and is often called Discursive Psychology (DP). Here, 'discourse' is understood to refer to a communicative interaction, and thus DP is concerned with the use of available cultural resources to achieve interactive ends (e.g. Potter & Wetherell, 1987).

We can see that both approaches to discourse analysis share some concerns and interests with IPA, but they clearly set out with a stronger and more singular commitment to social constructionism. To develop this further, let's draw on an example from Larkin et al. (2006) to consider how a research topic – in this case, 'love' – might be conceptualized by these different approaches. A DP study of 'love' might set out to identify the various constructions of love, as they are played out during a particular form of social interaction (e.g. speed dating), and might then focus on 'the functions of those constructions within the localised situation of *that interaction*' (2006: 109). An FDA approach might prefer to treat the record of such interactions as an indicative text, through which the 'bodies-of-knowledge that *constitute* "love" in a wider cultural environment might be accessed' (2006: 109). In the former case, the focus is performative, and *interaction* (identifying patterns of discursive action) is the topic. In the latter, the focus is structural, and *knowledge* (identifying discursive structures) is the topic. In both cases, discursive representations are the unit of analysis.

For an IPA researcher, however, the focus will be hermeneutic, idiographic and contextual (an interpretation of the meaning for a particular person in a particular context). Experience (shorthand for 'a person's relatedness to a given phenomenon' – i.e. love) is the topic, and the individual and their meanings are the units of analysis. IPA can be used to reveal something about a particular person's understanding of their experience of a phenomenon such as love. What it can reveal is that person's positionality in relation to love – love in their experience, their culture, language and locale. Thus, through IPA, we glimpse a person's current subjective mode-of-engagement with some specific context (e.g. a Greek wedding) or aspect of their world (e.g. ongoing involvement in an intimate relationship). These modes of engagement can be multiple or even paradoxical; they are not unitary or static.

To help clarify, it is worth pointing out that IPA subscribes to social constructionism but to a less strong form of social constructionism than discursive psychology and FDA. And Mead (1934), already discussed in relation to the relational self in Chapter 10, is a powerful theoretical touchstone. Mead argues that while humans come into and are originally shaped by pre-existing cultural forces, they have the possibility to rework the constitutive material, through symbolic or cognitive activity as part of developing as individuals:

> After a self has arisen, it in a certain sense provides for itself its social experiences, and so we can conceive of an absolutely solitary self ... who still has himself [sic] as a companion, and is able to think and to converse with himself as he had communicated with others. (p. 1934: 140)

Thus, while mind begins as a social phenomenon: 'There is nothing odd about a product of a given process contributing to, or becoming an essential factor in the further development of that process' (p. 226).

Mead's work, while generally neglected in psychology, does find echoes in a number of more recent theoretical perspectives:

> Self-identity is not a distinctive trait or even a collection of traits, possessed by the individual. It is the self as reflexively understood by the person in terms of her or his biography. Identity here still presumes continuity across time and space: but self-identity is such continuity as interpreted reflexively by the agent. (Giddens, 1991: 53–54)

See Smith (1994a, 2003) for more on this theoretical model of the person which usefully connects with the IPA perspective.

It seems that IPA does have the potential for fertile links with, in particular, Foucauldian discourse analysis, through shared concerns with how context is implicated in the experiences of the individual. While IPA studies provide a detailed experiential account of the person's *involvement* in the context, FDA offers a critical analysis of the structure of the context itself and thus touches on the resources available to the individual in making sense of their experience. A number of IPA studies have developed along these lines (Chadwick, Liao, & Boyle, 2005; Flowers, Duncan, & Frankis, 2000; Johnson, Burrows, & Williamson, 2004; Larkin et al., in press). These studies vary in the extent to which they explicate a connection between the two approaches, but on the whole the link remains implicit. Given the way that these approaches appear to come to the social world in *potentially* complementary forms, it would seem that there is value in a more explicit articulation of the relationship between them.

IPA has a strong intellectual connection with various forms of narrative analysis. IPA is centrally concerned with meaning-making and the construction of a narrative is one way of making meaning. Bruner's model of narrative (1987) as an interpretative meaning-making endeavour clearly resonates with the project of IPA. While narrative psychology has also developed from social constructionism (see Bruner, 1990), it has also connected with several aspects of phenomenological psychology during its development. This is particularly the case in the work of researchers who are interested in narrative as a mechanism for understanding life experience. For example, much of the work carried out by Crossley, Reissman and by various authors publishing in the *Narrative Study of Lives* series (edited by Josselson and Lieblich) has an experiential impetus. These researchers are primarily interested in the *content* of people's stories about various events (e.g. Crossley, 2000), and as such they obviously make contact with IPA researchers (e.g. Eatough & Smith, 2006a, 2006b; Shaw, 2004; Smith, 1994a) who have been interested in the use of narratives and/or the development of experiential accounts over time.

For example, in Eatough and Smith's (2006a) study of one woman's experiences of anger and aggression, the authors discuss the changes in the participant's self-narratives as a key component for understanding the impact of a series of counselling sessions on the participant's experience of herself as 'angry'. Having observed that the participant has long maintained a story which situates bio-chemical agents as the source of her anger, the researchers are struck by her subsequent struggle to *re-story* herself, in the light of the counselling. This reconstructive function is a key aspect of many counselling and psychotherapeutic approaches. The underlying principle is a narrative one; clients are encouraged to re-interpret their lived experiences so that their lives become more liveable.

Thus we would assert that telling the story of one's life has personal significance for the individual, indeed can be described as a central marker of what it is to have an identity, as suggested in the discussion of Mead above. Thus the storytelling is an occasioned activity but it is also more than this. As Eatough and Smith (2008) put it:

> When people tell stories of their lives, they are doing more than drawing on the culturally available stock of meanings. People may want to achieve a whole host of things with their talk such as save face, persuade and rationalize, but there is almost always more at stake and which transcends the specific local interaction. Rosenwald (1992: 269) poignantly notes: 'If a life is no more than a story and a story is governed only by the situation in which it is told, then one cannot declare a situation unlivable or a life damaged.' Amongst other things it seems to us that our personal accounts are also concerned with human potential and development, with *making* our lives by connecting the past with the present and future. (p. 185)

Of course, there are other narrative researchers who are more interested in the *structure* of people's stories (e.g. Gergen & Gergen, 1988), and who aim to explore the constraints and opportunities which these structures place upon human experience. This is a more explicitly constructionist endeavour, which shares some commonalities with discourse analysis. One can again, however, see the potential for a fruitful exchange with IPA. See, for example, Smith's

(1994a) paper illustrating how women's reconstructive narratives of the transition to motherhood draw on positively inscribed trajectories of either personal growth or continuity.

Embodiment and emotion

The phenomenon of embodiment has recently resurfaced across a range of critical and qualitative approaches to psychology (e.g. see Finlay & Langdridge, 2007; Nightingale & Cromby, 1999) and in the human sciences more generally (e.g. Burkitt, 1999; Wider, 1997). Much of the interest has been re-kindled or informed by phenomenological work, and by the philosophy of Merleau-Ponty, whose ideas were sketched briefly in Chapter 2, in particular. This development has come about partly as a response to a perceived shortfall in social constructionism's ability to deliver an adequate account of the body, that is, one which recognizes its experiential, social and political primacy. The fact that a significant proportion of IPA work has taken place in these very fields indicates the importance of embodiment to IPA researchers.

For phenomenologists embodiment has long been a central concern, because it is a central concern for human beings. The many dimensions of this concern are captured very effectively by Ainley (1989):

> A person's experiences of the world and self are bound up with her/his experience of her/his body ... The body anchors the individual in a world of things and other people ... A person's ties to her/his body are perhaps made most clear when something about the body goes awry ... Most people are aware then – whether they view their bodies as enabling or limiting – of both being and having a body. (pp. 21–22)

What this evokes is a body which is, meaningfully, more than appearance, or physiology, but which is nevertheless constrained by these factical matters. These limits are, however, complex and contextual. Bodies are different from one another (genetically, biologically, physically and apparently, but also *expressively* and *experientially*). As Ratner observes, when writing about emotions, these differences cannot be reduced to biology, and neither can their meaning: 'Biological processes – hormones, neurotransmitters, autonomic reactions – underlie (mediate) but do not determine emotional qualities and expressions. Particular qualities and expressions are determined by cultural processes and factors' (2000: 5). The body is a cultural and a biological entity then and it can be helpful to think, as Bruner (1990) does, of the biological body as a set of constraints and potentials, which are made meaningful through a person's engagement in the cultural and physical world.

To this end, Merleau-Ponty describes human beings as *body-subjects* (See Busch, 2008; Morris, 2008), because our intentionality *begins* with the body – reaches out from the body, even. We come to know the world partly through our bodily engagement with it – we have an *embodied knowing* of how to throw, walk, find the light switch in our kitchen. Becoming *aware* of ourselves as a body-subject, through, for example, some critical social judgement, or a physical illness, can be a very troubling but also a very illuminating experience.

For psychologists then, it is very important to understand embodied experiences, and also to be able to relate them (critically, constructively, and sometimes affirmatively) to other more reductive accounts of bodies. A large corpus of IPA research is focused on the body, and particularly the body when it appears to go wrong. The particular task of IPA is to examine how the individual attempts to make sense of this embodied experience. See Chapter 7 for more on this.

This does not mean that person and body are literally, exactly and phenomenologically coterminous. Embodiment is a sense of bodiliness which may exceed physical limits. Langdridge (2007) suggests that Heidegger's distinction between the corporeal (the physical) and the bodily (the sense of one's embodiment) is a useful place to begin here. The latter is a psychological or phenomenological sense of the body which transcends (but is grounded in) the physicality of the body. We might, for example, find that in the act of pointing, or dancing, our sense of embodiment seems to exceed the physical limits of the body. For Merleau-Ponty, this means that, 'Consciousness projects itself into the physical world and has a body, as it projects into a cultural world and has its habits' (1962: 137).

The body, then, brings us full circle – it reminds us of how experience is connected to the physical and cultural world. Through a further, phenomenologically-informed, field of work (e.g. Gallagher & Varela, 2001), it also connects IPA with the developing field of embodied cognition. Here cognition is understood to be an embodied, situated and intersubjective process of meaning-making. This is a model of 'thinking' which is amenable to IPA's insights (see Larkin, Eatough, & Osborn, submitted), and where IPA researchers may be able to make a very positive and complementary contribution to the developing experimental work in 'neuro-phenomenology' (Gallagher & Sørensen, 2006).

The body also reminds us about emotions. Emotions are absolutely central to our human understanding of experience, and to phenomenologists' understandings of intersubjective acts. From a phenomenological perspective, emotions and cognitions are closely interrelated (e.g. see Damasio, 1995) as aspects of our engagement in the world. Further, emotions are a powerful indicator of the personal resonance of culturally and physiologically influenced entities. Nancy Chodorow (1999) describes this well:

> Emotion words and emotional concepts must have individual resonance and personal meaning ... That thoughts and feelings are entangled and that thoughts are thought in culturally specific languages – these ideas do not mean that there is no private feeling or that any particular thought has only a public cultural meaning. Culturally recognizable thoughts or emotion terms can also be entwined in a web of thought-infused feelings and feeling-infused thoughts experienced by an individual as she creates her own psychic life within a set of interpersonal and cultural relations. (pp. 165–166)

Emotions – their embodied and intersubjective qualities, their cultural and cognitive dimensions – have been an important and recurring aspect of IPA work across a diverse range of topics (women's aggression; recovery from addiction; making social and relational decisions about risk; responding to distressing life events; coping with chronic and acute illnesses; and so on). Indeed, alongside identity development, emotional experience is probably one of the strongest prevailing themes in the IPA literature.

IPA in relation to other phenomenological approaches

Of course IPA is not the only articulation of a phenomenological approach to psychology and a number of people have developed particular forms of phenomenological psychology or phenomenological human science research. Among the primary exponents are: Ashworth (2003); Dahlberg et al. (2008); Finlay (2008); Giorgi (1997); Halling (2008); Todres (2007); Van Manen (1990). We can see this as a family of approaches, a fuzzy set where all share the basic tenets of phenomenology but each articulates an approach in a particular way. Rather than describe each of these different approaches here, what we will do is compare IPA to a small number of them, in order to help position IPA within the general conceptual map of phenomenological research.

First, it is helpful to think of IPA in relation to what is probably the longest established phenomenological psychology, that of Amedeo Giorgi, and through this we will see the similarities and differences between the two approaches. As with IPA, Giorgi (Giorgi & Giorgi, 2008) is attempting to operationalize a phenomenological approach for psychology, and, in a similar way to IPA, articulates the transformations which are necessary when moving from philosophy to psychology.

A significant difference between IPA and Giorgi's approach is that Giorgi is attempting as close a translation as possible of Husserl's phenomenological method, while, as indicated elsewhere, IPA draws from the wider corpus of phenomenology and is not attempting to operationalize a specific version of it. Relatedly, while IPA is avowedly interpretative, Giorgi (1997) emphasizes that his approach is descriptive.

Giorgi's method is primarily concerned with developing accounts of commonality in experience so that a complete and integrated eidetic picture (or the general structure) of a particular phenomenon can be built up. IPA, by contrast, has the idiographic aim of providing a detailed analysis of divergence and convergence across cases, capturing the texture and richness of each particular individual examined.

Because of the different emphases between Giorgi's phenomenological psychology and IPA, the outcome of research using the two approaches tends to look rather different. The result of a Giorgi study is most likely to take the form of a third person narrative, a synthesized summary statement outlining the general structure for the phenomenon under question. The result of an IPA analysis usually takes the form of a more idiographic interpretative commentary, interwoven with extracts from the participants' accounts.

IPA is also not alone in attempting to operationalize a hermeneutic phenomenology and it shares considerable common ground with related approaches. Van Manen (1990), in common with IPA, draws on and connects phenomenology and hermeneutics. Van Manen is particularly interested in the phenomenological investigation of everyday practice and gives detailed instances of how he has applied his approach to pedagogy and parenting. He describes how a hermeneutic phenomenological approach focused on understanding human beings within the context of their lifeworld is especially relevant to researchers in education, health and nursing. Van Manen also emphasizes the centrality of writing to the phenomenological endeavour. A related approach is exemplified in the collection edited by Benner (1994) which outlines and illustrates an approach which is particularly influenced by Heidegger and has been applied primarily in nursing.

A new addition to the array of phenomenological approaches in psychology is critical narrative analysis, as articulated by Langdridge (2007). Critical narrative analysis is strongly informed by Ricoeur and aims to include an identification of key narratives and an interpretation of suspicion to the analysis. The latter involves interrogating texts through the lens of social theory. Thus the emphasis of the analysis is different from that of IPA. It will be interesting to see research studies which emerge using this approach.

IPA and grounded theory

Finally we should discuss grounded theory, which is often seen as the main alternative method for someone considering IPA for a research study. Grounded theory has a strong trans-disciplinary identity. Thus it is not necessarily either experiential or psychological, but it can be used in this way. It has been around a lot longer than IPA, and, as a result, it now exists in a number of rather different forms. Grounded theory was originally developed in order to offer researchers a clear, systematic and sequential guide to qualitative fieldwork and analysis (e.g. see Glaser & Strauss, 1967). This was operationalized via a rather technical sounding vocabulary (e.g. 'co-axial coding') and a highly structured procedure for the development of theory. Taken together, these features probably account for its great success in making a space for qualitative research in social scientific disciplines which were largely dominated by positivism.

Grounded theory researchers generally set out to generate a theoretical-level account of a particular phenomenon. This often requires sampling on a relatively large scale, especially in comparison to IPA. There are several versions of this approach but constructivist grounded theory (e.g. Charmaz, 2006) is now probably the most widely used in psychology. Compared with other strands of grounded theory, the constructivist version appears to offer a greater flexibility of process, and a clearer epistemological position (see also Chapter 3).

Clearly there is considerable overlap between IPA and what grounded theory can do, and both have a broadly inductivist approach to inquiry. On the whole, however, an IPA study is likely to offer a more detailed and nuanced analysis of the lived experience of a small number of participants with an emphasis on the convergence and divergence between participants. By contrast, a grounded theory study of the same broad topic is likely to wish to push towards a more conceptual explanatory level based on a larger sample and where the individual accounts can be drawn on to illustrate the resultant theoretical claim. Of course grounded theory's grand aims mean that much that purports to be grounded theory is in reality more like grounded analysis – something on the way to grounded theory. It is also the case, as mentioned in Chapter 10, that it is possible than an IPA study could lead onto a subsequent grounded theory study.

The relation between IPA and grounded theory has some parallels with IPA's relation with Giorgi's phenomenological psychology. Both grounded theory and Giorgi's phenomenological psychology have grand ambitions – aiming to produce either mid-level theoretical accounts of psychosocial phenomena in the case of grounded theory, or a general structure of phenomena in the case of Giorgi's phenomenological psychology. By contrast, IPA is concerned with the micro analysis of individual experience, with the texture and nuance arising from the detailed exploration and presentation of actual slices of human life. It is partly about degree of focus and speed of generalization. IPA is not opposed to more macro level claims but it steadfastly asserts the value of complementary micro analyses, analyses which may enrich the development of more macro accounts.

THIRTEEN

Conclusion and reflections on future developments

We hope that readers will now have a sense of IPA as both a dynamic and a holistic entity. For those who are new to IPA research, we have tried to provide a solid platform – one from which a first project might set out. For those who are already involved in IPA work, we hope we have provided some inspiration and encouragement – perhaps to take a creative approach to design and data collection, to develop more interpretative analyses, to examine new topics, or to explore connections with related approaches.

Qualitative psychology requires the researcher to engage in data collection and analysis, and in IPA's case this means engaging with participants too. We began the book by presenting the theoretical inspirations for IPA, and in subsequent chapters we have been showing how IPA enacts these ideas. The philosophical sources outlined in Chapter 2 provide us with an important set of principles. For qualitative researchers, who so often have to accommodate the unexpected, such principles are more useful than the methodological protocols which inform other approaches. Nevertheless, these philosophical principles require some translation for praxis, and in this book, we have tried to draw out some of the possibilities without closing down too many alternatives. Thus we hope that readers will find further consonant ways to draw upon these ideas, to explore their implications and help them to solve problems in their own work.

For us, the structure of the book – much like the processes in IPA – works iteratively. We hope that the framework for conducting IPA research which we described in Chapters 3 to 6 is sufficienctly well structured to support and encourage the first-time researcher, but also flexible enough that more experienced readers will find plenty of opportunities to innovate and delve deeper. In the research examples in Chapters 7 to 10, we hope we have shown how some of the key theoretical ideas can be instantiated, and have also given a sense of where the typical practices of the IPA researcher might lead. And we hope that these outcomes demonstrate why IPA is so often appropriate for the 'real world' researcher. Finally, in the last two chapters we have considered current issues for IPA, and in particular have shown how IPA is currently in a dialogue with several other major approaches in psychology.

What expectations do we have for the future of IPA? We expect that dedicated IPA studies will continue to develop and appear in a range of exciting and stimulating subject areas, and indeed that the range of those areas will be ever increasing, and we hope that researchers will continue to find IPA to be an accessible, flexible and useful approach to understanding what something is like, from the perspective of the person who is trying to make sense of it. We expect to see that some of these studies will open up new avenues of design and data collection for IPA. Certainly, longitudinal studies working with small samples, systemic and multi-perspectival designs, and in-depth single cases are already becoming more common designs. Approaches to data collection which aim to engage with shared experiences (such as small group interviews), or to collect accounts from people who share experiences, but who are separated by some distance (such as on-line interviewing), are likely to become more common. We would also hope to see developments in the use of diaries and written materials. And we will be interested to discover whether the use of various experiential and mindful methods to 'train' or prompt participants to provide a different level of recall – a 're-imagining' or 're-living' or focusing of their experiences – will lead to a strand of IPA work which gets even more 'experience-close'.

Alongside these developments within IPA, we also expect to see some studies which expand IPA's connections to other qualitative approaches, along the lines described in Chapter 12. We welcome these developments as working towards a more mature, synthesized, qualitative psychology. We think it is crucial to what IPA might bring to such syntheses, however, that the core elements of IPA – concern with lived experience, hermeneutic inquiry, idiographic focus – remain central. We would also expect to hear of more IPA work operating within mixed methods (i.e quantitative and quantitative studies), because of its capacity for a dialogue with other levels of explanation. Again we welcome this, but again we would emphasize that this will only be a fruitful way forward if the core concerns of IPA are recognized and made manifest in the study design.

We also hope that researchers will respond to the challenge offered in this book to push interpretation further. We recognize that, for new researchers, doing experiential qualitative psychology can seem daunting and we understand the need for a notion of 'good enough'. However, we do wish to encourage more experienced IPA researchers to be bolder and to work with more interpretative analyses, and so to strive beyond 'good enough'. Fuller, deeper interpretation is not only consonant with IPA, it is often a marker of good quality work. The important thing is that interpretations should be clearly developed from the phenomenological core, from the concerns of the participants themselves. This is what we mean when say that interpretations should come from within, rather than from without. Interpretation in IPA is a form of *amplification* or *illumination* of meaning, which is cued or sparked by a close engagement with the data, and which requires creativity, reflection and critical awareness for its full development.

Indeed the question of what is actually involved in interpretation is central to IPA as well as to qualitative psychology more broadly. Yet the nature of the process of interpretation has been rather neglected in qualitative psychology. We think that IPA, as one particular instantiation of qualitative research, is well placed to contribute to hermeneutic theory through analyses of what is happening during interpretation.

Following on from this, the presence of more interpretative studies, and more awareness of what interpretation is, will help inform debates about what represents quality in qualitative research. As we have seen in Chapter 11, some of the existing guidelines are helpful in suggesting a range of ways of assessing the validity of a piece of qualitative research. This debate can be taken further forward by looking closely at pieces of qualitative work in general and IPA in particular and articulating what it is that makes a particular paper excellent whereas another paper, which does actually meet the established criteria of validity for qualitative research, remains mediocre rather than outstanding.

As the corpus of IPA studies grows, it will be interesting to see the emerging 'themes within the themes'. In Chapter 10 we noted that it is already apparent that identity appears as a key construct in much IPA research, and in Chapter 12 we have pointed to the affective domain as another significant emergent dimension in many IPA studies. We will have to see what other themes will come out of the growing body of work as particularly resonant and recurrent, and the elaboration and exploration of these issues in future review papers will be interesting.

On a related note, as more studies are conducted in particular areas, it will be possible to begin developing stronger theoretical statements, perhaps, for example, through the models of case law or analytic induction, which we described in Chapter 2, or perhaps through some of the frameworks for the 'meta-synthesis' of qualitative research which have been published in recent years. As an example, there is now a reasonable body of work using IPA to examine the lived experience of chronic pain. It will soon be possible to review this work to examine common features, and to explore variations across contexts and samples in the studies, and so to move to a broader claim about the phenomenology of pain.

We would expect then to see a number of reviews of IPA work in the next five years. So far, two reviews exist (Brocki & Wearden, 2006; Reid et al., 2005) and these offer useful overviews of the work up to that time. However, these are both methodological rather than substantive reviews. For the future, it will be valuable to see both further developments in the process of methodological reviewing as well as the emergence of reviews of IPA research in substantive areas.

For us, IPA provides a fascinating and very rich way of engaging with, and understanding, other people's worlds. Through it, we have learned about the complexity of individual lived experience. At times, it has provided us with insights into the lives of people whose voices might not otherwise have been heard, or whose experiences were ignored, or else constructed quite differently, by mainstream theoretical models. At other times it has afforded us illuminating perspectives upon personal relationships and processes, or professional interventions and contexts. We have found the process of doing IPA exhilarating, demanding and stimulating. We hope that you will feel encouraged and stimulated by what you have read in this book and that you find your experience of IPA to be as enjoyable, as rewarding, and as powerful as we have done.

| **Interpretative phenomenological analysis**

References

Ainley, S.C. (1989). *Day Brought Back My Night: Ageing and New Vision Loss.* London: Routledge.

Ajzen, I. & Fishbein, M. (1980). *Understanding Attitudes and Predicting Social Behaviour.* Englewood Cliffs: Prentice Hall.

Allport, G.W. (1951). *The Use of Personal Documents in Psychological Science.* New York: Social Science Research Council (Bulletin No. 49).

Allport, G.W. (1965). *Letters from Jenny.* New York: Harcourt.

Anderson, M.L. (2003). Embodied cognition: a field guide. *Artificial Intelligence, 149,* 91–130.

Andrews, M., Sclater, S.D., Squire, S., & Treacher, A. (2000). *Lines of Narrative: Psychosocial Perspectives.* London: Routledge.

Antonucci, T.C. & Mikus, K. (1988). The power of parenthood: Personality and attitudinal change during the transition to parenthood. In G. Michaels & W. Goldberg (Eds.), *The Transition to Parenthood: Current Theory and Research.* Cambridge: Cambridge University Press.

Arroll, M.A. & Senior, V. (2008). Individuals' experience of chronic fatigue syndrome/myalgic encephalomyelitis: an interpretative phenomenological analysis. *Psychology & Health, 23,* 443–458.

Ashworth, P.D. (2003). (Guest editor, special issue). Contingencies of the lifeworld: Phenomenological psychology from Sheffield, England. *Journal of Phenomenological Psychology, 34* (2).

Ashworth, P. (2008). Conceptual foundations of qualitative psychology. In J.A. Smith (Ed.), *Qualitative Psychology: A Practical Guide to Methods* (2nd edn). London: Sage.

Becker, C. (1992). *Living and Relating: An Introduction to Phenomenology.* Newbury Park: Sage.

Benner, P. (Ed.) (1994). *Interpretive Phenomenology.* Thousand Oaks: Sage.

Bentall, R. (2004). *Madness Explained: Psychosis and Human Nature.* London: Penguin.

Bhogal, S. & Larkin, M. (in preparation). Staff experiences of working with British Asian service-users and their families, in an Early Intervention Service for young people experiencing first-episode psychosis. Unpublished manuscript.

Binswanger, L. (1975/1963). *Being in the World.* London: Souvenir Press.

Birchwood M., Fowler, D.G., & Jackson, C. (Eds.) (2000). *Early Intervention: A Guide to Concepts. Evidence and Interventions.* John Wiley and Sons.

Birchwood, M., Trower, P., Brunet, K., Gilbert, P., Iqbal, Z., & Jackson, C. (2007). Social anxiety and the shame of psychosis: A study in first episode psychosis. *Behaviour Research and Therapy, 45,* 1025–1037.

Bohnsack, R. (2000). Group discussions and focus groups. In U. Flick, E. von Kardoff, & I. Steinke (Eds), *A Companion to Qualitative Research.* London: Sage.

Borkoles, E., Nicholls, A., Bell, K., Butterly, R., & Polman, R. (2008). The lived experiences of people diagnosed with multiple sclerosis in relation to exercise. *Psychology & Health, 23,* 427–441.

Boyle, M. (1990). *Schizophrenia: A Scientific Delusion?* London: Routledge.

Boyle, M. (2002a). It's all done with smoke and mirrors. Or, how to create the illusion of a schizophrenic brain disease. *Clinical Psychology, 12* (April), 9–16.

Boyle, M. (2002b). *Schizophrenia: A Scientific Delusion?* (2nd edn). London: Routledge.

British Psychological Society (BPS) (2000). *Recent Advances in Understanding Mental Illness and Psychotic Experiences.* Leicester: British Psychological Society.

Brocki, J.M. & Wearden, A.J. (2006). A critical evaluation of the use of interpretative phenomenological analysis (IPA) in Health Psychology. *Psychology and Health, 21,* 87–108.

Bromley, D. (1985). The case-study method as a basic approach to personality. Paper given to BPS London Conference.

Bromley, D. (1986). *The Case Study Method in Psychology and Related Disciplines.* Chichester: Wiley.

Bruner, J. (1987). Life as narrative. *Social Research, 54,* 11–32.

Bruner, J. (1990). *Acts of Meaning.* Boston: Harvard University Press.

Burkitt, I. (1999). *Bodies of Thought: Embodiment, Identity and Modernity.* London: Sage.

Burman, E. (1994). Interviewing. In P. Banister, E. Burman, I. Parker, M. Taylor, & C. Tindall (Eds), *Qualitative Methods in Psychology: A Research Guide.* Buckingham: Open University Press.

Busch, T. (2008). Existentialism: the 'new philosophy'. In R. Diprose & J. Reynolds (Eds), *Merleau-Ponty: Key concepts.* Stocksfield: Acumen.

Campbell, D.T. (1975). 'Degrees of freedom' and the case study. *Comparative Political Studies, 8,* 178–193.

Carradice, A., Shankland, M., & Beail, N. (2002). A qualitative study of the theoretical models used by UK mental health nurses to guide their assessments with family caregivers of people with dementia. *International Journal of Nursing Studies, 39,* 17–26.

Chadwick, P., Liao, L.M., & Boyle, M. (2005). Size matters: experiences of atypical genital and sexual development in males. *Journal of Health Psychology, 10,* 559–572.

Chamberlain, K. (2000). Methodolatry and qualitative health research. *Journal of Health Psychology, 5* (3), 285–296.

Charmaz, K. (1983). Loss of self: A fundamental form of suffering in the chronically ill. *Sociology of Health and Illness, 5,* 168–195.

Charmaz, K. (1989). The self in time. In N. Denzin (Ed.), *Studies in Symbolic Interaction, A Research Annual. 10. Parts A and B.* Greenwich, CT: JAI Press.

Charmaz, K. (1991). *Good Days Bad Days.* New Brunswick: Rutgers University Press.

Charmaz, K. (1995). The body, identity and self: adapting to impairment. *The Sociological Quarterly, 36,* 657–680.

Charmaz, K. (2006). *Constructing Grounded Theory: A Practical Guide through Qualitative Analysis.* London: Sage.

Charmaz, K. (2008). Grounded theory. In J.A. Smith (Ed.), *Qualitative Psychology: A Practical Guide to Methods* (2nd edn). London: Sage.

Chodorow, N.J. (1999). *The Power of Feelings.* New Haven: Yale University Press.

Cieurzo, C. & Keitel, M.A. (1999). Ethics in qualitative research. In M. Kopala & L.A. Suzuki (Eds), *Using Qualitative Methods in Psychology.* London: Sage.

Clare, L. (2002). We'll fight it as long as we can: Coping with the onset of Alzheimer's disease. *Aging and Mental Health, 6,* 139–148.

Clare, L. (2003). Managing threats to self: awareness in early stage Alzheimer's disease. *Social Science & Medicine, 57,* 1017–1029.

Cole, M. (1996). *Cultural Psychology: A Once and Future Discipline*. Boston: Harvard University Press.

Connop, V. & Petrak, J. (2004). The impact of sexual assault on heterosexual couples. *Sexual & Relationships Therapy, 19*, 29–38.

Conrad, P. (1987). The experience of illness: recent and new directions. *Research in the Sociology of Health Care, 6*, 1–31.

Coyle, A. & Rafalin, D. (2000). Jewish gay men's accounts of negotiating cultural, religious and sexual identity. *Journal of Psychology and Human Sexuality, 12*, 21–48.

Crossley, M.L. (2000). *Introducing Narrative Psychology: Self, Trauma and the Construction of Meaning*. Buckingham: Open University Press.

Dahlberg, K., Dahlberg, H., & Nystrom, M. (2008). *Reflective Lifeworld Research* (2nd edn). Lund: Studentlitteratur.

Dahlberg, K., Drew, N., & Nystrom, M. (2001). *Reflective Lifeworld Research*. Lund: Studentlitteratur.

Damasio, A. (1995). *Descartes' Error: Emotion, Reason and the Human Brain*. New York: Avon Hearst.

Daniel, E., Kent, G., Binney, V., & Pagdin, J. (2005). Trying to do my best as a mother: Decision-making in families of children undergoing elective surgical treatment for short stature. *British Journal of Health Psychology, 10*, 101–114.

Datan, N., Rodeheaver, D., & Hughes, F. (1987). Adult development and aging. *Annual Review of Psychology, 38*, 153–180.

de Visser, R. & Smith, J.A. (2006). Mister in between: A case study of masculine identity and health-related behaviour. *Journal of Health Psychology, 11*, 685–695.

de Visser, R. & Smith, J.A. (2007). Alcohol consumption and masculine identity among young men. *Psychology and Health, 22*, 595–614.

De Waele, J.P. & Harré, R. (1979). Autobiography as a psychological method. In G. Ginsburg (Ed.), *Emerging Strategies in Social Psychological Research*. Chichester: Wiley.

Dickson, A., Allan, D., & O'Carroll, R. (2008). Biographical disruption and the experience of loss following a spinal cord injury: An interpretative phenomenological analysis. *Psychology & Health, 23*, 407–425.

Dilthey, W. (1976). *Selected Writings* (H. Rickman, Ed., Trans. and Intro.). Cambridge: CUP.

Drummond, J. (2007). Phenomenology: Neither auto- nor hetero- be. *Phenomenology and the Cognitive Sciences, 6*, 57–74.

Duncan, B., Hart, G., Scoular, A., & Bigrigg, A. (2001). Qualitative analysis of the psychosocial impact of a diagnosis of chlamydia: implications for screening. *British Medical Journal, 5*, 165–185.

Dunne, E.A. & Quayle, E. (2001). The impact of iatrogenically acquired hepatitis C infection on the well-being and relationships of a group of Irish women. *Journal of Health Psychology, 6*, 679–692.

Eatough, V. & Smith, J.A. (2006a). 'I feel like a scrambled egg in my head': An idiographic case study of meaning making and anger using interpretative phenomenological analysis. *Psychology and Psychotherapy, 79*, 115–135.

Eatough, V. & Smith, J.A. (2006b). 'I was like a wild wild person': Understanding feelings of anger using interpretative phenomenological analysis. *British Journal of Psychology, 97*, 483–498.

Eatough, V. & Smith, J.A. (2008). Interpretative phenomenological analysis. In C. Willig and W. Stainton Rogers (Eds), *The SAGE Handbook of Qualitatitive Research in Psychology*. London: Sage.

Elliott, R, Fischer, C.T., & Rennie, D.L. (1999). Evolving guidelines for publication of qualitative research studies in psychology and related fields. *British Journal of Clinical Psychology, 38*, 215–229.

Erikson, E. (1980). *Identity and the Life-Cycle*. New York: Norton.

Finlay, L. (2002). Negotiating the swamp: the opportunity and challenge of reflexivity in research practice. *Qualitative Research, 2*, 209–230.

Finlay, L. (2008). A dance between the reduction and reflexivity: explicating the 'phenomenological psychological attitude'. *Journal of Phenomenological Psychology, 39*, 1–32.

Finlay, L. & Gough, B. (Eds) (2003). *Reflexivity*. Oxford: Blackwell Science.

Finlay, & Langdridge, D. (2007). Embodiment. In W. Hollway, H. Lucey, & A. Phoenix (Eds), *Social Psychology Matters*. Maidenhead: Open University Press.

Flowers, P. (2008). Temporal tales: The use of multiple interviews with the same participant. *Qualitative Methods in Psychology Newsletter, 5*, 24–27.

Flowers, P., Davis, M., Hart, G., Rosengarten, M., Frankis, J., & Imrie, J. (2006). Diagnosis and stigma and identity amongst HIV positive Black Africans living in the UK. *Psychology and Health, 21*, 109–122.

Flowers, P., Duncan, B., & Frankis, J. (2000). Community, responsibility and culpability: HIV risk management amongst Scottish gay men. *Journal of Community and Applied Social Psychology, 10*, 285–300.

Flowers, P., Duncan, B., & Knussen, C. (2003). Re-appraising HIV testing: An exploration of the psychosocial costs and benefits associated with learning one's HIV status in a purposive sample of Scottish gay men. *British Journal of Health Psychology, 8*, 179–194.

Flowers, P., Hart, G., & Marriot, C. (1999). Constructing sexual health: Gay men and 'risk' in the context of a public sex environment. *Journal of Health Psychology, 4*, 483–495.

Flowers, P., Knussen, C., & Duncan, B. (2001). Re-appraising HIV testing among Scottish gay men: The impact of new HIV treatments. *Journal of Health Psychology, 6*, 665–678.

Flowers, P., Marriott, C., & Hart, G. (2000). 'The bars, the bogs and the bushes': The impact of locale on sexual cultures. *Culture, Health and Sexuality, 2*, 69–86.

Flowers, P., Sheeran, P., Beail, N., & Smith, J.A. (1997). The role of psychosocial factors in HIV risk-reduction among gay and bisexual men: A quantitative review. *Psychology and Health, 12*, 197–230.

Flowers, P., Smith, J.A., Sheeran, P., & Beail, N. (1997). Health and romance: Understanding unprotected sex in relationships between gay men. *British Journal of Health Psychology, 2*, 73–86.

Gadamer, H. (1990/1960). *Truth and Method* (2nd rev. edn). New York: Crossroad.

Gallagher, S. & Sørensen, J.B. (2006). Experimenting with phenomenology. *Consciousness and Cognition, 15*, 119–134.

Gallagher, S. & Varela, F. (2001). Redrawing the map and resetting the time: phenomenology and the cognitive sciences. In S. Crowell, L. Embree, & S.J. Julian (Eds), *The Reach of Reflection: Issues for Phenomenology's Second Century*. Electronpress. Available at: pegasus.cc.ucf.edu/~gallaghr/G&V01.pdf (date of access: 31 January, 2008).

Gallagher, S. & Zahavi, D. (2007). *The Phenomenological Mind: An Introduction to Philosophy of Mind and Cognitive Science*. London: Routledge.

Gergen, K.J. (1987). Toward self as relationship. In K. Yardley & T. Honess (Eds), *Self & Identity: Psychosocial Perspectives*. Chichester: Wiley.

Gergen, K.J. (1991). *The Saturated Self: Dilemmas of Identity in Contemporary Life*. New York: Basic Books.

Gergen, K.J. & Gergen, M.M. (1988). Narrative and the self as relationship. In L. Berkowitz (Ed.), *Advances in Experimental Social Psychology, Vol. 21*. New York: Academic Press.

Ghaemi, S.N. (2001). Rediscovering existential psychotherapy: the contribution of Ludwig Binswanger. *American Journal of Psychotherapy, 55*, 51–64.

Giddens, A. (1991). *Modernity and Self-Identity: Self and Society in the Late Modern Age.* Oxford: Polity Press.

Gilligan, C. (1982). *In a Different Voice: Psychological Theory and Women's Development.* Cambridge, MA: Harvard University Press.

Giorgi, Λ. (1997). The theory, practice, and evaluation of the phenomenological method as a qualitative research procedure. *Journal of Phenomenological Psychology, 28,* 235–260.

Giorgi, A. & Giorgi, B. (2008). Phenomenology. In J.A. Smith (Ed.), *Qualitative Psychology: A Practical Guide to Methods* (2nd edn). London: Sage.

Glaser, B.G. & Strauss, A. (1967). *Discovery of Grounded Theory: Strategies for Qualitative Research.* Mill Valley, CA: Sociology Press.

Glasscoe, C. & Smith, J.A. (2008). Through a mother's lens: A qualitative analysis reveals how temporal experience shifts when a boy born preterm has cystic fibrosis. *Clinical Child Psychology and Psychiatry, 13,* 609–626.

Golsworthy, R. & Coyle, A. (2001). Practitioners' accounts of religious and spiritual dimensions in bereavement therapy. *Counselling Psychology Quarterly, 14,* 183–202.

Gregory, D.M., Way, C.Y., Hutchinson, T.A., Barrett, B.J., & Parfrey, P.S. (1998). Patients' perceptions of their experiences with ESRD and haemodialysis treatment. *Qualitative Health Research, 8,* 764–783.

Gubrium, J.F. & Holstein, J.A. (Eds) (2002). *Handbook of Interview Research: Context and Methods.* Thousand Oaks: Sage.

Hagren, B., Pettersen, IM., Severinsson, E., Lützén, K., & Clyne, N. (2005). Maintenance haemodialysis: patients' experiences of their life situation. *Journal of Clinical Nursing 14,* 294–300.

Halling, S. (2008). *Intimacy, Transcendence, and Psychology.* New York: Palgrave.

Hammersley, M. (1989). *The Dilemma of Qualitative Method.* London: Routledge.

Harré, R. (1979). *Social Being.* Oxford: Blackwell.

Harrop, C.E. & Trower, P. (2003). *Why Does Schizophrenia Develop at Late Adolescence?* Chichester: Wiley.

Heidegger, M. (1962/1927). *Being and Time.* Oxford: Blackwell.

Henwood, K. & Pidgeon, N. (2006). Grounded theory. In G. Breakwell, C. Fife-Schaw, S. Hammond, & J.A. Smith (Eds), *Research Methods in Psychology* (3rd edn). London: Sage.

Hermans, H.J. (1988). On the integration of nomothetic and idiographic research methods in the study of personal meaning. *Journal of Personality, 56,* 785–812.

Hollway, W. & Jefferson, T. (2005). Panic and perjury: A psycho-social exploration of agency. *British Journal of Social Psychology, 44,* 147–163.

Holmes, S., Coyle, A., & Thomson, E. (1997). Quality of life in survivors of bone marrow transplant. *Journal of Cancer Nursing, 1,* 106–116.

Hopf, C. (2004). Research ethics and qualitative research. In U. Flick, E. von Kardoff, & I. Steinke (Eds), *A Companion to Qualitative Research.* London: Sage.

Howes, H., Benton, D., & Edwards, S. (2005). Women's experience of brain injury: An interpretative phenomenological analysis. *Psychology and Health, 20,* 129–142.

Hunt, D. & Smith, J.A. (2004). The personal experience of carers of stroke survivors: an interpretative phenomenological analysis. *Disability & Rehabilitation, 26,* 1000 1011.

Husserl, E. (1927). Phenomenology. For *Encyclopaedia Britannica* (R. Palmer, Trans. and revised). Available at: http://www.hfu.edu.tw/~huangkm/phenom/husserl-britanica.htm

Husserl, E. (1970). *The Crisis of European Sciences and Transcendental Phenomenology* (D. Carr, Trans.). Evanston: Northwestern University Press.

Husserl, E. (1982). *Ideas Pertaining to a Pure Phenomenology and to a Phenomenological Philosophy* (F. Kersten, Trans.). Dordrecht: Kluwer.

IRIS (2006). Early detection in psychosis. Available at: http://www.iris-initiative.org.uk/

Jarman, M., Smith, J.A., & Walsh, S. (1997). The psychological battle for control: a qualitative study of health care professionals understandings of the treatment of anorexia nervosa. *Journal of Community & Applied Social Psychology, 7*, 137–152.

Jarman, M., Walsh, S., & De Lacey, G. (2005). Keeping safe, keeping connected: a qualitative study of HIV-positive women's experiences of partner relationships. *Psychology & Health, 20*, 533–553.

Johnson, S., Burrows, A., & Williamson, I. (2004). 'Does my bump look big in this?' The meaning of bodily changes for first time mothers-to-be. *Journal of Health Psychology, 9*, 361–374.

Johnstone, L. (2000). *Users and Abusers of Psychiatry* (2nd edn). Hove: Brunner-Routledge.

Josselson, R. (2004). The hermeneutics of faith and the hermeneutics of suspicion. *Narrative Inquiry, 14*, 1–29.

Kam, S. & Midgeley, N. (2006). Exploring 'clinical judgement': How do child and adolescent mental health professionals decide whether a young person needs individual psychotherapy? *Clinical Child Psychology and Psychiatry, 11*, 27–44.

Kidder, L.H. & Fine, M. (1997). Qualitative inquiry in psychology: A radical tradition. In D. Fox & I. Prilleltensky (Eds), *Critical Psychology*. London: Sage.

Kierkegaard, S. (1974). *Concluding Unscientific Postscript* (D.F. Swenson & W. Lowrie, Trans.). Princeton: Princeton University Press.

Kirschenbaum, D. (1991). Integration of clinical psychology into haemodialysis programs. In J. Sweet, R. Rozensky, and S. Tovian (Eds), *Handbook of Clinical Psychology in Medical Settings*. New York: Plenum Press.

Lamiell, J.T. (1987). *The Psychology of Personality: An Epistemological Inquiry*. New York: Columbia University Press.

Langdridge, D. (2007). *Phenomenological Psychology: Theory, Research and Method*. Harlow: Pearson.

Lanzoni, S. (2005). The enigma of subjectivity: Ludwig Binswanger's existential anthropology of mania. *History of the Human Sciences, 18*, 23–41.

Larkin, M. (2001). Understandings and Experiences: A Post-constructionist Cultural Psychology of Addiction and Recovery in the 12-Step Tradition. Unpub. PhD thesis. Nottingham Trent University.

Larkin, M., Clifton, E., & de Visser, R. (in press). Making sense of 'consent' in a constrained environment. *International Journal of Law & Psychiatry*.

Larkin, M., Eatough, V., & Osborn, M. (submitted). Interpretative phenomenological analysis and embodied active situated cognition.

Larkin, M. & Griffiths, M.D. (2002). Experiences of addiction and recovery: the case for subjective accounts. *Addiction Research and Theory, 10*, 281–311.

Larkin, M. & Griffiths, M.D. (2004). Dangerous sports and recreational drug-use: rationalizing and contextualizing risk. *Journal of Community and Applied Social Psychology, 14*, 215–232.

Larkin, M., Watts, S., & Clifton, E. (2006). Giving voice and making sense in Interpretative Phenomenological Analysis. *Qualitative Research in Psychology, 3*, 102–120.

Latif, S., Newton, E., & Larkin, M. (2004). Experiences of psychosis and Early Intervention: Asian service-users' perspectives. Paper presented to the Annual Interpretative Phenomenological Analysis Conference, July, Nottingham Trent University.

Lavie, M. & Willig, C. (2005). 'I don't feel like melting butter': An interpretative phenomenological analysis of the experience of 'inorgasmia'. *Psychology & Health, 20*, 115–128.

Lieblich, A. (1996). Some unforeseen outcomes of conducting narrative research with people of one's own culture. In R. Josselson (Ed.), *The Narrative Study of Lives: Ethics and Process in the Narrative Study of Lives*. London: Sage.

Macdonald, I., Sinason, V., & Hollins, S. (2003). An interview study of people with learning disabilities' experience of, and satisfaction with, group analytic therapy. *Psychology and Psychotherapy: Theory, Research and Practice, 76*, 433–453.

MacLeod, R., Craufurd, D., & Booth, K. (2002). Patients' perceptions of what makes genetic counselling effective: An interpretative phenomenological analysis. *Journal of Health Psychology, 7*, 145–156.

Martin, C.R. & Thompson, D.R. (2000). Prediction of quality of life in patients with end-stage renal disease. *British Journal of Health Psychology, 5*, 41–55.

McGorry, P.D., Edwards, J., Mihalopoulos, C., Harrigan, S.M., & Jackson, H.J. (1996). EPPIC: An evolving system of early detection and optimal management. *Schizophrenia Bulletin, 22*, 305–326.

Mead, G.H. (1934). *Mind Self and Society*. Chicago: University of Chicago Press.

Merleau-Ponty, M. (1962). *Phenomenology of Perception*. London: Routledge.

Michie, S., Hendy, J., Smith, J.A., & Adshead, F. (2004). Evidence into practice: a theory based study of achieving national health targets in primary care. *Journal of Evaluation in Clinical Practice, 10*, 447–456.

Michie, S., Smith, J.A., Senior, S., & Marteau, T. (2003). Understanding why negative genetic test results sometimes fail to reassure. *American Journal of Medical Genetics, 119A*, 340–347.

Mishler, E.G. (1986). *Research Interviewing: Context and Narrative*. Boston: Harvard University Press.

Mohanty, J.N. (1975). Review of *Edmund Husserl: Philosopher of Infinite Tasks* by M. Natanson. *Journal of History of Philosophy, 13*, 542–545. Available at: muse.jhu.edu/journals/journal_of_the_history_of_philosophy/v013/13.4mohanty.pdf

Moran, D. (2000). *Introduction to Phenomenology*. London: Routledge.

Moran, D. and Mooney, T. (2002). *The Phenomenology Reader*. London: Routledge.

Morgan, C. & Fearon, P. (2007). Social experience and psychosis insights from studies of migrant and ethnic minority groups. *Epidemiologia e Psichiatria Sociale, 16*, 118–123.

Morris, D. (2008). Body. In R. Diprose & J. Reynolds (Eds), *Merleau-Ponty: Key Concepts*. Stocksfield: Acumen.

Moss-Morris, R., Weinman, J., Petrie, K., Horne, R., Cameron, L., & Buick, D. (2002). The revised illness perception questionnaire (IPQ-R). *Psychology & Health, 17*, 1–16.

Much, N. (1995). Cultural psychology. In J.A. Smith, R. Harré, & L. Van Langenhove (Eds), *Rethinking Psychology*. Sage: London.

National Institute for Clinical Excellence (NICE) (2002). *Clinical Guideline 1. Schizophrenia: Core Interventions in the Treatment and Management of Schizophrenia in Primary and Secondary Care*. London: NICE.

Newton, E., Landau, S., Smith, P., Monks, P., Shergill, S., & Wykes, T. (2005). Early psychological intervention for auditory hallucinations: An exploratory study of young people's voices groups. *Journal of Nervous and Mental Disease, 193*, 58–61.

Newton, E., Larkin, M., Melhuish, R., & Wykes, T. (2007). More than just a place to talk: young people's experiences of group psychological therapy as an early intervention for auditory hallucinations. *Psychology and Psychotherapy: Theory, Research, Practice, 80*, 127–149.

Nicolson, P. (1986). Developing a feminist approach to depression following childbirth. In S. Wilkinson (Ed.), *Feminist Social Psychology: Developing Theory and Practice*. Milton Keynes: Open University Press.

Nicolson, P. (1989). Counselling women with post natal depression: Implications from recent qualitative research. *Counselling Psychology Quarterly, 2*, 123–132.

Nightingale, D. & Cromby, J. (1999). *Social Constructionist Psychology: A Critical Analysis of Theory and Practice*. Buckingham: Open University Press.

O'Connell, D.C. & Kowal, S. (1995). Basic principles of transcription. In J.A. Smith, L. Van Langenhove, & R. Harré (Eds), *Rethinking Methods in Psychology*. London: Sage.

Osborn, M. & Smith, J.A. (1998). The personal experience of chronic benign lower back pain: An interpretative phenomenological analysis. *British Journal of Health Psychology, 3*, 65–83.

Packer, M. & Addison, R. (1989). *Entering the Circle: Hermeneutic Investigation in Psychology.* New York: State University of New York Press.

Palmer, M., Larkin, M., De Visser, R., & Fadden, G. (in press) Developing an interpretative phenomenological approach to focus group data. *Qualitative Research in Psychology.*

Palmer, R. (1969). *Hermeneutics.* Evanston: Northwestern University Press.

Parker, I. (1992). *Discourse Dynamics: Critical Analysis for Social and Individual Psychology.* London and New York: Routledge.

Parkes, C.M. (1998). *Bereavement: Studies of Grief in Adult Life* (3rd edn). London: Penguin.

Penny, E., Newton, E., & Larkin, M. (in press). Whispering on the water: British Pakistani families' experiences of support from an Early Intervention Service for first-episode psychosis. *Journal of Cross Cultural Psychology.*

Pitt, L., Kilbride, M., Nothard, S., Welford, M., & Morrison, A.P. (2007). Researching recovery from psychosis: a user-led project. *Psychiatric Bulletin, 31*, 55–60.

Platt, J. (1988). What can case studies do? In R.G. Burgess (Ed.), *Studies in Qualitative Methodology: A Research Annual: Conducting Qualitative Research, Vol. I.* Greenwich, CT: JAI Press.

Plummer, K. (2001). *Documents of Life 2: An Invitation to a Critical Humanism.* London: Sage.

Potter, J. & Wetherell, M. (1987). *Discourse and Social Psychology: Beyond Attitudes and Behaviour.* London: Sage.

Rathwell, M. (2007). The Incredible Hulk television series page. Available at: www.incrediblehulktvseries.com/index.html

Ratner, C. (2000). A Cultural-Psychological Analysis of Emotions. *Culture & Psychology, 6*, 5–39.

Read, J. (2004). Poverty, ethnicity and gender. In J. Read, L.R. Mosher, & R.P. Bentall (Eds), *Models of Madness.* London: Routledge.

Read, J., Mosher, L.R., & Bentall, R.P. (Eds) (2004). *Models of Madness.* London: Routledge.

Reichsman, F. & Levy, N. (1972). Problems of adaptation to maintenance dialysis. *Archives of Internal Medicine, 130*, 859–865.

Reid, K., Flowers, P., & Larkin, M. (2005). Exploring lived experience: An introduction to Interpretative Phenomenological Analysis. *The Psychologist, 18*, 20–23.

Reynolds, F. & Prior, S. (2003). Sticking jewels in your life: Exploring women's strategies for negotiating an acceptable quality of life with multiple sclerosis. *Qualitative Health Research, 13*, 1225–1251.

Rhodes, J.E. & Jakes, S. (2004). The contribution of metaphor and metonymy to delusions. *Psychology and Psychotherapy: Theory, Research and Practice, 77*, 1–17.

Rich, A. (1977). *Of Woman Born.* London: Virago.

Richardson, W.J. (1963). *Heidegger: Through Phenomenology to Thought.* The Hague: Martinus Nijhoff.

Ricoeur, P. (1970). *Freud and Philosophy: An Essay on Interpretation.* New Haven: Yale University Press.

Riggs, E. & Coyle, A. (2002). Young people's accounts of homelessness: A case-study of psychological well-being and identity. *Counselling Psychology Review, 17*, 5–15.

Robson, C. (1993). *Real World Research: A Resource for Social Scientists and Practitioner-Researchers.* Oxford: Blackwell.

Roose, G.A. & John, A.M. (2003). A focus group investigation into young children's understanding of mental health and their views on appropriate services for their age group. *Child: Care, Health & Development, 29*, 545–550.

Rose, D. (2003). Collaborative research between users and professionals: Peaks and pitfalls. *Psychiatric Bulletin, 27*, 404–406.

Rosenwald, G.C. (1992). Conclusion: reflections on narrative understanding. In G.C. Rosenwald & R.C. Ochberg (Eds), *Storied Lives: The Cultural Politics of Self-Understanding*. London: Yale University Press.

Rubin, R. (2004). Men talking about Viagra: An exploratory study with focus groups. *Men and Masculinities, 7*, 22–30.

Salmon, P. (2002). How do we recognise good research when we see it? Anarchism, methodologism and the quantitative *vs* qualitative debate. *Psychologist, 16*, 24–27.

Sarbin, T. R. (1990). Toward the obsolescence of the schizophrenia hypothesis. *Journal of Mind and Behaviour, 11*, 259–284.

Sartre, J-P. (1948). *Existentialism and Humanism* (P. Mairet, Trans.). London: Methuen.

Sartre, J-P. (1956/1943). *Being and Nothingness*. New York: Washington Square Press.

Schleiermacher, F. (1998). *Hermeneutics and Criticism and other Writings* (A. Bowie, Trans.). Cambridge: CUP.

Schoenberg, M. & Shiloh, S. (2002). Hospitalized patients' views on in-ward psychology counseling. *Patient Education and Counselling, 48*, 123–129.

Shaw, R. (2004). Making sense of violence: A study of narrative meaning. *Qualitative Research in Psychology, 1*, 131–151.

Shinebourne, P. & Smith, J.A. (in press). Alcohol and the self: An interpretative phenomenological analysis of the experience of addiction and its impact on the sense of self and identity. *Addiction Research & Theory*.

Sloman, A. (1976). What are the aims of science? *Radical Philosophy, Spring*, 7–17.

Smith, J.A. (1993). The case study. In R. Bayne and P. Nicolson (Eds), *Counselling and Psychology for Health Professionals*. London: Chapman Hall.

Smith, J.A. (1994a). Reconstructing selves: An analysis of discrepancies between women's contemporaneous and retrospective accounts of the transition to motherhood. *British Journal of Psychology, 85*, 371–392.

Smith, J.A. (1994b). Towards reflexive practice: Engaging participants as co-researchers or co-analysts in psychological inquiry. *Journal of Community & Applied Social Psychology, 4*, 253–260.

Smith, J.A. (1996). Beyond the divide between cognition and discourse: Using interpretative phenomenological analysis in health psychology. *Psychology & Health, 11*, 261–271.

Smith, J.A. (1999a). Identity development during the transition to motherhood: An interpretative phenomenological analysis. *Journal of Reproductive and Infant Psychology, 17*, 281–300.

Smith, J.A. (1999b). Towards a relational self: Social engagement during pregnancy and psychological preparation for motherhood. *British Journal of Social Psychology, 38*, 409–426.

Smith, J.A. (2003). Shifting identities: The negotiation of meanings between texts and between persons. In L. Finlay & B. Gough (Eds), *Doing Reflexivity* (pp. 176–186). Oxford: Blackwell.

Smith, J.A. (2004). Reflecting on the development of interpretative phenomenological analysis and its contribution to qualitative research in psychology. *Qualitative Research in Psychology, 1*, 39–54.

Smith, J.A. (2007). Hermeneutics, human sciences and health: Linking theory and practice. *International Journal of Qualitative Studies on Health and Well-Being, 2*, 3–11.

Smith, J.A. (ed.) (2008). *Qualitative Psychology* (2nd edn). London: Sage.

Smith, J.A., Brewer, H., Eatough, V., Stanley, C., Glendinning, N., & Quarrell, O. (2006). The personal experience of juvenile Huntington's Disease: An interpretative phenomenological analysis of parents' accounts of the primary features of a rare genetic condition. *Clinical Genetics, 69*, 486–496.

Smith, J.A., Flowers, P., & Osborn, M. (1997). Interpretative phenomenological analysis & health psychology. In L. Yardley (Ed.), *Material Discourses & Health*. London: Routledge.

Smith, J.A., Harré, R. & Van Langenhove, L. (1995). Idiography and the case study. In J.A. Smith, R. Harré, & L. Van Langenhove (Eds), *Rethinking Psychology*. London: Sage.

Smith, J.A., Michie, S., Stephenson, M., & Quarrell, O. (2002). Risk perception and decision-making processes in candidates for the genetic test for Huntington's Disease: An interpretative phenomenological analysis. *Journal of Health Psychology, 7*, 131–144.

Smith, J.A. & Osborn, M. (2003). Interpretative phenomenological analysis. In J.A. Smith (Ed.), *Qualitative Psychology: A Practical Guide to Methods*. London: Sage.

Smith, J.A. & Osborn, M. (2007). Pain as an assault on the self: An interpretative phenomenological analysis. *Psychology and Health, 22*, 517–534.

Smith, J.A. & Osborn, M. (2008). Interpretative phenomenological analysis. In J.A. Smith (Ed.), *Qualitative Psychology: A Practical Guide to Methods* (2nd edn). London: Sage.

Stall, R., Coates, T., & Hoff, C. (1988). Behavioural risk reduction for HIV infection among gay men and bisexual men. *American Psychologist, 43*, 878–885.

Styles, J. (1979). Outsider/insider: researching gay baths. *Urban Life, 8,* 135–152.

Swift, T.L. & Wilson, S.L. (2001). Misconceptions about brain injury among the general public and non-expert health professionals: An exploratory study. *Brain Injury,* 15, 149–165.

Thompson, A.R., Kent, G., & Smith, J.A. (2002). Living with vitiligo: Dealing with difference. *British Journal of Health Psychology, 7*, 213–225.

Timotijevic, L. & Breakwell, G.M. (2000). Migration and threat to identity. *Journal of Community and Applied Social Psychology, 10*, 355–372.

Tipton, S. (2003). Comics 101: Driven By Rage. http://www.moviepoopshoot.com/comics101/17.html (source of comic image).

Todres, L. (2007). *Embodied Enquiry: Phenomenological Touchstones for Research, Psychotherapy and Spirituality*. London: Palgrave Macmillan.

Touroni, E. & Coyle, A. (2002). Decision making in planned lesbian parenting: An interpretative phenomenological analysis. *Journal of Community and Applied Social Psychology*, 12, 194–209.

Trevarthen, C. & Aitken, K.J. (2001). Infant intersubjectivity: research, theory, and clinical implications. *Journal of Child Psychology and Psychiatry, 41*, 3–48.

Turner, A., Barlow, J., & Ilbery, B. (2002). Play hurt, live hurt: Living with and managing osteoarthritis from the perspective of ex-professional footballers. *Journal of Health Psychology, 7*, 285–301.

Van Manen, M. (1990). *Researching Lived Experience: Human Science for an Action Sensitive Pedagogy*. Albany: Sate University of New York Press.

Vandevelde, P. (2005). *The Task of the Interpreter*. Pittsburgh: Pittsburgh University Press.

Von Eckartsberg, R. (1986). *Life World Experience*. Lanham: University Press of America.

Warnock, M. (1987). *Memory*. London: Faber.

Watnick, S., Kirwin, P., Mahnensmith, R., & Concato, J. (2003). The prevalence and treatment of depression among patients starting dialysis. *American Journal of Kidney Disease, 41*, 105–110.

Wetherell, M., Taylor, S., & Yates, S. (Eds) (2001). *Discourse Theory and Practice*. London: Sage.

Wider, K.V. (1997). *The Bodily Nature of Consciousness: Sartre and Contemporary Philosophy of Mind*. Ithaca: Cornell University Press.

Wilkinson, S. (2003). Focus groups. In J.A. Smith (Ed.), *Qualitative Psychology: A Practical Guide to Methods*. London: Sage.

Wilkinson, S., Joffe, H., & Yardley, L. (2004). Interviews and focus groups. In D.F. Marks & L. Yardley (Eds), *Research Methods for Clinical and Health Psychology*. London: Sage.

Willig, C. (2001). *Introducing Qualitative Research in Psychology: Adventures in Theory.* Buckingham: Open University Press.

Willig, C. (2008). *Introducing Qualitative Research in Psychology* (2nd edn). Maidenhead: Open University Press.

Wyer, S.J., Earll, L., Joseph, S., & Harrison, J. (2001). Deciding whether to attend a cardiac rehabilitation programme: An interpretative phenomenological analysis. *Coronary Health Care, 5,* 178–188.

Yardley, L. (2000). Dilemmas in qualitative health research. *Psychology & Health, 15,* 215–228.

Yardley, L. (2008). Demonstrating validity in qualitative psychology. In J.A. Smith (Ed.), *Qualitative Psychology: A Practical Guide to Methods* (2nd edn). London: Sage.

Yin, R. (1989). *Case Study Research: Design & Methods* (2nd edn). Beverly Hills: Sage.

Index

experience *cont.*
  pure, impossibility of 33
  shared, disclosure of 66
experimental psychology 192

Finlay, L. 25, 42, 200, 202
first-person processes 15, 166
focus groups 57, 71–3
fore-conception 25
fore-projection 26
fore-structures 25, 26, 100
fore-understanding 25, 26, 29
Foucault, M. 44, 195, 196
free imaginative variation technique 14
freedom of choice 20

Gadamer, H. 25–9, 34, 35, 37
Galton, Francis 31
gaze 12, 15, 20, 26
generalizability/generalizations 4, 29
Gergen, K.J. 172
Gilligan, C. 172
Giorgi, A. 200, 202
Glasscoe, C. 134
Goethe, J. W. von 31
grammatical interpretation 22
Gregory, D.M. 122
Griffiths, M.D. 52–3
grounded theory 43, 44, 201–2
  health and illness study 122, 129

haemodialysis treatment, study of psychological
      impact 121
  alienation of patient 124, 125, 126
  analysis 123–9
  background 122–3
  dreams 128–9, 131
  home treatment 126, 127, 131
  hospital regime 124, 125, 127, 128, 130
  identity as patient 124
  method 123
  self, assault on 126, 127, 130
  stages in response to treatment 122
Hagren, B. 123
Halling, S. 32, 202
harm, avoiding in research 53
Harrison, J. 132–3
health and illness 121–34
  cardiac rehabilitation programme, attending 132–3
  carer, psychology of being 133–4
  chronic fatigue syndrome, experience of 132
  coping strategies 133
  decision making 133
  dialysis and undermining of identity 122–31
  haemodialysis treatment *see* haemodialysis
      treatment, study of psychological impact
  response to treatment, stages 122, 123
  self regulation model of health behaviour 133
Health Belief Model 136
health psychology, and IPA 4
Heidegger, M. 187, 194
  embodiment 199
  hermeneutics 23–5, 26, 28–9, 34, 35

Heidegger, M. *cont.*
  and Husserl 17
  and Merleau-Ponty 18
  phenomenology 16–17, 21, 24–5, 28
  writing style 17
hermeneutic circle 27–8
  see also hermeneutics
  concept 28
  emergent themes, developing 91
  health and illness, personal experience 121
  and interviews 64
  and IPA 29
  and levels of interpretation 103
  and research process 35
  whole and part relationship 28, 35, 38,
      81, 131
  and writing up of analysis 110
hermeneutics 21–9
  dialogue 109
  double hermeneutic 3, 35, 36, 80, 187
  of empathy 36, 105
  Gadamer 25–7, 28–9
  health and illness, case study 131
  Heidegger 23–5, 26, 28–9, 34, 35
  hermeneutic turn 34–7
  history and development 21
  interpretation 22
  and IPA 3, 28
  and metaphor 155–9
  and phenomenology 24, 28, 201
  and qualitative psychology 22, 27
  of questioning 36
  Schleiermacher, F. 22-3, 25, 27, 29
  and starting of research project 41
  of suspicion 36, 105
  as theory of interpretation 3, 21
history of interpretative phenomenological
      analysis 4–5
HIV
  as global public health issue 136
  meaning of relationships to HIV-positive gay
      men *see* HIV-positive gay men, study of
      meaning of relationships to
  risk management 138, 139, 143
  women's experience of living with 143–4
HIV-positive gay men, study of meaning of
      relationships to 83, 84–8, 89, 137–42
  background 136–7
  condom use 137, 138, 139, 141, 142
  discussion 142–3
  method 137
  relational language of risk 140–2
  relational language of sex acts 138–9
  unstructured interviews 70–1
homelessness, impact on identity 173–4
homogeneous sampling 3, 49–50, 54
homosexuality
  and decision making 146
  and HIV *see* HIV-positive gay men, study of
      meaning of relationships to
  and religion 145
Howes, H. 159
Hunt, D. 133

Qualitative Psychology

A Practical Guide to Research Methods • *Second Edition*

Edited by Jonathan A. Smith, Birkbeck University of London

Covering all the main qualitative approaches now used in psychology, the **second edition** offers readers a step-by-step guide to carrying out research using each particular method with plenty of pedagogical advice. All chapters are written by international experts – many of them key figures in either the inception or development of their chosen method.

Key features of the **second edition** include:

- updated and extended chapters
- examples of good research studies using each approach
- text boxes and further readings.

Contents:

2008 • 288 pages
Paperback: 978-1-4129-3084-0
Hardcover: 978-1-4129-3083-3

Find out more and order online at
www.sagepub.co.uk